Dan Mason

Dan Mason

*From Vaudeville to Broadway
to the Silent Screen*

JOSEPH P. ECKHARDT

McFarland & Company, Inc., Publishers
Jefferson, North Carolina

LIBRARY OF CONGRESS CATALOGUING-IN-PUBLICATION DATA

Names: Eckhardt, Joseph P., author.
Title: Dan Mason : from Vaudeville to Broadway to the silent screen / Joseph P. Eckhardt.
Description: Jefferson, North Carolina : McFarland & Company, Inc., Publishers, 2021 | Includes bibliographical references and index.
Identifiers: LCCN 2020052182 | ISBN 9781476683416 (paperback : acid free paper) ∞
ISBN 9781476641812 (ebook)
Subjects: LCSH: Mason, Dan, 1853–1929. | Actors—United States—Biography. | Theater—United States—19th century—History. | Theater—United States—20th century—History. | Vaudeville—United States—History. | Motion pictures—United States—20th century—History.
Classification: LCC PN2287.M54235 E34 2021 | DDC 792.02/8092 [B]—dc23
LC record available at https://lccn.loc.gov/2020052182

BRITISH LIBRARY CATALOGUING DATA ARE AVAILABLE

ISBN (print) 978-1-4766-8341-6
ISBN (ebook) 978-1-4766-4181-2

© 2021 Joseph P. Eckhardt. All rights reserved

No part of this book may be reproduced or transmitted in any form or by any means, electronic or mechanical, including photocopying or recording, or by any information storage and retrieval system, without permission in writing from the publisher.

Front cover: Dan Mason as Pop Tuttle, the character he invented for the Plum Center Comedies in 1922. The photograph is inscribed to his co-star and close friend, Wilna Hervey (Gelfand Collection)

Printed in the United States of America

McFarland & Company, Inc., Publishers
Box 611, Jefferson, North Carolina 28640
www.mcfarlandpub.com

For Dan and Jennie Gelfand

Table of Contents

Acknowledgments — viii
Preface — 1

Part One: Dan Mason on Stage

1. The Dutch Boy from Syracuse — 5
2. The Trouper — 11
3. The Traveling Family Man — 24
4. The Two Dans — 37
5. Broadway — 43

Part Two: Dan Mason on Screen

6. The Pictures — 57
7. The Toonerville Trolley — 70
8. Plum Center — 81
9. Hollywood — 91
10. "Characters, Comic or Otherwise" — 101
11. The Idle List — 121

Appendix A. Afterpieces, Plays and Scenarios by Dan Mason — 129
Appendix B. The Crowded Hotel by Dan Mason and Dan Sully — 131
Appendix C. Dan Mason, Raconteur — 135
Filmography — 141
Chapter Notes — 173
Bibliography — 185
Index — 189

Acknowledgments

I am very grateful to the dedication's Daniel Gelfand of Woodstock, New York, for granting me unlimited access to Dan Mason's personal papers and memorabilia during the four years it took to research and write this work. Without the ability to explore Mason's unique and fascinating time capsule, and do so at my own pace, this book would not have been possible.

I also want to thank film historian Steve Massa for help in identifying the forgotten faces of many of the obscure actors in Dan Mason's old production stills and for his description of Mason's final film, *Hop Off*.

I also owe a debt of gratitude to the late film historian Robert Birchard for sharing with me his rare copy of Dan Mason's film *Pop Tuttle's Movie Queen* (1922) and to actor and film archivist Stan Taffel for digitizing that film for me. My thanks as well to Joann Margolis and Andrea Newman-Winston of the Historical Society of Woodstock for providing me a copy of Dan Mason's manuscript for his play *Via the Coal Hole* and to J. Flint Baumwirt for sharing anecdotes about her grandfather, film director Robert Eddy.

Finally, my special thanks to my partner, Brent, for his constant encouragement, feedback, and enthusiasm for this project.

Preface

From the 1880s to the 1920s, Dan Mason was one of the most popular figures in American show business. Over a career that spanned six decades and paralleled the rise of the American entertainment industry itself, he performed in variety, vaudeville, musical comedy, Broadway shows, early silent comedies, and Hollywood feature films. He was auditioning for his first "talkie" when he died. With no training in the profession he pursued, Mason launched his career in 1872 with an incomplete eighth grade education, an uncanny knack for mimicry and improvisation, and a compelling need to support his family the only way he knew how. That he managed to maintain his success for fifty-seven years in the rapidly evolving and fickle arena that was the American entertainment industry speaks of his talent, resourcefulness and forbearance.

My initial encounter with Dan Mason came in 1989 when I saw four of the Toonerville Trolley silent comedies he made for the Betzwood Film Company in the Philadelphia suburbs in the early 1920s. I had recently established the Betzwood Film Archive at Montgomery County Community College in Blue Bell, Pennsylvania, to preserve the history of this once-famous movie studio. Among the first copies of surviving Betzwood films we acquired for the collection were the Toonerville comedies. As I watched these vintage films, I was immediately captivated by Mason's performance as the shambolic and scheming old "Skipper" who pilots the decrepit Trolley. Everything about his evocation of this eccentric character was hilarious, from his disheveled appearance to his crotchety demeanor and abrupt gestures to his comical facial expressions that revealed so much about the Skipper's free-spirited personality. I was instantly a fan. Equally amused by his antics, as it turned out, were the audiences of the Betzwood Silent Film Festival that I hosted for twenty-seven years. The Toonerville films became our movie patrons' favorites and they roared with laughter at the Skipper's adventures just as his original fans had done back in the twenties. Dan Mason was a largely unknown figure in the 1980s, but the quality

Preface

of his work in the Toonerville comedies motivated me to find out more about him. Where had the Betzwood Film Company found this actor, and where did he go when the studio closed in 1921?

In 2012, while working on another book, I learned that a large private collection of Dan Mason's personal effects survived in the care of an artist living in Woodstock, New York. The memorabilia had been discovered in the Woodstock home of Mason's daughter, Nan, when she died in 1982. Rescued by two local artists, Daniel Gelfand and his wife Jennie, the collection had been in storage at the Gelfands' home and studio ever since. While in Woodstock to give a lecture in the summer of 2016, I visited Dan Gelfand and asked to take a look at Mason's memorabilia. I was stunned by the scope of what the intrepid old trouper had left behind—a treasure trove of vintage playbills, newspaper clippings, hand-written scripts, scrapbooks, hundreds of photographs, movie lobby cards, theater programs, stacks of letters, and the beginnings of a memoir Mason never lived to finish. As I dug deeper into this time capsule, marveling at each new discovery, Dan Gelfand suggested that maybe I should just take the whole lot home with me and write a book about Dan Mason.

So I did.

While Mason's story was well documented by the artifacts he had saved, his memorabilia collection raised as many questions as it answered. For help in fleshing out his narrative, I turned to the multiple newspaper archives that have arisen online in recent years. I wondered if any old newspapers might have some mention of him. The answer was a resounding "Yes." There were well over ten thousand hits. It was quickly obvious that Mason had been a popular actor whose career went all the way back to the 1870s and continued into the late 1920s. In addition to advertisements for Mason's many vaudeville appearances, there were multiple articles about him with revealing anecdotes, and hundreds of reviews of his performances in plays, musicals, and movies. To put this wealth of raw material in context, I consulted a series of books and articles detailing the history of variety, vaudeville, turn-of-the-century theater, and the early motion picture industry. The various online archives, books, and articles I utilized in my pursuit of Dan Mason's story are listed in the bibliography. I also sought out and viewed as many of Mason's surviving films as I could gain access to. These are listed in the filmography. Unfortunately, with the vast majority of all silent films lost forever, this is one gap in the story of Dan Mason's career that will never adequately be filled.

Dan Mason's partial memoirs, numerous interviews, and surviving personal letters made it possible to see his world through his eyes and

Preface

report the unfolding of his career in his own words. I have tried to use these resources to give a living sense of this talented, resourceful, and ferociously determined man who lived to make people laugh. Reviews and detailed descriptions of his stand-up routines, afterpieces, touring musicals, Broadway plays, and early films—all long since vanished and forgotten—made it possible to envision the milieu Mason moved in and gain a sense of the popular tastes of middle-class Americans in that era when almost everyone got their entertainment in local theaters.

While a large number of early motion picture players had roots in the theater, few other performers enjoyed so many full and varied years of success on stage before exploring the possibilities of the cinema. By the time Dan Mason stepped in front of a movie camera in 1913, he was already sixty years old, and his reputation for clever comedy was well established; the mere appearance of his name on a poster was all it took to pack a theater. He had entertained legions of fans for forty years, not only as a German dialect comedian and character actor but also as a singer, dancer, playwright, director, and erstwhile impresario. The unique and colorful saga of this once popular entertainer has been overlooked until now. It is my hope that this work will help re-establish Dan Mason's place in the annals of American show business.

PART ONE: DAN MASON ON STAGE

1

The Dutch Boy from Syracuse

Born Daniel Grassman, on February 9, 1853, in Syracuse, New York, Dan Mason was the third of seven children born to Jacob Grassman and Nancy McMullen Grassman. Both of his parents were immigrants; his father was a native of Worms, Germany, and his mother had been born in Bushmills, Ireland.[1] While Nancy Grassman spoke with an Irish lilt that added a certain charm to her spoken English, Jacob Grassman's heavy German accent could be a challenge to interpret. The speech patterns of both of his parents would have a significant influence on the content and style of Dan Mason's stage performances.

Dan Mason's long career as an entertainer began years before he ever set foot in a theater, let alone on a stage. A natural born mimic and incorrigible extrovert, young Dannie Grassman could not resist comically imitating his father's tangled Teutonic syntax and torrents of mispronounced English words. Herr Grassman's opinion of his son's impersonations is unknown. Dannie's friends, on the other hand, were amused enough to recruit him to appear in the neighborhood shows the children cobbled together in a barn owned by the father of one of the boys. These shows, for which local youngsters lined up to pay one cent for admission, were quite ambitious, with Dannie and his friends writing scripts, building scenery, and even printing their own programs on a small printing press. "It was in such an environment that ... the taste for theatricals developed in me," Mason remembered. Years later he would recall with a certain pride that he was the only one of his childhood friends who "stuck to my guns and became a trouper," while the other amateur thespians went on to be bankers, newspapermen and lawyers.[2]

In the early 1860s, the elaborate entertainments staged by the children in the Grassmans' neighborhood served to distract the youngsters from the anxieties they felt with so many of their fathers, uncles, older brothers and cousins away from home, fighting in the Civil War. One of the twelve thousand men from Syracuse and the surrounding Onondaga County who served in the Union army was Jacob Grassman, a member of the Lafayette

Part One: Dan Mason on Stage

Grenadiers. After the war, Jacob returned to his work at the Excelsior Salt Mill, one of the many such firms making up the booming salt industry for which Syracuse was famous in those days. In May 1868, Jacob was severely injured by an accident at work and died two days later. Only fifteen years old at the time of his father's untimely death, Dannie Grassman was forced to grow up fast. With the family suddenly in dire financial straits and in danger of losing their house, he quit school to help his mother support the family. "At an early age I had to get out and hustle," he recalled. "I obtained a position in a drug store."[3]

At Kenyon and Porter's wholesale drug store, young Grassman's first job was the tedious but essential task of grinding compounds together with a mortar and pestle. He would work at this for several years, rise to the rank of a compounding chemist, and even consider at one point becoming a druggist himself. For recreation, in between working and helping his mother, the energetic teenager enrolled in a gymnasium. When the gym began to sponsor amateur shows, Dannie immediately volunteered to participate, elaborating on and refining the act he had once performed in his neighborhood barn shows. With the help of a friend who taught him a few dance steps, he began to spend every lunch hour, as well as those stray moments when the boss was away, in an empty room above the pharmacy improvising a song, dance, and story-telling sketch that was well received by all who saw it. "At these entertainments, I was pretty good," he later recalled. "At least my friends said so, … so I believed it."[4]

His salary, while modest, allowed Dannie Grassman to attend his first professional performances in real theaters, of which Syracuse had several. Along with the ubiquitous traveling minstrel companies that were popular attractions in such notable Syracuse venues as Shakespeare Hall or Wieting's Opera House, there were also many touring variety shows and in one of them he caught an act that helped point the direction of the rest of his life: The "Dutch" routine of comedian J.K. "Fritz" Emmett. Clad in a stereotypical German immigrant outfit that included knee breeches and wooden clogs, Emmett sang songs in fractured English, danced, and told stories in a "Dutch" dialect. As he peered down from the cheapest seats in the gallery high above the stage, Dannie watched in amazement as Emmett marched around the stage, singing his signature hit, "Ven I Valk Dot Broadvay Down," getting paid for doing that same kind of routine the aspiring young entertainer had long performed for free. Inspired and encouraged, it wasn't long before young Grassman had assembled his own "Dutch" outfit and begun perfecting his own dialect comedy act with an eye to making his debut on the stage. He didn't have long to wait.[5]

1. The Dutch Boy from Syracuse

Dannie Grassman's first break in show business came in the form of a traveling extravaganza called Washburn's Last Sensation, which arrived in Syracuse for a one-night stand in the late summer of 1872. The owner and proprietor of this large and ever-changing variety show with circus overtones was E.S. Washburn, a garrulous impresario who prided himself on finding and developing new acts. Unaware of Washburn's reputation as a talent scout beforehand, however, Dannie was actually surprised when the tall and imposing showman not only listened to the stage-struck youngster who approached him at the stage door but even arranged for an audition after the show. Impressed by what he saw and heard, Washburn asked the boy's age, then offered him a position in his company, so long as his mother approved.

Providing the lad with a list of his engagements for the next several weeks, Washburn told him to join up with the show on the road when he could. Both elated and apprehensive, Dannie rushed home to tell his mother who, predictably, reacted with horror and refused her permission. "Who could blame her?" Dan Mason recalled. "There I was, a young fellow in my teens, unsophisticated, knowing nothing of the world, wanting to take up an occupation tabooed by a large majority of people." In the end, after weeks of the sort of stubborn persistence Mason would come to be known for, Nancy Grassman reluctantly gave her consent, on one condition; her son must not disgrace his family by using their surname on stage. So it was that Dannie Grassman ventured forth into the limelight as "Dan Mason, the Dutch Boy from Syracuse."[6]

Totting a flimsy cardboard trunk with a change of clothes, Dan Mason boarded a train and caught up with the Washburn company in Binghamton, New York, in the fall of 1872. He was immediately sent to the theater to rehearse with the orchestra and there got his first dose of showbiz reality. "From the outside [the theater] had much the appearance of a livery stable," Mason remembered. "Inside, the auditorium was just a level floor with a gallery across one end." The footlights were kerosene lanterns.

That evening, as the orchestra played his cue and Mason made his entrance onto the low stage, he tripped over a scenery cleat he had not noticed in the dim light and fell. As he struggled to his feet, he momentarily forgot the words to his song and floundered badly before getting his bearings. Utterly demoralized, Dan ran back to the hotel and sat alone in his room, convinced he had made a terrible mistake in leaving home. It took all his courage to go down to breakfast in the morning and face Washburn and the rest of the dancers, gymnasts, ballad singers, Indians, and animal trainers who had not fallen on their faces the night before. To his surprise,

Part One: Dan Mason on Stage

his affable boss greeted him pleasantly and didn't seem at all annoyed at his disastrous debut. Taking him aside, Washburn demonstrated the skills he had used to develop many a previous young performer. Assuring the youngster, "I think you have it in you," he critiqued his routine, recommended rehearsals of dancing every day, and commented wryly that a trouper needs to learn "how to get on and off the stage."[7]

Traveling with Washburn's Last Sensation proved to be an ordeal but also a valuable education that Dan Mason would never forget. Whatever fantasies he might have once entertained about traveling the country as a stage performer, the reality was soberingly different. Very seldom did they play big cities with large theaters of the sort he was familiar with in Syracuse. Washburn specialized in bringing entertainment to small towns and remote communities where many of the performance venues were as bad as the hall where Dan made his awkward debut. A few were even worse. On occasion, they played houses that were no more than glorified saloons, with no footlights or scenery whatever on the simple platform they called a stage, and where the main point of the performers being there was to keep the crowd sufficiently entertained so they would stay longer and drink more. Leaving these concert saloons after the show, the male performers carried lanterns and made sure to accompany the girls in groups back to their hotel.[8]

Washburn's Last Sensation moved by rail when they could, but more often by wagon when their destinations were not accessible by train. As a newcomer and one of the younger members of the troupe, Mason was assigned a seat atop the bandwagon beside the driver as they traveled. In summer, when it rained, the wheels got mired in the mud on the unpaved roads. In winter, when it snowed, the wheels were replaced by runners so the struggling horses could drag the show to the next town. In the cold, Dan's feet would freeze, compelling him to jump down and jog alongside the rig to regain his circulation. Always a curious and careful observer, the youngster soon learned how to handle the reins himself and could give the teamsters a break when they got weary. Because of the horses and other animals, the show only stayed at "farmer's hotels" where both man and beast could be accommodated. The beds were cheap, stuffed with cornhusks (and, in one memorable instance, corn stalks), and often in short supply, requiring the performers to sleep two to a bed. Sanitation was primitive and in winter washing up sometimes meant breaking the ice atop the buckets of water set aside for that purpose in an unheated room behind the hotel manager's office. Everyone used the same "continuous" towel. Dan's salary for his first tour as a professional trouper was $10 a week (the modern

1. The Dutch Boy from Syracuse

equivalent of more than $200) plus room and board and transportation. He sent all of it home to his mother.[9]

Regardless of any inconveniences or difficulties the company encountered on tour, whether at theaters, hotels, or railway stations, E.S. Washburn proved endlessly resourceful, positive-minded and unflappable. Not only was he the consummate showman but a skilled diplomat as well, whose abilities to "quell any argument or dispute that arose in the company" Mason came to admire, and eventually emulate. In addition to providing sound advice regarding Mason's performances, the veteran showman would become a role model that served him well in later years when "Dan Mason and Company" toured the country and encountered similar situations.[10]

Making its way throughout New England, New York and Pennsylvania, the Washburn show often changed from one week to the next as entertainers and acts came and went from the company. Washburn had, in fact, hired Dan Mason partly because his previous German dialect comedian, George S. Knight, with the Last Sensation for several years, had abruptly gone off on his own. When the ever-morphing troupe included minstrels, the first act on the Washburn program was a minstrel show, with the now-infamous blackface routines which have long since been judged irredeemably racist but were considered the height of entertainment in the nineteenth century. After an intermission, the second act was an "olio," a series of variety acts that could include acrobats and trapeze artists, Irish clog and jig dancers, stand-up comedians in several dialects, contortionists, female impersonators, innumerable vocal offerings, dancing midgets, and an "Indian" princess of dubious

Dan Mason in 1873. When the twenty-year-old entertainer returned home to Syracuse after his first year of touring as a German dialect comedian, he was dressed in a stylish new set of clothes. His proud mother showed him off to the neighbors.

Part One: Dan Mason on Stage

heritage. It was in this part of the program that young Dan Mason did his German dialect songs, stories, and dance routines, accompanied by the company's orchestra. The third act of the show was always an "afterpiece," in which many if not all of the performers participated. Before the afterpiece, Washburn himself would make an appearance before the curtain (if there was one) in his most splendid attire, briefly address the audience and grandly announce the "laughable extravaganza" that his "excellent players" had devised for their pleasure.[11]

Dan Mason traveled with Washburn's Last Sensation for about a year. His reasons for leaving late in 1873 are unknown. Throughout his career, Mason would exhibit a fine instinct for knowing when to join and when to quit the various enterprises with which he became involved. Perhaps buoyed by his success on stage thus far, he decided to take his chances elsewhere. Returning to Syracuse, Dan was greeted by his mother with enthusiasm. In addition to his obvious success as an entertainer—he had sent home a substantial amount of money—he had been transformed. The teenager who left home pale and scrawny was now a bit taller, fleshed out thanks to the three robust meals a day he wolfed down at the farmer's hotels, and had good color from riding atop the band box in the open air. He was also well dressed, his sole indulgence with the money he had made. Nancy Grassman never again cast doubt on her son's career choice. In fact, she made a point of showing him off to the neighbors who had been talking behind her back about her scandalous son. "From then on, she was ever my champion," Dan wrote.[12]

2

The Trouper

His first taste of life as a traveling performer reinforced Dan Mason's decision to make entertainment his chosen profession and whetted his appetite for more. After a brief rest at home and reunion with friends, Mason was soon back on the stage, at first at several theaters in Syracuse where he took a kind of homecoming victory lap, and then back out on the road as a solo act. From watching Washburn he had gleaned the basics of booking appearances in advance. Armed with this knowledge, a parcel of railroad maps and train schedules, and his self-admitted tendency to "hustle," the novice entertainer always had something lined up weeks ahead. At first, however, getting a foot in the door required some resourcefulness:

> It was the custom then to book direct with managers. There were no booking agents collecting a percentage for so doing.... I found it a handicap in not being known, but it was overcome through the kindness and good fellowship that existed among the variety actors, and the willingness of managers to help along anyone who might make good. My fellow actors would endorse my letters or write to managers I wished to book with, when they knew them, recommending me. Or I would get the manager to endorse my letters. In that way I got through until I became known.[1]

With the memories of some of the dismal venues he found himself in while traveling with Washburn still vivid in his brain, Dan Mason made an effort to avoid the concert saloons and promote himself to actual theaters or some of the newly opened "Variety Halls." While still mostly catering to all-male audiences, many of these increasingly popular variety houses were beginning to host special matinees for the ladies, temporarily banishing the gentlemen and their cigars for an afternoon. This trend would continue and ultimately help usher in an era of "clean" vaudeville theaters where women and children were welcomed as regular patrons. That Mason had entered show business in the 1870s, when a movement to upgrade public entertainment was already underway, worked to his advantage. His reputation for performing a routine of "good clean fun," universal in its appeal, enhanced his marketability.[2]

Careers such as Dan Mason embarked upon in the second half of

Part One: Dan Mason on Stage

the nineteenth century were boosted by the rapid growth of the railroads and the telegraph, which spread across the continent in tandem, making it easy for entertainers to travel quickly to new bookings and communicate with theater managers hundreds of miles away. In his first year out as a solo act in 1874, the intrepid young Dutch comedian traveled more than fifty-five hundred miles by rail before coming home to Syracuse for a rest. By the time he settled in Hollywood in the mid–1920s, Mason had logged over four hundred thousand miles, a distance sufficient to circumnavigate the globe sixteen times. While he would eventually take advantage of the ever-improving Pullman sleeper cars when traveling long distances, in his youth Dan slept sitting up in his coach seat, unwilling to waste hard earned dollars on an actual sleeping berth.

Most theaters were illuminated by natural gas during the first twenty or so years of Dan Mason's career. Although the danger of fire was ever-present (literally hundreds of theaters burned down in the nineteenth century, including one in which Mason was scheduled to perform), gas lighting was standard equipment. By using a mounted set of stopcock valves and levers known as a "gas table," a forerunner of the modern switchboard, the house lights could be dimmed while the stage lights and foot lights (unless the latter were lime lights) were brought up. The gas fixtures had a tendency to hiss and flicker and the heat produced in a theater illuminated by hundreds of burning gas jets was considerable. In larger upscale theaters, it was sometimes the case that the rising heat was vented through openings in the ceiling or at the top of the walls, creating a draft that pulled cooler air in through vents lower down. Even in a house with good circulation, however, oxygen levels would fall and the temperature would rise considerably during a performance. The gas fumes combined with cigar and cigarette smoke and the various aromas emanating from the audience in an era of limited personal hygiene lent a distinctive atmosphere to the average theatrical experience. There was a good reason why so many theaters chose to go dark for the summer season.[3]

Similar in format to the shows Mason had already experienced on stage in Syracuse and while traveling with Washburn, the variety shows he joined on the road in the 1870s usually began with a minstrel or comedy sketch, followed by an olio in the second act, and concluded with an afterpiece. If the house had an orchestra, a musical prelude preceded each act. Surviving theater programs show that Dan often participated in all three acts, sometimes appearing on stage as many as four times in one evening. It was not unusual for his first stint of the night to be a blackface routine as one of the end men, "Mr. Bones" or "Mr. Tambo," singing and telling jokes

2. The Trouper

in the minstrel skit. But it was in the olios, and soon the afterpieces as well, that Dan Mason began to make a name for himself.

Billed variously as "the Popular Dutch comedian," "the great Teutonic comedian," "the Popular Dutch specialty artist," and several other variations on the same theme, Dan clattered out in front of the olio curtain in his wooden clogs on stages throughout the Midwestern, Middle Atlantic and New England states through the 1870s. Assuming the persona of a recently arrived German immigrant, he

Dan Mason's youthful ambition and hustle are evident in this 1878 variety playbill from The New National Theater in Hartford, Connecticut. Besides participating in the Minstrel Scene, he took the stage twice in the Olio—as a solo act and in his own skit, "The Dutch Agency"—and performed in the Afterpiece as well, appearing a total of four times in one evening. Note that he was also the stage director.

Part One: Dan Mason on Stage

offered up quaint viewpoints about the world around him. He reminisced about "der Faderland," told droll stories about the misadventures of fictitious friends and family, and recited humorous poems, some of which were original and others quite familiar to the audience, like his fractured version of Poe's "The Raven". He also sang witty songs in dialect, and danced as nimbly as his heavy wooden shoes would permit. Though he had never studied music, Dan personally wrote many of the songs he performed, indicating the melodies with letters that corresponded to the notes of the musical scale scribbled in the margins. House musicians, charged with the job of playing for newly arrived performers, cringed when presented with his latest "compositions."[4]

While he worked hard to perfect his dialogue, comic timing, and delivery, not all of the laughs Dan provoked were of his own making. On one occasion in Chicago, his scheduled slot in the olio came so soon after his role as "Mr. Bones" in the minstrel skit that he didn't have time to change clothes and remove his burnt cork makeup, leaving him no choice but to go on stage to do his Dutch routine in blackface. The leading entertainment trade journal of the day, *The New York Clipper*, dryly reported that he had performed "Dutch negro songs."[5]

During the olio, stagehands in carpet slippers quietly set up scenery and props behind the curtain, preparing for the show's concluding afterpiece. Most performers signing on to appear in variety halls and theaters were encouraged if not expected to appear in the afterpiece, though some were more adept than others at doing so. Taking the form of a broad farce that might lampoon a popular play or satirize current events, the afterpieces often had very loose scripts and might involve some improvisation on the part of the participants. From the start of his career, Dan Mason threw himself into these spirited affairs with enthusiasm and was much appreciated, by both the audiences and his fellow performers, for his quick-witted resourcefulness. In time his suggestions for stage business and comic dialogue came to be relied upon and he was increasingly asked to write up outlines and plots for new sketches. By 1876, his ability to craft clever afterpieces became, along with his German dialect routine, a valuable calling card when promoting himself to distant theater managers.

In early 1876, while on a swing through the south, Mason was stunned to find himself face to face with his alter ego in female attire. Miss Flora Frawley, German dialect comedienne, was a popular attraction on the stage of Myers' Opera House in Memphis, Tennessee, and had been receiving enthusiastic ovations night after night since her debut at age eighteen the previous year. How impressed Dan was with Miss Frawley's professional

2. The Trouper

talents and personal charms can be judged by the fact that, in short order, he not only suggested they combine their acts but also proposed marriage. Flora Frawley was happy to accept both offers and officially became Mrs. Dan Mason on March 28, 1876, in Little Rock, Arkansas.[6] By June they had perfected their new act and began making the rounds as "Dan and Flora Mason, Teutonic Comedians."

Unable to contain his excitement over what he considered his amazing good fortune, both professionally and personally, Mason took his young bride home to Syracuse to meet his family in July. Just what Nancy Grassman, or Dan's siblings, thought of the new Mrs. Mason is unknown, but when the young troupers took their new act onto the stage of Baries Opera House in Syracuse that summer, they were a big hit, with Flora singled out for special attention in the local press.[7]

For the rest of the summer and into the fall, the Masons, performing solo, together, and in Dan's afterpieces, played weeklong engagements in a series of theaters and variety halls throughout Ohio, Michigan, Illinois, and Indiana. In several cases they were invited back months or even weeks later to the same theaters, a sign that their efforts were well received and in demand. Even so, they occasionally found themselves living close to the edge. During a swing through the South, they arrived in New Orleans with just fifteen cents to their names only to find that the St. Charles Theater, where they were scheduled to perform, had suddenly closed. Dan left Flora in the hotel and made the rounds of the local concert saloons until he made sufficient money to get them to the next town. The couple finished out 1876 by opening a week's engagement on Christmas Day at the Theatre Comique in Toledo, Ohio.[8] With the New Year, it was back on the road, returning yet again to some of the theaters that had welcomed them months before and adding new stops in Ohio and Pennsylvania. It was a grueling schedule that left little time for anything but performing, rehearsing, booking engagements, consulting train schedules, and traveling on to the next stop. If being constantly in each other's company brought each a clearer understanding of the other's talents and performance quirks, their appreciation of each other as husband and wife does not seem to have advanced beyond their initial infatuation.

By the autumn of 1877, the partnership of Dan Mason and Flora Frawley Mason was faltering for reasons that are unclear. Did one or both of them come to the conclusion that they could do better professionally on their own? Did married life fail to provide a sense of security and support for their careers? Were they struggling financially? Was Flora's health, known in retrospect to have been failing, an issue? The abrupt end of their

Part One: Dan Mason on Stage

seemingly successful variety act, after only nineteen months on the road, raises all sorts of questions that can never be answered.

Dan and Flora Mason performed together for the last time at the Atlantic Garden Theater in Fort Wayne, Indiana, on October 20, 1877. When that gig was up, they parted company: Dan left for a new booking in Detroit, while Flora took the train to Chicago. The Two Teutonic Comedians would never meet again. In September 1878, while appearing at Crone's City Garden in Indianapolis, Dan Mason went to court and officially divorced Flora Frawley, quipping to a local reporter that he was now "a free Mason." Three months later, Flora Frawley Mason died of "consumption" in Kansas City, Missouri. She was only twenty-one years old. It is possible that neither one of them suspected that she was fatally ill while they were still performing together. Tuberculosis, undiagnosed and untreated, can prove fatal within a year's time. Dan likely learned of the former Mrs. Mason's passing via *The New York Clipper*, which published a death notice in January 1879. His reaction is unknown.[9]

Four months after the death of Flora Frawley, Dan Mason appeared onstage at Parmele's Novelty Theater in Louisville, Kentucky, with a new performance partner, the Irish actor and comedian, Dan Sully. The two men had met the previous November when they found themselves on the same

Dan Mason at age thirty in 1883. Early hair loss ran in the Grassman family and Dan began losing his hair at age twenty-one. As it turned out, his eventual baldness worked to his advantage as an actor. As he constructed his endless stream of new characters, it was easier to fake a full head of hair when needed than it was to convincingly fake a bald head.

2. The Trouper

program at the Coliseum in Cincinnati. Appraising each other's acts and appearing together in the afterpiece—one of Dan Mason's own sketches, *The Dutch Shoemaker*—the two dialect comedians quickly arrived at a mutual appreciation for each other's talents and began discussing a possible collaboration. After finishing out the commitments they had already made for early 1879, they agreed to meet up in Louisville for what was to be an extended partnership and long-term friendship.[10]

Born Daniel Sullivan in Rhode Island in 1855, Dan Sully made his show business debut at age seven, as an acrobat with a traveling circus. In 1875, at the age of twenty, he went on the stage as an Irish comedian, offering stories and songs in a broad Irish brogue. Though he had not yet begun to write any of the several plays for which he would eventually be famous, Dan Sully was, at the time of his first encounter with Dan Mason, widely known in the profession for a real life melodrama of his own making: In 1877 he seduced a young singer who followed him from town to town and subsequently killed herself when he rejected her.[11]

Beyond romantic disasters, the two Dans had much in common and enjoyed an easy personal chemistry both in person and on stage. Similar in stature and build (at least as youths; Sully would gain significant weight as time went on), both were for the most part self-taught, having received limited formal educations. Both had learned early on to keep their eyes and ears open and absorb what they could from other performers. Their respective stage performances were somewhat similar in that each man sang, danced, and told wry stories in a dialect. Both were resourceful and relentless in their pursuit of better spots on the program and better publicity on the playbills. There were differences, of course, and chief among them was a decidedly different approach to handling money that Dan Mason would eventually discover about his friend the hard way.

The first iteration of Mason and Sully as a team lasted from April 1879 till the end of 1880. During the twenty months they toured together, they performed their individual routines and also appeared together in the short afterpieces that were the focus of their collaboration. The program they played in Buffalo the last week of May 1880 was typical of the shows in which they appeared:

"Dan Sully in Irish songs and dances, etc.;
Foster and Hughes in Negro eccentricities;
Dan Mason in Dutch songs-and-dances;
Laura Bennett & Capitola Forrest in duets, medleys & skip-rope dances;
Raymond and Murphy in Irish songs and dances;
Lynn Sisters in songs and recitations;

Part One: Dan Mason on Stage

Mlle. De Granville in feats of strength;
W. Henry Rice in burlesque ballads and comical sayings..."

The program concluded "with a sketch called 'Unneighborly Neighbors' by the entire company with Messrs. Mason and Sully in the principal roles."[12]

Dan Sully's budding interest in writing afterpieces and plays, and his skill at doing so, were an inspiration to his performance partner. With his encouragement, Dan Mason advanced from writing quick spontaneous sketches to constructing longer, more structured and more ambitious farces. These one-act plays, featuring stereotypical Irish and German characters specifically designed to fit the talents of the two Dans, became an increasingly important part of their appeal as an entertainment team. The fact that the duo would arrive with a ready-made afterpiece, complete with scripts and necessary props, in addition to their own routines, often tipped the balance in their favor as distant theater managers made decisions for future bookings. Once their short plays began to garner positive reviews, and word went out that they had helped pack the house, the team of Mason and Sully found they had no trouble booking engagements well in advance. In some cases, they were able to stay multiple weeks in large cities. They packed them in for six weeks at Philadelphia's Grand Central Theater to close out 1879. Among those enjoying the show in Philadelphia was former president Ulysses S. Grant, for whom a special matinee was staged on December 20.[13]

In each new theater they played, the afterpieces took on new cast members, drawing from the bill of entertainers booked for that week. In addition to several of the vocalists appearing on the program, the cast might include the cross-dressing contortionist trapeze artist, the clog dancer who performed with a barrel over his head, or the forty-year-old midget who performed bicycle tricks dressed as a baby. In the afternoon before their evening performances, each participant would be handed a small hand-bound copy of his or her specific part, written out long hand and coded with the spoken cues they needed to respond to. With little time to learn their lines by heart, and largely unaware of the plot line of the piece since the only master copy of the whole script was in Dan Mason's possession and not easily accessible, many hapless thespians had no choice but to venture out on stage for the afterpiece reading from their scripts. Flubs were common and many of the best laughs were generated by one of the two Dans adlibbing to keep the plot moving along.[14]

As fragments of two plays—*The Crowded Hotel* and *Unneighborly Neighbors*—co-written by Mason and Sully have survived, it is possible to get a glimpse into the nature of their creative partnership as well as what

2. The Trouper

audiences enjoyed when the two Dans came to town. In *The Crowded Hotel* (the better preserved of the two) Dan Mason utilized his personal experiences as a traveling trouper and his keen observations about the kinds of people he encountered along the way to construct the circumstances of his play. Due to a shortage of hotel rooms, the two characters, Gottlieb Schoffer (Mason) and John Brady (Sully), are not only forced to share a room but a bed as well, a circumstance Mason had encountered more than once. The rapid-fire exchanges in dueling accents between the two unwilling roommates echoed Mason's memories of spirited disagreements between his German father and Irish mother. The immediate antipathy of the German and Irish characters reflected the chronic tensions among immigrant groups in late nineteenth century America and is framed in simple-minded and stereotypical terms of ethnic prejudice. The Irish character, John Brady, is immediately suspicious of the African American porter, Pete, and worries he will steal his valise. (See Appendix B for a reconstructed scene from this play.) As for his reaction to the German guest, Jacob Schofer, Brady tells the landlord: "If I sleep with that Dutchman I'll get up tomorrow morning and I'll be talking German, 'nix come a rouse from the Dutchman's house,' and 'wee gates' and all them kinds of things." He also advises the German to "go out and take a Turkish bath" before getting into bed. The mutual suspicion that fuels much of the comedy may also reflect Mason's occasional experiences on the road when some of the strangers he encountered in hotels or boarding houses made it clear that they had no time for "theater folk."[15]

An anecdote Mason liked to tell in later years was rooted in one of his several unpleasant encounters with fellow lodgers while on tour. Arriving in a small town in the Midwest, Mason found himself the only actor in a hotel filled with protestant ministers and deacons in town for a conference. The atmosphere was noticeably chilly when the entertainer was seated at the common table by the host. Noses went up and conversation ceased when it was learned that Mason was appearing in a local theater. At one point the actor asked the reverend closest to him to please pass the pepper. "Do you take me for a waiter, sir," the man sniffed in self-righteous indignation. "No," Dan sweetly replied. "I took you for a gentleman."[16]

In mid–December 1880, Mason and Sully, by then twenty-seven and twenty-five, closed out a two-week engagement at the Knickerbocker Theater in Louisville and, with the applause of the audience that had packed the house to see *The Crowded Hotel* still ringing in their ears, announced that they were dissolving their partnership. Dan Sully's desire to write longer and more serious plays was the likely reason for their cordial parting. For his part, Dan Mason was content for the moment to continue the trajectory

Part One: Dan Mason on Stage

of the previous year, performing his Dutch routines and writing new comic farces to cash in on the rising success of his and Sully's previous pieces. By now their two plays had received the ultimate compliment of being used in unauthorized performances, a circumstance that led the authors to

Daniel Sully (left) and Dan Mason in an unidentified afterpiece, c. 1880. The witty exchanges in dueling accents between their German and Irish characters echoed Mason's memories of spirited conversations between his immigrant parents. Mason and Sully would team up a second time in the 1890s.

2. The Trouper

copyright both *The Crowded Hotel* and *Unneighborly Neighbors* and to issue warnings against plagiarism in *The New York Clipper*. While he would craft many more skits, plays and scripts over the years, *The Crowded Hotel* would long be regarded by Dan Mason as one of his best efforts. Thirty years later, with a few adjustments, it would inspire the plot for one of his first motion pictures.[17]

Only a week after his final performance with Sully, Dan Mason was onstage with another Irish comedian, John D. Griffin, at the Theatre Comique in Providence, Rhode Island. To continue successfully marketing himself and his afterpieces required a partnership with an Irish comic who would learn the parts of the plays and who also had a polished dialect routine of his own. Griffin, who performed an act not unlike that of Dan Sully, with the added gimmick of impersonating an old Irish woman who sang ballads, fit the bill. His almost immediate hook up with Griffin suggests that as he and Sully discussed parting company, Dan Mason had hastened to look for and recruit another Irish comic.[18]

Mason's and Griffin's solo acts, and Dan's afterpieces, were so well received at the Theatre Comique in Providence that they were invited to stay for a forty-week engagement, during which they presented two of Dan's newly written farces, *Our Uncles*, and *All Fools' Day*. As with *The Crowded Hotel*, Dan Mason's *All Fools' Day*, a one-act play in five scenes, would thirty years later find its way onto the silver screen.[19]

The extended stay at the Theatre Comique also brought Mason a brief affair with a beautiful young woman named Mollie Wilson, a popular serio-comic vocalist. Miss Wilson, petite and shapely with quick movements and dark flashing eyes, was an audience favorite and had a reputation for being called back for two, three, and even four encores. She also had a keen talent for mischief, stirring up unwelcome melodrama everywhere she went. Six years earlier, Mollie had been dismissed from one theater for spreading vicious rumors about a romantic rival. She had also staged a bogus suicide attempt, which, after generating the publicity she craved, she totally denied. Having already divorced two husbands, one recently in Philadelphia the year before she met Dan, Mollie decided that their little fling in Providence rendered her eligible to become the second Mrs. Dan Mason. She even announced to *The New York Clipper* that the nuptials were imminent. The lessons learned from his impetuous marriage to Flora Frawley still fresh in his mind, however, Dan demurred.[20]

When their long engagement at the Theater Comique came to an end in November of 1882, Dan Mason, John Griffin, and the intrepid Mollie Wilson were all hired to perform their specialties and Dan's afterpieces in

Part One: Dan Mason on Stage

a combination show assembled by famed impresarios, Tony Pastor and Michael Bennett Leavitt. When the touring company reached Philadelphia, Mollie decided to save money on a hotel room by arranging a rendezvous with her ex-husband, Henry Harrison. In a fit of drunken jealousy, fueled in part by seeing Dan escort Mollie to the trolley stop after a performance, Harrison proceeded to shoot his ex-wife in the head. Fortunately for Mollie, Harrison's inebriated condition badly affected his aim and her wound proved superficial; she was back on stage again just a few months later, albeit with a wig artfully hiding her scar. This episode proved sufficient to end Dan's affair with Mollie Wilson once and for all.[21]

Leavitt and Pastor's interest in Dan Mason, John Griffin, and Mollie Wilson was likely based as much on Dan's afterpieces as on the individual routines of the three performers. Dan's sketches, which had evolved into short plays in several acts, were growing in popularity and receiving positive reviews. Tony Pastor, often cited as the "Father of Vaudeville" for his efforts to clean up variety and welcome women and children to his theaters, had an abiding interest in afterpieces but was reportedly finding it difficult in 1882 to find writers who could produce the pieces. During the six months that Mason and his fellow troupers stayed with the Leavitt-Pastor Combination, Dan's play *Dinkle and Maginty's Racket* was the featured afterpiece for the majority of the performances. When the ever-changing combination show—by now consisting of a dog circus, a trio of acrobats, and Professor Wallace the "Bird Man," in addition to the usual dancers, comedians and vocalists—played the Park Theater in Detroit in March 1883, *Dinkle and Maginty's Racket* was the hit of the evening. So much so, in fact, that Dan Mason's instinct for knowing when a better opportunity had come along kicked in and he was able to convince his Irish partner that they could make more money on their own. Leaving Leavitt and Pastor, the team of Mason and Griffin began booking their own appearances. They would tour together until the autumn of 1883.[22]

In September 1883, Dan Mason seized upon a major opportunity that redefined his career. Learning that Charles Atkinson, a Boston theatrical manager, was about to produce a musical comedy based on the popular stories by George Wilbur Peck, known collectively as "Peck's Bad Boy," Mason landed a major role in the upcoming show. Taking the part of Max Schultz, the beleaguered German Grocer perpetually tormented by the mischievous "Bad Boy," he created the first in the long series of stage characters for which he would become nationally famous.

Peck's Bad Boy, destined to become one of the biggest theatrical successes of the 1880s, hit the road in January 1884, with the premiere

2. The Trouper

performances given in the Chelsea Academy of Music, just outside Boston. The standing room-only crowd gave the play an enthusiastic reception and Mason's efforts were deemed a "decided success" by a critic for the *Boston Herald*. In particular, the burlesque ballet that his character, Schultz, performed with an Irish cop, "convulsed the audience, and was the cleverest hit of the evening." During the months that Dan Mason toured with the Atkinson production of *Peck's Bad Boy*, from Washington, D.C., through the deep south and back north again, he consistently garnered rave reviews everywhere they played. Comments like "Mr. Dan Mason ... gives a splendid characterization which approaches the artistic" and "[His] new Teutonic dance ... is an extravagantly funny example of the terpsichorean art" were typical of the reception Dan received.[23]

Mason's portrayal of Max Schultz would become the standard by which subsequent performances by other actors in that role would be judged. The nearly yearlong tour of *Peck's Bad Boy* ended in late June 1885, with a two-week engagement at the Sans Souci Theater in Providence, where the antics of the grocer and the incorrigible bad boy once again brought down the house.[24] Now "at liberty" for the first time in a year, Dan Mason hastened from Providence to New York City for a rendezvous with a lovely young singer and burlesque entertainer he had met while on tour the previous November. Her name was Millie La Fonte, and she was seven months pregnant with Dan Mason's child.

3

The Traveling Family Man

Millie La Fonte, whose real name was Millicent Page, was only about twenty-four in 1884, but had already been on the stage for over a decade. Born in San Francisco and orphaned before she reached her teens, Millie had survived by her wits, utilizing her good looks, a sweet singing voice, and a talent for using both. By 1874, she had been gathered into the protective embrace of the De Angelis Family, a troupe of San Francisco-based minstrel entertainers, with whom she toured the country for several years, appearing in a variety show that showcased her blossoming talents. Along with benefiting from the protection and performance coaching provided by her adoptive family, Millie suffered hard times with them, at one point being reduced to near starvation. In 1875, while traveling in a wagon across the prairie headed to California, the De Angelis troupe found themselves in a barren landscape devastated by a recent plague of grasshoppers that left the residents of the

Millie La Fonte (Millicent Page), c. 1880. One of the most popular serio-comic singers of the day, Millie appeared in variety and burlesque and was a featured performer in Sullivan and Hart's "Female Mastodons" touring extravaganza. The faded and battered appearance of this photograph is a sign of Dan Mason's devotion to his beloved second wife. He carried this portrait with him everywhere he went for forty-five years, from the time they met until the day he died.

3. The Traveling Family Man

many little farm towns uninterested in frivolous entertainments and unable to afford them in any case.[1]

By the time Millie La Fonte set out on her own in her late teens, she was tough, resourceful, and self-possessed to an extent that belied her diminutive size and charming smile, a fact that some found out the hard way. In 1882, while traveling on a train from Pittsburgh to Youngstown, Ohio, Millie leapt from her seat in the parlor car and scolded the formidable Civil War general and governor-elect of Massachusetts, Benjamin Butler, to his face when she witnessed Butler refuse to shake the hand of an amputee Union army veteran who approached him. When the press, much amused by this story, began to print the episode in papers all over the country, the chastened General Butler wrote Millie a note of apology, sent her his photograph, and made sure his act of contrition was reported to the press.[2]

In the year just before she met Dan Mason, Millie La Fonte traveled with Sullivan and Hart's Female Mastodons, a combination minstrel show and burlesque extravaganza that substituted lovely ladies on velvet swings for the standard blackface comedians. Traveling to each new engagement by train, it was the usual practice of the Female Mastodons to herald their arrival in town with a parade from the station to the theater where they were scheduled to perform. A brass band led the entire company in costume, which in the case of the girls consisted of nothing more than form-fitting pink tights. The sight of these scantily clad beauties in broad daylight was often the very first lesson in sex education that local adolescent boys received. A poem "Dedicated to Millie La Font," in an 1884 newspaper clipping saved by Millie in her scrapbook, reflects the show's heavy reliance upon the voyeuristic appeal of the young beauties:

> Who's that young lady passing by
> With charming beauty and golden hair,
> Whose gorgeous style and fancy gait
> Would cause your heart to stare?
> A youth stood by on a cracker box
> In a choking voice responds—
> You bet your life she's a fly young gal,
> She's one of the female mastodons![3]

Beyond the fact that they must have conceived their child in mid–November 1884, it is impossible to determine exactly how and where Dan Mason and Millie La Fonte might have met. The movements of both popular entertainers were well documented in *The New York Clipper* as they moved from one engagement to another in the early 1880s, with both of their names

Part One: Dan Mason on Stage

often mentioned on the same page. However, finding a time when the two troupers were even in the same state, let alone in the same city or theater, has proven problematic. A close reader of every week's new issue of the *Clipper*, Mason may well have heard of Millie La Fonte years before meeting her in person. She was well known throughout the United States, enough so that by 1884 Millie's photo was being used in Opera Puff and Little Beauty cigarette advertisements and her portrait, seated on a velvet swing, would soon appear in the illustrated book *Theatrical and Circus Life*.[4]

In the months immediately following his fateful tryst with Millie La Fonte, Dan continued his tour with *Peck's Bad Boy*, while simultaneously writing another play, *The Tigers*, and recruiting a cast to perform in it when the tour ended. For her part, Millie spent the holiday season of 1884 touring the South, where gold and diamonds were lavished upon the popular singer as New Year's gifts. She then traveled north to Minnesota for an extended engagement in St. Paul's Theatre Comique. It was during her three-month stay at the Comique that Millie realized she was pregnant and somehow got word to Dan Mason.

In contrast to the somewhat cavalier attitude he had displayed toward both Mollie Wilson and the unfortunate Flora Frawley, Mason took full responsibility for Millie's situation and suggested they meet up in New York City, when their scheduled commitments ended, to await the birth of their child. On August 29, 1885, Millie La Fonte gave birth to a baby boy. The couple named him Daniel Mason Grassman. Two days later, using their given names, Daniel Grassman and Millicent Page were married at New York's City Hall.[5] Despite the haphazard circumstances of their beginnings as a couple, Dan and Millie Mason would prove to be remarkably devoted spouses for thirty-four years.

With the birth of her son, the newly minted Millicent Mason withdrew from show business for a time to devote herself to her new roles as wife and mother. When Dan Mason headed out on tour with a new play only three weeks after his son's birth, Millie remained behind in Manhattan. In October, while her husband was in Kansas, performing in his new play, *The Tigers*, Millie took baby Dannie to a photographer for a portrait. She inscribed the back "to my Papa from Dannie," and mailed it to her husband as a memento of the family he now had waiting for him back home.

To appear opposite him in *The Tigers*, Dan Mason enlisted yet another Irish comedian, John T. Kelly. Described by reviewers as a "mass of music, dancing, and nonsense," and "a string of wild absurdities," *The Tigers*, like so many of Dan Mason's plays, revolved around misunderstandings among a group of strangers staying in a boarding house, in this case a resort located

3. The Traveling Family Man

at the seaside. The plot, such as it was, primarily sufficed as an excuse for a series of variety acts. It was Mason's most ambitious production to date and the troupe traveled with a suite of special scenery and at least one mechanical effect—"Dizzy, the Dancing Elephant." Included in the cast, as *The Tigers* toured through the fall and winter of 1885, was one Edwin ("Eddie") Foy. Not yet famous but destined to become a vaudeville and Broadway legend, Foy played an English detective and a Chinese laundryman. His dancing was praised on more than one occasion. *The Tigers* played twenty-one cities from Boston to Topeka, logging four thousand miles in the space of four months. By the end of the year, however, Mason realized he had been making more money with *Peck's Bad Boy*, abandoned *The Tigers*, and quickly went back to playing the excitable grocer Max Schultz.[6]

To put into context the frequent and rapid pivots Dan Mason made from one show to another and back again, one must keep in mind the extent to which he was a self-made man who came from meager circumstances. Mason was always haunted by the memory of the frightening aftermath of his father's sudden death, when the family of six found themselves with no income and on the verge of being evicted from their home. Dan's lifelong frugality and relentless no-nonsense quest for more money was rooted in that experience; he was determined to never again find himself or his family in such desperate straits. He had no formal education beyond the eighth grade, a fact reflected in the many spelling errors in his letters and hand-written manuscripts. There had been no training in the theatrical arts he now pursued. There had been no dancing teachers, no music instructors, no voice or dialect coaches, and no one, aside from Dan Sully, himself a novice writer, to guide his efforts as a would-be author. He had only his keen talent for mimicry which served him well all his life as he watched, listened, learned, applied and even appropriated the examples of other performers whose skill and success he admired or envied. Furthermore, he had nothing else to fall back on. Any opportunity for ongoing income had to be seized without hesitation before it was lost in a robustly competitive business. On occasion, even after appearing in a long running play as the featured star, Mason had no qualms about temporarily going back to variety performances in a third-rate theater to keep the dollars flowing in. As he himself once put it: "The actor who is not above carrying his art into the common affair of life need never walk the ties or make precarious tours on freight trains."[7]

The Atkinson Company, still touring with *Peck's Bad Boy*, was more than happy to welcome back the prodigal groceryman. The first stop on Dan Mason's third tour as Max Schultz was Chicago, and this time he

Part One: Dan Mason on Stage

decided to take Millie and infant son Dannie along rather than be separated from them for another extended period of time. However, if the rigors of a long train trip in winter were hard enough on Millie, who was now expecting their second child, they proved fatal to the Masons' baby. Tragically, on February 11, 1886, while *Peck's Bad Boy* was playing at Grenier's Lyceum Theater in Chicago, little Dannie Mason Grassman died of pneumonia in his parents' hotel room. He was just over five months old.[8]

Faithful to the long standing creed of troupers—"The show must go on!"—Dan Mason performed the night of Dannie's death, cavorting, mugging, singing and dancing, giving the audience the full measure of what they paid to see. A day later, heartbroken, he left the show so that he and Millie could accompany their child's remains back to New York for burial. As Dan and Millie Mason returned to their modest New York apartment after the funeral, dazed and demoralized, taking time off to grieve was not an option. Within days, Dan Mason was in rehearsal for the part of Captain Dietrich in a revival of the celebrated 1874 musical comedy *Evangeline, or the Belle of Arcadia*, then enjoying one of its longest and most successful runs at the Fourteenth Street Theater in Manhattan. Though the popular farce, often cited as the first widely successful American musical comedy, was slated to go on the road in May, stepping into the local production in March allowed Dan two precious months to spend at home with his grief stricken and pregnant wife. It also brought Dan Mason's name to Broadway for the first time.[9]

Mason's evocation of Captain Dietrich is the first of his roles for which we have specific details of the costume and makeup he employed in crafting a character, a talent for which he would ultimately gain considerable recognition both on stage and in the movies. As with his many other theatrical skills, Mason's proficiency with the craft of costuming and makeup had been acquired by observing and consulting fellow performers in the dressing rooms and experimenting in his hotel rooms. In a play that often included the spoofing of current events, it had become customary for any actor playing Dietrich to disguise himself as General Benjamin Butler, or at least the popular newspaper cartoon versions of Butler's facial features, and Mason followed suit, using as his guide the photograph that the embarrassed general had sent to his critic Millie La Fonte five years earlier. The *Chicago Tribune* wrote: "He distorts his shapely nose with French paste until it looks like the nasal organ that comic artists accredit to Mr. Butler. Then he places small bladders under the eyes, and over the lids he places pieces of pasteboard...." Mason was pleased enough with the final results—prosthetic hooked nose, hooded eyes, moustache, and partial wig—that he

3. The Traveling Family Man

had himself photographed in costume and makeup while playing the part of Dietrich in Chicago later that year. It was the first of his roles to be photo documented.[10]

In May 1886, after completing a record run in New York, *Evangeline* began its road tour in Philadelphia, accompanied by a train car loaded with musical instruments, costumes, elaborate scenery, and the apparatus for several scenic effects, including a balloon ascension. Mason was with the show for fourteen months altogether, most of it on the road. It was one of his longest associations with any production. In June 1886, while performing at Hooley's Theater in Chicago, where *Evangeline* packed the house for a record one hundred two nights, Dan received a telegram from Millie telling him that she had given birth to their second child, a boy they named Clinton Winford Mason. He would not meet his new son until the show returned to New York City ten months later in April 1887.[11]

On the road, the weekly schedule of performances every night and matinees on Wednesday and Saturday allowed ample time for Dan Mason to scrutinize the latest issue of *The New York Clipper* in search of new potential opportunities, write letters (at least one a day to Millie), send telegrams, and most importantly, write up his latest ideas for new plays. A man whose idea of a good time was one beer after the show and early to bed, Mason rose early every morning and made good use of his unencumbered hours. That he had been busy writing during the long run of *Evangeline* became evident as the show neared the end of its tour in May and reports began to surface in the press that Mason planned to "star" the next season in his own three-act comedy, *The Sideshow by the Seaside*. However, this play and four others trotted out in late 1887 and early 1888 failed to gain any traction and were soon abandoned, forcing Mason to return briefly to the vaudeville stage with his German dialect routine.[12]

Meanwhile, despite the fact that her son Clinton was only two years old, and had recently suffered a bout of serious illness, Millie, now billing herself as Millicent Page, was eager to resume her career, spend time with her husband, and not incidentally, add her income stream to the couple's finances. Though Dan is on record as having "put aside some money" by this time, Millie shared her husband's chronic sense of insecurity when it came to money. In August 1888, the Masons found an excellent opportunity for both of them, securing the leads in a touring production of *Over the Garden Wall*, a popular 1884 musical farce by Scott Marble. Under the management of vaudeville impresario F.F. Proctor, who had just begun to build his legendary circuit of clean and inexpensive theaters, *Over the Garden Wall* had been making the rounds for four years before Dan and Millie took

Part One: Dan Mason on Stage

over the starring roles. They would tour in *Over the Garden Wall* for nearly a year, following a hectic schedule that often saw them playing in as many as four towns in five days.[13]

Playing the part of Julius Snitz, a "poet-politician and husband" who hates babies and is driven to drink by chaos surrounding the surprise appearance of his nephew's child in his home, Mason received mostly good reviews for his efforts. For her part, Millie's return to the stage also received favorable comment. However, even as he and Millie played their new parts for the first time in Manhattan's Novelty Theater, Dan Mason had begun to plan for the next show that would inevitably follow when *Over the Garden Wall* had run its course. With two solid incomes now expanding his bank account, Mason decided this might be an ideal time to "break into the theatrical producing line" and become his own boss by forming his own troupe in which he would serve as producer, director, writer and featured actor. Accordingly, he spent most of the eleven months that he and Millie toured with *Over the Garden Wall* rewriting *The Tigers*, adding among other things a flamboyantly gay character called "Pansy" and renaming the play *A Clean Sweep*. Putting together the team he would need to take the show on tour, Mason engaged seven more cast members, several of whom would play multiple parts. He also hired a business manager/advance man to do the bookings, as well as a musical director, a properties manager, and a lithographer to handle the production of playbills. Based on the reception he was getting from the audiences in Proctor's theaters, Dan was able to convince Proctor to send the ambitious production of *A Clean Sweep* out on his theater circuit when the tour of *Over the Garden Wall* came to an end in July 1889.[14]

After a scant two weeks of rehearsals and preparations, *A Clean Sweep* made its debut on August 26, 1889, at the Lyceum Theater in Brooklyn. Following the successful format of *Evangeline* and nearly every other musical farce on the road at that time, the plot merely served as an excuse to present humorous exchanges and a string of variety entertainments. The thin story line involved a hotel where a mischievous waiter mixes up people and room numbers until "every man imagines that his wife belongs to somebody else, and every woman is in doubt whether she is married to her own husband or to some other lodger." In one scene, much enjoyed by several critics, Dan Mason's character, Julius Winkle, believing himself to be climbing into bed with his wife, encounters the whiskers of another male guest who has been tricked into the wrong room. Millie's waltz with "Dizzy," the dancing elephant, was also a crowd pleaser.[15]

A Clean Sweep played for two seasons. The first tour, starting in the

3. The Traveling Family Man

fall of 1889, met with limited success. Dan Mason's antics as Winkle were consistently applauded and praised, with a Philadelphia critic stating that "Mason is taking a very high place among the interpreters of farce comedy," but the overall show itself was often found wanting. "With all due respect to Mr. Mason," the *Kansas City Globe* pointedly observed, "the sooner he gets some play better than 'A Clean Sweep' the better off he will be in pocket and reputation." With mixed reviews and low turnout on occasion, the expense of the show was not matched by ticket sales. Nevertheless, after the summer hiatus of 1890, during which both Dan and Millie played vaudeville in the summer park circuit to keep the dollars flowing in, *A Clean Sweep* ventured out for a second season in the fall of 1890. Despite advertising "new songs, new dances, new faces, new specialties," the show did not generate interest equal to the hype, and the box office continued to suffer. Within the first month of the second tour, Mason found it expedient to conserve his resources by withholding payments to his cast and crew. They soon revolted. In Newark, New Jersey, the constable was called to the Opera House to stop the show and attach the box office receipts, forcing Mason to pay his disgruntled thespians. One account of this episode suggested that there was more than just financial discontent within the cast. Ever devoted to his beloved Millie, Dan was giving her such prominence in the show that others felt eclipsed. The fact that Millie, described the previous year as "pretty and plump," had more recently been criticized as "too robust for her part," may have fueled the perception that Dan Mason's leadership of the troupe was not always based on sound judgment.[16]

A Clean Sweep cut short its second season and closed in Harlem in mid–January 1891, amidst reports that "the company had been playing to poor business for some time." Decades later, Dan Mason would recall with his customary ironic humor that his attempt to break into the world of theatrical production had resulted in a "clean sweep" of his bankroll. However, if he was discouraged by the *Clean Sweep* misadventure, he would not be for long. Within a year, he would launch an even more ambitious production. This one, however, would not only end in disaster but tragedy as well.[17]

Three days after the final performance of *A Clean Sweep* in Harlem, Dan Mason stepped onto the stage of the Theatre Vendome in Nashville, Tennessee, joining the cast of Lew Rosen and Scott Marble's musical farce *The Hustler*. With his usual nimbleness, and constant scanning of *The Clipper* for new opportunities, Dan had scored another substantial role for himself in a major production even as he stumbled along in the ruins of his own self-destructing venture. In *The Hustler*, a tale of an Irish con man living in a New York hotel, Mason assumed the part of Aniser Busch, a German

Part One: Dan Mason on Stage

capitalist who gets snookered by the title character. The sudden presence of Dan Mason in the show gave the play, which had been losing patronage, a substantial boost at the box office. The press celebrated Mason's appearance in the cast. Typical of the reception Dan got was the critic in Pittsburgh who wrote approvingly that Mason's "facial expressions had simply captivated the audience," and, somewhat tellingly, that he had "made more of the part than was intended when the play was written."[18]

One measure of Mason's success with German characters is the fact that as many times as he created a new persona for a play, each was distinctive and different in some way from the rest. He not only created new costumes and makeup but new physical and vocal mannerisms as well, and gave each character his own distinctive set of facial expressions. It is worth noting that while Dan's performances over the years were not without criticism by those reviewing his shows (some thought that his singing voice was not exactly the greatest and others complained of his tendency to milk some routines for more than they might be worth), not once in his forty years onstage did anyone complain that the characters he portrayed were derivative or stale or reminiscent of any previous effort.

Just how popular Dan Mason had become as an entertainer was made clear when *The Hustler* reached Philadelphia in March 1891. Despite sheets of rain gusting through the streets on the night of March 9, the venerable Walnut Street Theater was packed to the rafters. Inside the gas-lit theater, where the likes of Edwin Forrest and Edwin Booth had once trod the boards, a capacity crowd overflowed into the aisles and stood twenty deep at the back of the balcony. As soon as Dan Mason stepped onto the stage in the first act, his entrance touched off such a sustained roar of applause and laughter that the actor had to pause in place and wait for the uproar to die down before he could begin his lines. The fact that he had adjusted his wig, whiskers, and makeup so as to resemble the mayor of Philadelphia, Edwin Henry Fitler, helped prolong the enthusiastic reception he received.[19]

The Philadelphia press was as receptive as the audiences during Dan's run at the Walnut Street Theater, interviewing him and publishing some of the humorous anecdotes he relayed. While not all the reviews were enthusiastic—in Buffalo a critic sniffed, "'The Hustler' is a variety hash ... composed largely of warmed over fragments"—the show proved a hit in most venues they played and Dan stayed with the show until the end of the season in May.[20]

When the five-month run of *The Hustler* came to an end, Mason immediately returned to his dream of breaking into the big time with his own production. Determined to achieve recognition as an uber-versatile

3. The Traveling Family Man

performer who could write, direct, and act in his own work, and undaunted by the difficulties and financial losses he had suffered with *A Clean Sweep* only twenty weeks before, Dan began assembling an even more ambitious production he called *An American Boy*. Hoping to avoid some of the logistical and personnel issues he had encountered with his previous venture, Dan put the business and managerial duties for the planned tour in the capable hands of George W. Heath, the agent/manager who handled Mason and Kelley's 1885 tour with *The Tigers* and after that guided the Atkinson company of *Peck's Bad Boy*. While *An American Boy* was a typical musical comedy of the sort popular at the time, it was decidedly different from Dan Mason's previous attempts at writing comedies. Instead of his usual hectic and thinly plotted farce based on mischief and mistaken identities in a hotel/boarding house/resort, and intended for adult audiences, Dan contrived a more defined and plausible plot that he described as "full of clean fun from beginning to end." Set in a country store in New Jersey, the story line involved an unmarried German grocer, Peter Blatz (played by Mason), who also serves as the village postmaster. The title character, Johnny Potts, a fifteen-year-old boy who hangs out at the store and helps out on weekends, is described as a "good natured lad." However, while the boy "does not lie or steal, he is not a goody goody boy, but a bright manly fellow who is ever ready for fun and frolic." As the story plays out, with some romantic sidebars, and the temporary disappearance of a large sum of money, it is revealed that young Johnny, the adopted son of the Widow Potts, is actually the long-lost nephew of Peter Blatz. In the end, Blatz marries the widow and Johnny becomes his son as well.[21]

One reason for Mason's strenuous emphasis, in every advertisement, on the wholesome and appealing nature of the "American Boy," Johnny Potts, was that this show was to mark the stage debut of his own five-year-old son, Clinton.[22] Though provided with only a simple walk-on part with no lines for his first appearance as a novice trouper, Clinton would be immersed in the show night after night. Like most children, the boy could be relied upon to start repeating the lines he heard, especially if they got laughs, and his father wanted to make sure that the boy saw and heard nothing "improper."

Dan's new show was assembled in Boston, George Heath's home base, with two weeks of rehearsals beginning on August 9, 1891. After a debut in Concord, New Hampshire, on August 17, and two weeks of trial runs before packed houses and excellent reviews in New England, Heath sent the company of *An American Boy* to the Midwest for a tour that started in Chicago, then headed for Kansas, Iowa, Nebraska, and Utah. Shrewdly

Part One: Dan Mason on Stage

keeping the show mostly in "popular price" houses that catered to middle- and low-class audiences, Heath heavily advertised the imminent arrival of the show and emphasized that "women and children are welcome." Though these tactics managed to generate packed houses, there were, tellingly, very few reviews afterward and those that were published were not exactly encouraging. One Iowa paper suggested that "the show had some redeeming features, but only a few and needed all it had," while a snide Chicago critic dryly observed "a fair audience bore the piece patiently." By late November *An American Boy* was reported to have "died" in Sterling, Idaho, and scattered notices of the show's cast members being "at liberty" began to appear in *The New York Clipper*. A short time later, Dan and Millie were reported to be back on stage performing their old variety acts.[23]

Nothing if not determined, and with his professional reputation on the line, Dan Mason defiantly and stubbornly planned a reduced budget revival of *An American Boy*, which he would manage himself, to be staged at Salt Lake City's Wonderland Theater, in the spring. He had invested too much time, energy, emotion, ego, and money to give it up. The plan was to arrive in Salt Lake City in March and present variety shows at Wonderland for a month while recasting and rehearsing *An American Boy* for its Utah debut. All the while they would aggressively advertise and try to build anticipation for the opening of Dan's extravagant musical comedy, which was now to include a circus parade featuring Dizzy, the reconfigured dancing elephant. With the entire original cast of the show gone on to other shows, Dan prevailed upon his stalwart Millie, now five months into her third pregnancy and more "robust" than ever, to take a leading role and filled in the rest of the parts with members of the Wonderland's resident stock company.[24]

Opening night for the weeklong stand of *An American Boy* was set for April 14, 1892, and ads and press releases were sent to all of the city's major newspapers. Dan looked forward to getting his show back on track. However, the show would not be presented as scheduled. During a grueling thousand-mile trek from Omaha to Salt Lake City in March, a two-day plus ordeal by train through the Rockies, Dan and Millie's son, Clinton, became seriously ill with a bladder infection. By the time the Masons arrived at the Valley House Hotel in downtown Salt Lake City, the boy was in such serious condition that the local doctor was summoned. He could offer no hope. As the child lingered near death, the first performances of *An American Boy* were postponed. On April 17, 1892, Clinton Mason, five years and ten months old, died of uremic poisoning.[25]

This time there was no talk of "The show must go on." All performances of *An American Boy* in Salt Lake City were cancelled. The musical

3. The Traveling Family Man

Clinton Winford Mason at age five, c. 1891. After losing their first son, Dannie, Dan and Millie hoped that their second boy, Clinton, would follow in their footsteps on the stage. Dan even included a part for him in his production of *An American Boy* in 1892. Clinton's sudden death only months after this photograph was taken left his parents devastated.

comedy Dan had written with his little son in mind would never be performed again. In the aftermath of her son's death, Millie suffered a complete collapse. Heartbroken and fearing for the mental and physical well being of his distraught and pregnant wife, Dan had the undertaker store

Part One: Dan Mason on Stage

Clinton's remains in a temporary vault in Salt Lake City until such time as he could arrange to ship the coffin back east for burial. Dan and Millie headed south to Galveston, Texas, where Dan hoped the peaceful atmosphere of a hotel overlooking the Gulf of Mexico would help them both recover their senses.[26]

4

The Two Dans

In August 1892, four months after the death of their son Clinton, Millie gave birth to the Masons' third child in New York City. She named the little boy Harry Grassman Mason. As she had after the birth of Clinton some six years earlier, Millie sent a telegram to Dan, informing him of the new baby's safe arrival. Two thousand miles away, in Montana with the Daniel Sully Company, Dan Mason was appearing in two of Sully's popular plays, *Daddy Nolan* and *The Millionaire*. He would not see Millie or meet his new son for eleven months.

Having lost money on the financial disaster that was *An American Boy*, and with no other immediate source of income, Dan and Millie had found themselves forced to make a difficult choice when they returned to New York after the death of Clinton. A timely and generous invitation from Dan Sully, now a successful playwright, for Dan Mason to join his company on tour, offered not only financial security for a time but an opportunity as well for Mason to restore some of his professional reputation that had suffered in the debacle of his own show. However, Sully's tour began in July and headed west for the better part of a year. This meant that Millie, still grieving for her recent loss, would have to face another childbirth without the close support and comfort of her husband. In the end, with no comparable professional prospects to be found in New York, Dan accepted Sully's offer.[1]

Daniel Sully (as he now styled himself) and Dan Mason had experienced an unexpected reunion in March 1892, when both of their touring companies wound up performing in St. Joseph, Missouri, during the same week. The spirited dinner conversations they enjoyed that week helped pave the way for the two Dans to team up once again. During the twelve years since they had last seen each other, Sully had achieved national recognition as an actor and playwright, appearing in six new plays of his own authorship. He had also achieved a bit of notoriety when he was arrested on stage at Tony Pastor's Theater in New York during a performance, charged

Part One: Dan Mason on Stage

by his first wife with abandonment and desertion. Though much reported in the press, the episode doesn't seem to have diminished his appeal in the eyes of the theater-going public.[2]

Both of the "serio-comic" musical plays Sully took out on the road for his seven- thousand-mile, ten-state, cross-country tour in 1892—*Daddy Nolan* and *The Millionaire*—had German dialect parts that were perfect for Dan Mason. Sully had recruited his old friend knowing he was capable of enriching both roles. Neither Sully nor his audiences were disappointed. In *Daddy Nolan*, Mason played a German newspaper editor, Frederick Eichler, a portrayal that, with his eccentric dancing during one song routine, often won him more applause than anyone else in the play. In *The Millionaire*, a drama about the building of a railroad, Mason played Baron von Steinberger, a scheming German businessman. Of his rendering of the Baron, the *Duluth Evening Herald* wrote, "Dan Mason has the most difficult role and takes it well," while *The Detroit Free Press* called his efforts "one of the most artistic bits of acting which the local stage has offered this season" and praised his "perfect dialect, quiet humor, and admirable characterization."[3]

This tour with Sully brought Mason for the first time into a series of upscale theaters that had recently replaced their gas lighting systems with electric. Starting in the early 1880s, the overall transition to electrical theater lighting in America was erratic and fraught with alarming episodes like bursting bulbs and inexplicable mid-performance blackouts, but once it began, it was inexorable. While many of the popular price houses would take years more to acquire the funding needed to make the switch, the bigger theaters in larger towns and cities were mostly electrified by the early 1890s. The transformation wrought by electric theater lights was for the most part welcomed by theater managers, audiences, and entertainers alike. Not only were the theaters safer, cooler, and fresher, but the stage and everything on it could now be seen more clearly then ever before. Traveling troupes used to performing in gaslight often found it necessary to make adjustments when confronted with this new modern technology; cheap or shabby scenery had to be upgraded and makeup reevaluated. The kinds of grease paint enhancements formerly needed to make a face visible to the back row, when viewed in gaslight, now appeared grotesque to the denizens of the first row who saw the faces illuminated by electric.[4] For Dan Mason, whose makeup kit had morphed into a small trunk that grew heavier each season, such adjustments were just one more improvisation.

By now Mason was commanding a princely salary for his talents, enough so that in one instance the cost of hiring him was used as a promotional gimmick. From notes Mason kept throughout the yearlong tour with

4. The Two Dans

Sully, we know that Sully paid his co-star $65 a week for his efforts, a comfortable amount of money in an era when the average factory worker was lucky to make a dollar a day. In today's money, his salary would equate to approximately $1800 a week or about $95,000 a year. Most of this money was wired back to New York City where Millie, after meeting her household expenses, salted the rest of it away in their savings account. If Dan's prolonged absence from his family was fraught with hardships for all concerned, there was at least the consolation that it was worth it, financially. It came as a great disappointment, therefore, and a major annoyance when towards the end of the tour Sully found himself increasingly unable to make payroll. He was a month behind when the company gave their final performances in Providence in late May and handed his featured player a promissory note for his back wages in the amount of $250 (about $6000 in today's money). Since the show had been doing well, it was not easy to explain where the money had gone. While Sully's talents as an actor, playwright, and impresario had greatly expanded over the years, his ability to manage his theatrical company as a business had not kept pace. Financial problems would increasingly plague Daniel Sully in the years to come.[5]

While the promissory note was satisfied within five months as promised, the unwelcome disruption to his income stream discouraged Dan Mason from venturing out on Sully's next tour in the fall of 1893. Instead, as he spent the summer with Millie and his new son, Harry, in New York, Dan teamed up with Irish comic Dan Kelley to appear in W.C. Anderson's production of *Jolly Old Chums*, another musical comedy devoid of plot and justified by wisecracks, beautiful girls, splendid costumes, and clever "specialties." Their four-month, six-thousand-mile tour of mostly one-night stands took them to Oregon and back again, only to grind to a premature halt in February 1894 when Anderson found himself unable to meet his payroll. Another similar venture followed that fall, with Mason as the featured and much heralded star of *Duffy's Blunders*, another farce offering "new music, new songs, new dances, new funny lines and situations," but no plot. *Duffy's Blunders* played the East Coast and Midwest until the two co-authors had a major falling out that led to the dissolution of their partnership and the cancellation of the show.[6]

The abrupt end of these two shallow confections, which had permitted Dan Mason no artistic input or control and did nothing for his professional reputation, led him back to Daniel Sully once again in September. Joining the road tour of Sully's newest comedy, *A Social Lion*, Mason took up the role of an eccentric German newspaper editor, to almost immediate stellar reviews. The reunion of the two old friends caught the attention of the *St.*

Part One: Dan Mason on Stage

Paul Globe during their successful two-week engagement in the twin cities. Their enduring friendship, as well as their individual and joint careers, were recounted in glowing terms. A week later it was reported that the two Dans were once again collaborating on a new play. Significantly, as both auteurs sought to expand their professional horizons, the new work would be a play and not another musical comprised of fluff glued together by a mindless plot. After a long dry spell, punctuated by frustration and tragedy, Dan Mason felt that his life was back on track, and not just professionally.[7]

While it is unknown whether Millie traveled with Dan as he toured in *Jolly Old Chums* and *Duffy's Blunders*, we know that she and their very healthy three-year-old son, Harry, accompanied him when he went back on the road with Sully in September. In October 1895, during their extended stay in Minneapolis/St. Paul, Millie became pregnant with her fourth child. The tour of *A Social Lion* took the Sully/Mason troupe across the continent to Oregon and California. Along the way, Dan Mason, who apparently wrote most of the new play, *A Day in June*, finalized his work. The company then began rehearsals, intending to cautiously debut the new comedy in a remote location: Anaconda, Montana. The play, which recycled some of the same elements the two had used with success twenty years before in *All Fool's Day*—erroneous impressions, amorous widows, and misplaced babies in a fashionable boarding house—was well enough received to be added to their repertoire. Under a new title, *A Bachelor's Wives*, the comedy was performed in Sacramento and San Francisco as part of a trilogy that included Sully's plays *Daddy Nolan* and *A Social Lion*. That these and subsequent performances did well and brought in a comfortable amount of money is clear from a detailed list of box office receipts tallied, down to the last cent, by Dan Mason as the troupe traveled in California then headed back east across the prairie states.[8]

Mason's reason for keeping close track of the money supposedly flowing into the company's coffers was simple; he wasn't being paid his full salary. Once again promised $65 a week as the show's featured star (after Sully himself), Dan was coming up short and apparently suspicious of whatever explanations the Irish comedian was giving him, especially since his previous stint with Sully had ended with his receiving a promissory note. That this was happening again, even as they performed a play that Mason had written himself, was especially galling. With Millie headed back to New York, pregnant and unable to cope with the exhausting schedule of six or seven one-night stands per week, Mason had little else to focus on but his suddenly precarious financial situation.

There were eleven actors and actresses in Sully's company. While we

4. The Two Dans

don't know what they were paid or whether Sully officially paid himself a specific amount, it is possible to estimate that, even allowing for generous salaries to all, Sully's weekly obligation to his stock company likely totaled no more than $600. If the weekly proceeds Dan Mason recorded were typical ($994, $1825, and $1075 for three successive weeks in January 1896) Sully should have been able to make payroll without any difficulties. Combined with the knowledge that the author of *The Millionaire* was notorious for not paying for many of the services he purchased (the printing of posters and programs for instance), one has to wonder where the money was going. Dan Mason certainly wondered, and confronted Sully with the evidence he had collected in late April. In May, unsatisfied by Sully's response, he left the tour of his own play, this time without a promissory note. He would never collect the back wages his erstwhile friend and collaborator owed him. Two years later, after a relentless barrage of letters, Mason was finally offered a pennies-on-the-dollar resolution, not by Sully but by Sully's manager, and then only if he could provide proof "in black and white to show your claim." The two Dans never met or spoke again. In May 1899, his long downward financial spiral finally complete, Daniel Sully was forced to file for bankruptcy. He claimed to have only thirteen dollars left to his name.[9]

Dan Mason spent the rest of 1896 performing his old German dialect vaudeville routine in theaters throughout the Midwest, while scouring the trade publications in search of a lucrative new gig. Whether or not he was in New York for the July birth of his fourth child, a daughter he and Millie named Anna, is unknown. Anna arrived on the seventeenth and Millie, now coping with a rowdy five-year-old son and breast feeding an infant, would not soon be willing to endure another siege of one-night stands in cheap hotels. For the foreseeable future, Dan would be on his own as he traveled back and forth across the country. Aside from the birth of his daughter, the year 1896, with its financial losses and professional frustrations, would not be fondly remembered by Dan as one of his best.

Nor did 1897 show much promise at first. Reprising his old role as Captain Dietrich in yet another touring company of *Evangeline*, Dan and his forty fellow cast members found themselves stranded in March 1897, when the show imploded, leaving all of them with no wages for six weeks of work. However, the year that began so dismally would in retrospect turn out to be one that held a life-changing milestone. In late March, during a vaudeville engagement in St. Louis, Dan saw flashing before his eyes in the darkened Grand Opera House a vision of his professional future. Closing out the show that night was "The Biograph," a clattering hand-cranked

Part One: Dan Mason on Stage

device that threw a beam of light upon a screen, producing an effect that astonished the audience. "Life Motion Pictures," they called them—photographs that moved. Though only a few were inclined to take this crude novelty seriously at first, Motion Pictures would soon catch the imagination of the public and grow exponentially into a major phenomenon within the American entertainment world. In this new medium, Dan Mason would eventually score his greatest success as a character actor.[10]

5

Broadway

In May 1897, two months after watching the flickering images of President McKinley's inauguration, Dan Mason was doing his standard vaudeville routine at Washington, D.C.'s Bijou Theater when he received an urgent telegram from New York. The actor playing a German character in a newly opened Broadway comedy, *The Man from Mexico*, was struggling with the role and the producers desperately needed a dependable actor with good comic timing who could do a believable accent. Dan took the next train back to Manhattan.

In addition to providing a rare opportunity to spend at least a little time in New York City with his wife and children, taking on the role of Von Bulow Bismarck Schmidt placed Dan in a Broadway theater opposite one of the most popular comedic actors of the day—Willie Collier. It was a major boost to his career, and the role of Schmidt would pave the way for his landing several other significant roles in Broadway productions in the next fourteen years.[1]

The Man from Mexico, a farce by prolific playwright H.A. Du Souchet, starred Collier as Benjamin Fitzhew, a wealthy society swell who is sentenced to a month in jail after a night out gone very wrong. Before secretly reporting to serve his time, he covers his embarrassment by telling his wife that he must make an emergency trip to Mexico. Fitzhew's misadventures in jail, where he encounters the excitable Schmidt, a German poet who has been wrongly imprisoned, and his inability to answer simple questions about Mexico when he finally returns home, provided two hours' worth of comedy that contemporary audiences found irresistible. After a long run in New York's Hoyt Theater, the play went on the road and except for the summers of 1897 and 1898, continued to tour and play to packed houses for nearly two years. Crossing the continent twice in twenty-three months, *The Man from Mexico* frequently returned to cities where it had previously enjoyed success, staged encore performances and consistently received rave reviews. While Collier's trademark deadpan wit and droll manner won him

Part One: Dan Mason on Stage

approval from the critics, Dan Mason garnered praise for the way he provided Collier an animated counterpart. The *Sacramento Daily Union* called his evocation of Schmidt "one of the best bits of character acting seen on the stage for a long time." *The Pittsburgh Press* advised its readers that "one of the strong features of 'The Man from Mexico' is Dan Mason's impersonation of the much-abused German poet Von Bulow Bismarck Schmidt," and called the actor "one of the best German dialect comedians on the stage today." *The Man from Mexico* kept Dan away from his family's West 24th Street Manhattan apartment for the better part of two years. Once again, the considerable income he enjoyed as a prominent cast member of a successful show helped justify his long absence from home.[2]

Willie Collier subsequently offered Mason the role of Dolt, the German butler in *Mr. Smooth*, the next play he took out on the road in 1899. However, while the show got decent reviews, it soon closed, leaving Dan free to accept the call to join the cast of the George H. Broadhurst comedy *Why Smith Left Home* when the actor playing the role of Count von Guggenheim abruptly quit. While playing the elegant and amorous Count, who flirts with the hapless Smith's wife, Dan was able to remain in New York for several months before the show went out on tour. Once again his efforts won consistent praise from critics: The comment that "Dan Mason's Count von Guggenheim is one of the

Dan Mason as the eccentric German poet Von Bulow Bismarck Schmidt in the Broadway comedy *The Man from Mexico* (1897). Mason's morose and agitated portrayal of Schmidt was the perfect foil to the droll and relaxed affect of the play's central character, Benjamin Fitzhew, played by popular actor Willie Collier.

5. Broadway

most comical German characters ever seen on the stage" was typical of the responses he got. Dan stayed with *Why Smith Left Home* until the show ended its successful run in the spring of 1900.[3]

By the fall of 1900, Mason had landed another German character role in *Naughty Anthony*, a comedy by noted actor, writer, and impresario David Belasco. At first glance the play seemed to promise him an opportunity to continue the upward trend of his previous three engagements. However, though Dan's portrayal of Otto Chillingheim, a nervous and talkative importer of fancy women's hosiery, was judged "worth of special mention" by one critic, his efforts along with those of the rest of the cast went largely unnoticed in the press thanks to a "scandalous" moment in the third act when a lovely young hosiery model removed her stockings on stage in full view of the audience. With reviewers focusing most of their attention on this risqué glimpse of normally hidden female flesh, all else was eclipsed. In the end, the entire play was itself overshadowed by the poignant one-act afterpiece presented with *Naughty Anthony* at each performance. Also written by Belasco, this brief and delicate little tragedy based on a story by John Luther Long, *Madame Butterfly*, quickly became the main focus of critics sent out to review the Belasco show. Largely ignoring or even dismissing *Anthony*, the critics lavished praise on the beautifully staged *Butterfly*, in which the same actress who played the brazen hosiery model demonstrated her range of talents by playing the tragic Japanese maiden as well. Long after *Naughty Anthony* had been forgotten (and it didn't take very long) the story of Cio Cio San and her Pinkerton would live on, immortalized in the opera by Giacomo Puccini who approached Belasco for the rights to the play even before the run of *Anthony* and *Butterfly* had ended.[4]

In the summer of 1901, playwright George Broadhurst recruited Dan Mason for his next project, a musical comedy called *Rudolph and Adolph*, set to hit the road that fall. The two title characters, Rudolph Dinkelspiel, a horse doctor, and Adolph Dinkelspiel, a women's tailor, though unrelated and unacquainted, are identical in appearance. When they both move to new apartments across the hall from each other, chaos ensues with their friends, their servants, and even their wives mistaking one for the other, creating a series of humorous situations.[5]

Broadhurst's show was not without its shortcomings. There was nothing especially new about the "mistaken identities/jealous wives" plot, some of the fractured language exchanges between the two main characters seemed drawn out and derivative of a Weber and Fields show that had recently made the rounds, and the entire third act, which had nothing to do with the first two, appeared to have been arbitrarily added on to provide

Part One: Dan Mason on Stage

Dan Mason as Count von Guggenheim in the Broadway comedy *Why Smith Left Home* (1900). Dan's inspiration for the moustache sported by the elegant and flirtatious Count was German Kaiser Wilhelm II, at the time a popular figure in the United States.

5. Broadway

Dan Mason as Rudolph Dinkelspiel in the musical farce *Rudolph and Adolph* (1901). Mistaken identities, jealous wives, fractured dialogue, and a horse doctor moonlighting as a ladies' tailor were just a few elements of this wildly successful show that packed theaters coast to coast for two years.

more opportunities for the song and dance specialties, of which there were far too many. In addition, while the plot depended on the notion of two men constantly mistaken for each other, Dan Mason's co-star, Charles Mason (no relation), was in fact noticeably taller and heavier. However, none of this mattered to the audiences of the popular price houses into which Broadhurst astutely booked the show. Gleefully suspending disbelief and standing in the aisles when necessary, thousands of patrons packed theaters from coast to coast to see the show during its two-year run. Many performances stretched well beyond the scheduled two-hour running time thanks to the constant demand for encores, as many as three or four in a row, and the prolonged waves of raucous laughter that brought the action to a standstill. Eager to stoke this enthusiasm to even greater heights, Dan Mason wrote up a series of humorous anecdotes about himself and his co-star and had the press agent release them in advance to the newspapers in towns they were about to play. (See Appendix C.) On occasion, demand for tickets was so heavy that extra matinees were added at the last minute. By the time the Broadhurst company had finished their second season's tour in 1904, they had traveled 41,582 miles and played 596 performances in 253 cities. Second rate farce though it was, a fact pointed out in vain by a few lone critics along the way, it proved to be a smash hit. Even reviews disinclined to offer praise for *Rudolph and Adolph* agreed that the primary reason for the show's unlikely success was its star, Dan Mason. Some questioned why he

Part One: Dan Mason on Stage

had agreed to appear in such a crude production at all. The answer to that question was a simple one: *Rudolph and Adolph* made a small fortune for George Broadhurst and for his featured star.[6]

During the 1902 summer hiatus between the two seasons of *Rudolph and Adolph*, Dan and Millie Mason took their two children, now ages ten and six, to Atlantic City, New Jersey, for a rare vacation. Millie had long loved the resort city that had been her summer refuge in the years before she met Dan. Now, straining to cope with the reality of endless months alone with the children while her trouper husband was on extended tours, Millie suggested that they give up the apartment in Manhattan and invest some of their savings in a house in Atlantic City. Playing to her frugal husband's ironclad practicality, Millie further suggested that the house be large enough to allow her to operate a boarding establishment catering to tourists. It would provide another source of income, and not incidentally, also provide her with adult companionship and something to do while Dan was hoofing it back and forth across the continent. Dan agreed and he and Millie became the new owners of a spacious home at 2005 Pacific Avenue. "The Lilas," only a block from the boardwalk and in time known for its cordial hostess and excellent food, would be the Mason family's base of operations for at least the next ten years.[7]

After his association with *Rudolph and Adolph* came to an end in the spring of 1903, Dan Mason once again fell back on his standard German dialect routine and returned to the summer vaudeville circuit. First, however, in search of fresh material to enliven his old act, he presented himself to the business manager of *Nancy Brown*, a lively musical comedy running at the Bijou Theater in Manhattan, and requested complimentary tickets to see the show. A common courtesy in the theatrical world, Dan's request to "pass the profesh," would have been routinely granted had he not been so forthright about his reasons for wanting to see the performance. One particular song and dance routine had piqued his interest, he cheerfully explained, and he wanted to learn the routine so as to incorporate it into his own act before he went on tour. Not only did Dan fail to get the free tickets he requested, he found his "brazen" request written up in the theater gossip columns of several New York City newspapers. "Dan Mason ... apparently does not intend to fall out of the procession through any lack of nerve," the *Morning Telegraph* commented. In response, the comedian who everyone in the theatrical world knew had just spent two years being mistaken for his double in *Rudolph and Adolph* offered the tongue-in-cheek explanation that it was another case of mistaken identity; someone in disguise must have been impersonating him.[8]

5. Broadway

This inauspicious event was an omen of sorts and the start of a two-year drought devoid of the kinds of stellar opportunities that had flowed Mason's way in the previous five years. After several months in vaudeville, he toured briefly as Hans Pumpernickel in the vacuous and forgettable musical farce *Alphonse and Gaston* before landing a part in the musical comedy *A Trip to Egypt* in the summer of 1904. Taking on an unspecified role in the Egypt story, Mason embarked on yet another grueling tour of one night stands across the country, playing in small houses in towns not known for their connoisseurship of fine theater. Reviews were few and far between and mostly mediocre. That his salary was as uninspiring as the reviews is suggested by the fact that, after six months with the show, Dan determined that he could make more money by going back to vaudeville and did so.[9]

In the summer of 1905, Dan Mason's professional drought ended when he negotiated a multi-year contract with noted theatrical manager Gus Hill, an impresario who had achieved the very goal that had thus far eluded the unsuccessful producer of *A Clean Sweep* and *An American Boy*. Hill had started out as a performer, invested his earnings into his own production company, and ultimately established himself as a successful manager of a series of shows under his name. Hill immediately cast Mason as the featured player in a revival of the musical farce *Gay New York*,[10] scheduled that fall to tour the Midwest and East Coast before heading to Broadway the following year. Taking on the role of Hermann Schultz, a well to do tailor whose loss of his hat during a night on the town leads to a series of complicated misunderstandings and mistaken identity situations, Mason once again devised an appealing and believable German character that audiences responded to with enthusiasm. One reviewer praised his portrayal of Schultz as a "clever combination of naturalness with ... effective comedy exaggerations," adding: "The merit of this part is the backbone of the performance." Mason had three songs in the show, including the novelty song "Hinkey Dee," which closed out the second (and final) act. His spirited rendering of this catchy tune and dance routine regularly brought down the house, creating a demand for multiple encores. In one instance he was obliged to reprise the song ten times before the audience would let the curtain fall. Midway through its nine-month run, *Gay New York* played eight performances at the Murray Hill Theater in Manhattan in February 1906. The audiences were large and appreciative, and the reviews were good. Mason reveled in the fact that after playing so many lower-class theaters in recent years he had garnered enthusiastic applause in a Broadway theater.[11]

Part One: Dan Mason on Stage

Dan Mason as Hermann Schultz in the musical comedy *Gay New York* (1905). Schultz's desire to explore New York City's fabled nightlife while his wife is away brought him more adventures than he was prepared for. His hangover was not the worst of his problems. Dan's "Hinkey Dee" song and dance routine in the show's finale brought down the house every night.

5. Broadway

In the summer of 1906, at age fifty-three, Dan Mason did something he had never done before; he took the whole summer off. Exhausted from his exertions in *Gay New York* (he had suffered two bouts of ill health while on tour) and well satisfied with the income he had brought in, Mason decided against immediately going out on the vaudeville circuit as he had in summers past. He would relax with his family at The Lilas, Millie's boarding house in Atlantic City. He had not seen his wife, nor their children, now aged fourteen and ten, in nine months. It wasn't in his nature to be completely idle, of course. There was the upcoming 1906/1907 season to consider. Scanning *The New York Clipper*, he took note of a rumor that Lew Fields, who had been on the road with his long running Broadway hit *It Happened in Nordland*, was not returning to the tour in the fall.

Fields had produced the Victor Herbert musical *It Happened in Nordland* at his eponymous theater in New York in December 1904; the appearance in the show of the popular German impersonator was one of the several reasons for its success. However, as the second season for the show came to an end, Fields was ready for another gambit and looking to hand off the plum role of Hubert Peepfogel, even as he sent the show out for a third year with most of the original cast in place. It is unknown who approached whom, but in mid–August 1906 it was announced that Dan Mason would replace Fields in the show when the next season of *Nordland* got under way. Taking on the role of Hubert Peepfogel, Mason confronted the high expectations established in the past two years with Lew Fields in the role. Nearly every review of Dan's efforts compared him to Fields, but all were in agreement that Fields had handed over the part to a consummate professional. A reporter for the *Leavenworth Post* summed up the actor's performance this way:

> The German on the stage today is largely an exaggerated, tiresome representation, the humor of which is generally eclipsed by the strained effort of the actor to be funny at the expense of the person depicted. Mason was well within himself and able to amuse without straining. His humor was penetrating.

However, *Nordland*, back in some theaters for the third time in as many years, was in fact running out of steam and losing patronage. Despite getting positive reviews to the very end, the Lew Fields Theatre Company abruptly ended its third season tour three months early, in February 1907, leaving Dan Mason once again "at leisure" and available to take on what would become one of his most memorable roles.[12]

In the spring of 1903, when impresario Henry W. Savage first produced his Broadway success *The Prince of Pilsen*, he hoped to recruit Dan Mason for the central role of Hans Wagner, the German-American brewer from Cincinnati who is mistaken for the Prince of Pilsen while on vacation in

Part One: Dan Mason on Stage

Dan Mason (left) as Hubert Peepfogel with Gus Vaughan as Dr. Blotz in Victor Herbert's musical *It Happened In Nordland* (1906). A homeless waif brought to Nordland as a child, Peepfogel became the assistant to Dr. Blotz, a traveling dentist. When Hubert complained of bodily aches, Blotz asked Hubert when and where he felt his pain. Hubert replied: "Vell, I tink it vas in de mittel of de night."

5. Broadway

the French city of Nice. Mason, then touring in *Rudolph and Adolph*, very much wanted the part, but in the midst of a successful show was unable to get out of his contract with George Broadhurst; he thus missed out on a major opportunity. Since that time, the highly popular *Prince of Pilsen* had gone through four more productions on Broadway and repeatedly toured the entire country, often with more than one company on the road at a time. It was during preparations for the sixth annual tour of *The Prince of Pilsen* in the fall of 1907 that Henry Savage and Dan Mason were finally able to align their plans and agree to a contract that put Mason in the show when it opened in Chicago in August.

Mason's evocation of the good natured and jovial brewer became one of his most popular roles and one for which he would be long remembered. His catch phrase, often repeated during the show, "Vas you effer in ZinZinnati?," echoed for days afterward as a running joke in communities where *The Prince* had played. The scene in which Wagner attempts to sober up by sloshing around in a public fountain delighted audiences. "When he fell in the fountain of real water, and stood under the spray, and walloped in the basin and threw water on himself until his clothes were thoroughly saturated, the house went wild," one critic reported. One has to wonder how many changes of clothing were necessary to keep Mason ready for his next performance and how they managed to dry his suits while on the road. Unfortunately, Mason's tenure with *The Prince* was cut short by a side effect of the play's long running success. In early 1908, Henry Savage staged a production of the popular play in Paris and decided that his current American company was the perfect unit to send on an extended tour of Australia. When Mason and most of the rest of the cast balked at the notion of leaving the United States for upwards of a year, Savage disbanded the company and boarded a ship to Europe to drop in on his Paris production.[13]

By the summer of 1908, Dan Mason had starred in nine major productions in ten years. In addition to the trunks full of scripts, costumes, wigs, and props he kept stored away in his Atlantic City home, he carried around in his head countless pages of dialogue and lyrics along with well rehearsed bits of business, and established schemes for makeup, all ready to be retrieved on short notice. This allowed Dan, once he got wind of a possible revival of one of his previous plays, to preempt potential competition for the part by assuring producers that he was ready to step immediately into the new production, take on the lead role and energize the show. His experience with directing his own shows and his established reputation for being able to stabilize and enliven a faltering production with his performances enhanced his chances.

Part One: Dan Mason on Stage

Thus, when two young entrepreneurs, Charles C. Barton and Louis C. Wiswell, leased the rights to staging Gus Hill's play *Gay New York* in the summer of 1908, Mason seized the opportunity to reprise the role of Hermann Schultz. He also managed to get his wife the part of Mrs. Schultz. The supposedly retired Millicent Page, apparently still missing her former life as a trouper, was eager to spend time with her husband in a show slated to head to the west coast. She placed her boarding house in the hands of Dan's widowed sister, Jane, who had recently moved in with them, and packed her trunks for a return to the stage, once again billing herself as Millie La Fonte. The venture was short lived, however. After playing a series of small popular price houses in New Jersey, Maryland, and Pennsylvania, complaints that the show was awful—except for its star—brought the tour to a close two thousand miles short of the west coast. As Millie went back to her boarding house, her husband pivoted from this fiasco to Broadway, reprising his role as Von Bulow Bismarck Schmidt in Willie Collier's revival of *The Man from Mexico* at Manhattan's Garrick Theater. The show ran for sixty-four performances with Dan Mason once again receiving high praise for his efforts.[14]

In late summer 1909, Henry W. Savage chose Mason for the role of Herr Beckman in *Miss Patsy*, an adaptation of the German farce by Franz von Schoenthan. The play opened in Binghamton, New York, in September before heading on to Chicago for the start of the New Year. A decided success, *Miss Patsy* ran for one hundred nights at Chicago's Opera House. The show then toured a series of midwestern theaters before pausing for the summer hiatus. In late August 1910, *Miss Patsy* reopened on Broadway at Nazimova's 39th Street Theater, to further acclaim. Though Dan's part as the "nerve worn factotum to the stage director" was relatively small, Savage promoted the veteran actor's presence in the play and sent out a press release that referenced Dan's many previous successes with German characters. His part in *Patsy* was hailed as the "best part of a long and successful career." Promotional hype aside, Mason's evocation of the frazzled and excitable Beckman delighted audiences. "Mr. Mason's work is thoroughly satisfying," commented *The Washington Post*. After leaving New York, *Miss Patsy* toured the East Coast until mid–October when the show closed in Philadelphia.[15]

The fall of 1910 found Dan Mason unemployed and at work once again on a return to Vaudeville in an eighteen-minute, one-act play, *The New Chauffeur*, a show he wrote, starred in and directed. Never tiring of the mistaken identity device, and assuming, correctly, that audiences in the popular price theaters had not as well, Mason concocted a three-person farce in

5. Broadway

which a German immigrant, Otto Schmidt, seeking to apply for a job as a chauffeur, accidentally falls into the coal chute of the house of his prospective employer. When he finds his way upstairs, he is at first mistaken for a burglar by the wife and then a romantic rival by the jealous husband. He ends up having to fight a duel with swords before all is resolved. *The New Chauffeur* would become one of Mason's most successful creations, a vindication of sorts after the failure of *A Clean Sweep* and the tragedy of *An American Boy*.[16]

The New Chauffeur opened in Kingston, New York, in early January 1911. After a one-week tryout, the piece was picked up by United Booking Offices for a twenty-week tour packaged with several other acts, among them a mind reader and a strong man who juggled cannon balls. In most instances, Mason's farce was the headliner act and advertised as such. After a successful twenty weeks, the contract was renewed and the Dan Mason Company continued to tour, wending their way across the continent and spending the summer months playing vaudeville houses in Washington, Montana, Minnesota, and parts of Canada where more theaters tended to stay open in the warmer months. By fall, *The New Chauffeur* was headlining in San Francisco and Los Angeles before making its way back across the country by way of Wisconsin and Michigan and Pennsylvania before heading up into New England.

By the time Dan Mason decided to take a break in the summer of 1912, and return to his stalwart and long suffering

Dan Mason as Otto Schmidt in his own one-act play *The New Chauffeur* (1910). After falling down the coal chute of the house where he had gone to apply for a job, the hapless Schmidt was mistaken for a burglar by the wife and a romantic rival by the husband. He had to fight a duel with swords before finally landing the job as the new chauffeur.

55

Part One: Dan Mason on Stage

Millie in Atlantic City, he had been away on tour for a total of sixteen months; his children, Harry and Anna, had turned twenty and sixteen in his absence. By September, *The New Chauffeur* was back on the vaudeville circuit, this time, however, venturing only as far away as New York and New England for its final eight-month tour. During the long run of *The New Chauffeur*, a variety of actors and actresses played the wife and husband caught up in the chaos brought on by the multiple layers of mistaken identity that Mason had crafted. The show also went through occasional tweaks as the author often used changes of cast as an opportunity to rewrite comic bits. Dan would continue to rework *The New Chauffeur* for years to come and like so many of his written efforts it would reappear many years later with a new title.[17]

PART TWO: DAN MASON ON SCREEN

6

The Pictures

When the long successful run of *The New Chauffeur* ended in Boston in April 1913, Dan Mason was exhausted and fighting a lingering cold that caused him to lose his voice. It was not by any means the first time that his grueling schedule had resulted in a serious bout of laryngitis. He had gone on stage barely able to speak during his tours with *Gay New York*, *Rudolph and Adolph* and *Over the Garden Wall*, a fact noted with dismay by reviewers in each instance. This time, however, the condition was so stubborn that it forced Mason to make one of his rare and reluctant visits to a doctor who advised him to take some time off to recover. The cigar-a-day habit the actor had acquired over the years was a likely contributor to his frequent throat irritation. It was by now such a facet of his public persona that a brand of cigars had been named after him, with his portrait emblazoned on the box. However, if the doctor addressed this issue at all, any advice given was completely ignored.[1]

Before making his way back to Millie and their children, Mason stopped in New York City to see an old acquaintance, C.J. Williams. Williams, who had appeared with Mason in *Rudolph and Adolph* twelve years earlier, was now a director of motion pictures at the Edison motion picture studios in the Bronx. Dan would later claim that it was Williams who convinced him to make his own entrance into the movies, with his severe bout of voicelessness helping to prompt the decision. In fact, his interest in the movies was not entirely new. In 1909/1910, Mason had written, directed and likely appeared in three short comedies for the Selig Polyscope Company of Chicago, using a couple of his old afterpieces as scenarios. At least two of these films seem to have been produced during his long engagement there with *Miss Patsy*. The number of nickelodeons raking in coins across America and the fact that motion pictures were featured on the programs of every vaudeville house where *The New Chauffeur* had played during his recent two-year tour might have helped convince Mason that this increasingly popular form of entertainment was the wave of the future. If the veteran of forty years on stage felt any lingering ambivalence about entering

Part Two: Dan Mason on Screen

pictures during his visit to the Bronx, it would have been dispelled when his discussion with C.J. Williams turned to the topic of potential salary; the movies, in fact, paid extremely well. By the time Dan left the studio in the Bronx that afternoon in the spring of 1913, he had signed a contract to appear in Edison films.[2]

In a way, Mason's several past bouts of laryngitis on the road had foretold a future successful career as a silent movie comedian. In a telling commentary in August 1901, *The Richmond Times*, reporting on a performance of *Rudolph and Adolph*, noted that "Dan Mason was suffering from a severe cold and at times could scarcely be heard," but pointed out that, even so, "in facial expression and action he was better than his co-star." Mason's ability to project his character's persona, if not his voice, to the proverbial last row in the balcony, combined with his makeup and costuming skills refined by forty years as a trouper, would serve him well as he embarked on his new career in the cinema.[3]

Dan Mason's two-year association with Edison began with the one-reel comedy *Professor William Nutt*, in which the sixty-year-old actor played the title role of a devout vegetarian who brings pockets full of his own food—peanuts, prunes and carrots—when invited to dinner. Upon its release the first week of June, the film was well received, with one paper calling it "one of the most enjoyable offerings of the season." This first of Mason's Edison films was followed by at least fifty-four additional movies, and an undetermined number in which he appeared as an extra, at the rate of two or three a month through the rest of 1913 and into the spring of 1915. Sadly, fewer than half a dozen of these films survive today, some only as fragments. For the most part we are left with photos, film bulletins and occasional reviews to get a sense of the range of characters he played. While he keenly missed the stage and the immediacy of getting laughs from a live audience, Dan found working in film to be liberating in one regard; it allowed him to explore new characters beyond his usual German stereotypes. After forty years of playing the German on stage, Mason's Teutonic persona had become so much a part of his identity that he occasionally lapsed into accented speech in everyday conversation. Sometimes he did it just to amuse himself and those around him, but now and then, when he was tired, his alter ego came through unconsciously. However, the "Dutch comedian" phase of his life was now over, and not only because of the new roles the movies made possible.[4]

In late summer of 1914, the First World War began in Europe and reports of the German onslaught in Belgium and France stirred up public sentiment in the United States against anything German. So intense was the

6. The Pictures

public outrage over reports of German atrocities in Belgium that some high schools stopped teaching the German language, many restaurants rechristened sauerkraut as "Liberty Cabbage," and owners of Dachshunds found it prudent to refer to their pets as "Liberty Hounds." In this overheated atmosphere, Mason's droll German routines would have landed with a thud. It was an opportune time to step away from the act that had made him famous. He would, in fact, never do his old dialect routines again.

"I know of no broader field for character study than the movies," he told a reporter from *Motion Picture Magazine* in 1915. "The pictures have afforded me an opportunity for quite a range of characters." At Edison these new non-Teutonic roles included a country simpleton, an ardent prohibitionist, curmudgeonly fathers and indulgent uncles, a janitor, a bartender, a butler, and a miser. Not all of the parts were comedic. Mason played an attorney in *The Witness to the Will*, a drama written by Rex Ingram during his brief sojourn at Edison, and an old family retainer in a Civil War piece.[5]

As he had in his early days in Variety when he offered his own afterpieces to theater managers, Dan Mason soon began writing up scenario ideas and submitting them to the Edison directors. While the studio was pleased to announce that the famous stage comedian was writing his own material, only three of these scripts were actually accepted for production. The first to be filmed was *The Janitor's Quiet Life*, a split reel comedy in which a gang of street urchins, chased from the street in front of the apartment building, get revenge by staging a circus with goats in one of the building's

Dan Mason in the Edison comedy *The Janitor's Flirtation* (1914), a film for which he also wrote the scenario. The much put upon Janitor was one of Dan's favorite character portrayals at Edison and one that he played several times.

Part Two: Dan Mason on Screen

empty flats. The second film, *The Janitor's Flirtation*, was also a split reel. Inspired by a vaudeville act he had encountered in 1895—a routine billed as "Fat Ladies on Bicycles" that was disrupted when one of the performers fell on her bike and destroyed it—Mason penned a tale of a hapless janitor lured into a flirtation by a cross dressing prankster. When the janitor's enormous wife chases him and the "girl" down a flight of stairs, she falls and lands on them; it takes the fire department to set them free. Dan's third scenario, *Dinkelspiel's Baby*, a serio-comic tale in which the title character adopts an abandoned baby and tricks his wife into accepting it, was the only one of Mason's known Edison scripts to be filmed as a full reel. The surviving typescript, with detailed synopsis and scene-by-scene plot line shows that Dan Mason had quickly learned the art of writing for the movies.[6]

As Mason settled into the production routine at the Edison studio, he settled into a new lifestyle as well, one that for the first time in his life did not entail year-long tours away from home. Now, a brisk walk or short trolley ride was sufficient to bring the actor home at night to a domestic arrangement he had only sporadically experienced in his twenty-nine years of married life. Leaving Atlantic City, where the onset of heart disease had forced her to give up her boarding house, Millie joined her husband in a rented house on Marion Avenue in the Bronx, only a few blocks from the studio. Their seventeen-year-old daughter, Anna, who now preferred to be called Nan, came with her. Their son, Harry, now twenty-one, left his job as an electrician and soon followed, lured by his father's promise to get him a job at the Edison studios. Dan Mason's reluctance to leave Millie for long periods of time now that she was ill cannot be discounted as another reason for his decision to settle down into an acting job that didn't require travel. In fact, Dan would not stray far from home, even as he jumped from one movie studio to another, for the remainder of Millie's life.[7]

With the whole Mason family now living together on an ongoing basis, tensions that had been brewing for years came to the surface. Having spent limited time with his son Harry during his formative years and done little actual bonding and parenting, Mason didn't really know or understand the tall young man with the thick mop of chestnut hair who towered over him in their frequently strained encounters. While his daughter Nan adored her father and doted on him, Harry's independent personality was a challenge for Dan to deal with. Millie, much to her distress, often found herself caught in the middle. True to his promise, however, Dan introduced Harry at the studio where his son was employed first as an electrician, and soon after as an actor and assistant director. Dan and Harry even appeared together in one film, *An Up to Date Courtship*, in which they played rivals

6. The Pictures

for the hand of an attractive widow. The emblematic photo used to promote the film shows father and son glowering at each other in an image ironically symbolic of their tense relationship.[8]

"There is an old theatrical saying, 'Looking the part is half the battle,'" Mason explained to a reporter in 1915. "If that is true of the stage, it is doubly so in Motion Pictures, where looking the part counts for much." However, looking the part in a movie presented a new challenge for the former stage performer, as the rules of movie makeup were somewhat different from those of the theater. For one thing, the kind of facial enhancements needed to be seen at a distance in a theater looked ghastly in movie close-ups and had to be toned down. In addition, thanks to the slow black and white orthochromatic film stock in use at that time, many colors registered as either too dark or too light. Freckles, for instance, looked black, while a pale complexion looked downright cadaverous. To look "natural" on screen, movie players had to appear before the cameras looking

In the Edison comedy *An Up to Date Courtship* (1914), Dan Mason (right) and his son Harry Mason played rivals for the hand of an attractive widow. It was a case of "Art Imitates Life," since father and son were often at loggerheads off screen as well.

Part Two: Dan Mason on Screen

decidedly unnatural, with faces tinted yellow or lavender and accented with green or red eyeliner and lipstick. Seen in natural light, the effect could be startling. On one occasion, while working on location, Dan was waiting on the sidelines for his cue to enter a scene when an old Irishman in the crowd of onlookers noted his odd yellow complexion and asked, "What ails you?" Ever ready to entertain himself as much as his audiences, Dan sadly told the man that he had the jaundice, evoking expressions of sympathy from the gentleman.[9]

With each new role he was given in his new career as a photoplayer, Mason spent many an evening at home experimenting with makeup, wigs, and facial hair, as he conjured up a new persona. With Millie and Nan as his captive audience, he went through a series of "looks" and facial expressions until he got the reaction he wanted: "If I can make them laugh, I figure the audience will laugh too."[10]

By the time Dan Mason's last film for Edison, *That Heavenly Cook*, was released in March 1915, he had already left Edison and begun working on a series of "Cameo Comedies" for the Colonial Motion Picture Corporation in Manhattan. While his specific reasons for leaving the Edison studios are unknown, it would have been obvious to him that the Edison Motion Picture Company, at the center of a federal anti-trust lawsuit, was in steep decline and the future employment of everyone there would soon be in jeopardy. He may have also reasoned that, based on the experience and recognition he had acquired at Edison, his skills were now more marketable elsewhere. His move to Colonial, however, turned out to be a less than stellar decision. He appeared in three largely ignored "Uncle Dudley" comedies, was not credited for his work and quickly moved on. Neither films nor stills remain of the comedies Mason made for Colonial/Cameo.[11]

The next stop was the Eastern Film Corporation where Mason was hired on as both actor and director. With their studios located in Providence, Rhode Island, taking up a position with Eastern required a four-hour train ride from the Bronx, a distance he apparently felt was close enough to his ailing wife to warrant accepting the job. None of the undetermined number of films Mason made for Eastern has survived, though extant photos and synopses allow us a glimpse of the one-reel comedies. In at least one of the films, *Hearts and Harpoons*, Mason co-starred with George Bunny, brother of the famed comedian, John Bunny. Of special note is the film *An All Fools Day Affair*, which Mason wrote, appeared in, and possibly directed as well. Surviving stills suggest that the scenario was based on Mason's 1881 afterpiece *All Fools Day*. The films Mason made for Eastern in 1915 were delayed in release and not seen by the public until 1917

6. The Pictures

Millicent Page Mason (left) and daughter Nan Mason in Atlantic City shortly before the family moved to the Bronx in 1913. Millie and Nan were often Dan's captive audience as he tried out costumes and makeup for new characters he was developing for Edison comedies.

Part Two: Dan Mason on Screen

and 1918, at which time they were variously billed as "Sparkle Comedies" or "Jaxon Comedies." While Mason's photograph was used in promotions for the films, his name was not.[12]

Leaving Eastern sometime in early 1916, Mason once again hit the vaudeville circuit with his comedy *The New Chauffeur* for a few months before accepting the first of a series of roles he would take on for the Fox Film Corporation at their studios in Fort Lee, New Jersey. It was here, only a short journey by rail and ferry across the Hudson River from his home in the Bronx that, working under directors Carl Harbaugh and William Nigh, Dan Mason would achieve his first significant recognition as a motion picture character actor.

Dan Mason's first role in a Fox feature film earned him this critical review: "He was horrible." It was meant as a compliment. A veteran of forty years of playing comical characters, Mason had never played a

The final scene from *An All Fools Day Affair*, one of the several films Dan Mason made for Eastern Film Corporation in 1915. In addition to appearing in the film, Mason (second from right) wrote the scenario based on his 1881 afterpiece *All Fool's Day* and likely directed it as well. However, when the film was released as a Jaxon Comedy in 1917, no credits were given for writing or direction and cast members were not identified. Thus, the other players in this photograph remain unknown.

6. The Pictures

A scene from *Toodles*, another of Dan Mason's films for Eastern Film Corporation in 1915. It was released as a Sparkle Comedy in 1917. Though this promotional still from the film shows Dan, his name was never used in publicity. His co-star in this film is unknown.

villain before. Yet the part that he was assigned in director Carl Harbaugh's alarmingly free adaptation of Hawthorn's *The Scarlet Letter* was that of Roger Chillingworth, the vengeful elderly husband of Hester Prynne. In Harbaugh's overwrought version of the story, Chillingworth tries to get his unfaithful wife burned at the stake as a witch and ends up being kidnapped by pirates and forced to walk the plank. Embracing the opportunity to expand his repertoire of characters, Mason devised an appearance that would subtlety conjure the malice of Chillingworth. Never happy with the artificial look of stage beards, Mason constructed his character's beard literally one strand at a time. The end result looked completely natural, as surviving photos reveal, but took so many hours to accomplish that the actor opted to craft the beard the night before production was to begin and wear the beard to bed rather than take time to create it at the studio. Beyond his appearance, Mason's demeanor and mannerisms as he portrayed the cunning and devious Chillingworth won him considerable praise. One critic suggested that while the performances of Stuart Holmes and Mary Martin, playing the roles of Arthur Dimmesdale and Hester Prynne, were dramatic

Part Two: Dan Mason on Screen

and moving, "Dan Mason was the most effective member of the cast." *The Scarlet Letter* was released in early February 1917 and was well received by the public and critics alike.[13]

Dan Mason's initial association with Fox, at Fort Lee, spanned twelve productions over two and a half years. Over the course of his career, Fox would provide him a steady source of parts at their studios on both coasts. While the majority of the roles Mason took on were comedic, a few were serious dramatic parts and one role, that of Mynheer de Haas in *Every Girl's Dream*, was described as a "rare mixture of comedy and villainy." Co-starring with George Walsh in *Jack Spurlock, Prodigal*, Mason played the wealthy and exasperated father of a ne'er-do-well son he is attempting to bring into the family grocery business. A critic for *Motography* commented that "Dan Mason plays Spurlock, Sr., with a naturalness that borders on the perfect," adding perhaps knowingly, "in fact it strikes one that Mason may have had the experience in real life."[14] Pleased with the reception the

Dan Mason as Roger Chillingworth in the Fox Film Corporation's production of *The Scarlet Letter* (1917). The critic who wrote, "He was horrible" meant it as a compliment. It was the first of Dan's ventures into serious dramatic roles, and it scored a considerable success.

6. The Pictures

versatile actor was getting from the public and critics alike, Fox promoted several of its films by including in their press kits talking points that highlighted Mason's appearance in the cast:

> "Dan Mason, without a peer as a character actor, plays the humble but picturesque Walt Collins, a 'bum.'"—*The Derelict* (1917)

> "Dan Mason, playing the crabbed old mill owner, needs little introduction. As a master of subtle comedy he is without a peer on the screen. Dan is sure to bring a laugh just when needed."—*The Broadway Sport* (1917)

> "Dan Mason is there, too. He can't jump from roof to roof anymore but on level ground he can cover some territory and keep you smiling the entire time he is on the way."— *Brave and Bold* (1918)

Sadly, none of the films Mason made for Fox survives today. All were lost in a devastating fire at Fox's film storage vault in Little Ferry, New Jersey, in July 1937. Detailed synopses, production stills, and reviews attest to the magnitude of that loss.[15]

By the spring of 1919, Dan Mason had appeared before the cameras at virtually every motion picture production center in the metropolitan New York City area. While it is unclear exactly how Mason obtained his initial part with the Fox studio in Fort Lee, his subsequent engagements at the other studios were the result of his engaging the services of a talent agency, the George M. Perry Motion Picture Service in Manhattan. Long opposed to the notion of paying someone else to

Dan Mason as the devious scoundrel Walt Collins in the Fox Film Corporation's production of *The Derelict* (1917). After helping a drunken father fake his own death, Walt tried to seduce the man's young daughter. The father found out and strangled him.

Part Two: Dan Mason on Screen

do something he thought he could do himself, Dan resisted hiring an agent until the realties of the rapidly expanding film production industry made further resistance futile. With more than a dozen movie studios in and around New York City, and scores of new film projects being announced every month, it became impossible to keep abreast of each new opportunity let alone successfully compete for parts. Working with an agent solved that problem and permitted the veteran trouper, who had a long history of quickly pivoting from one job to another in pursuit of better salaries, to find work at other nearby studios. In the fall of 1917, Mason landed parts in at least three films produced by the Astra Film Company working out of the former Pathé studios in Jersey City and one film for the Clara Kimball Young Film Production Corporation, which had taken over the old Thanhouser studio in New Rochelle. In 1918 he found himself in films produced by short-lived Rex Beach Pictures at their Manhattan studio, the Goldwyn studio in Fort Lee, and Famous Players on West 26th Street in Manhattan.

As the Reverend Timothy Neal in Astra Film's *Over the Hill* (1917), Dan Mason played the poignant dramatic role of a naïve and kindly grandfather in decline. Gladys Hulette, with whom he had appeared in several Edison films, played Dan's granddaughter and caretaker.

6. The Pictures

By the end of 1918, Dan Mason had been seen by the public in twenty-two features released by six studios over a period of twenty-four months, as well as in the several short comedies finally released two years after their production by the Eastern Film Corporation. He had appeared with Will Rogers, Stuart Holmes, John Barrymore, Mae Marsh, Clara Kimball Young, Fannie Ward, and George Walsh. Whether co-starring or in supporting roles, Mason's character turns were well received: "Dan Mason ... has a part made to order for him and runs the star a close race for honors" was typical of sentiments expressed by critics. The name and multiple faces of the veteran stage actor were now better known to American movie audiences than they ever were to the crowds that once packed variety halls, vaudeville houses and Broadway theaters to see his stage appearances. His reputation as a movie character actor was growing rapidly and was about to be enhanced in an important way.[16]

7

The Toonerville Trolley

In the summer of 1918, when Dan Mason went to the Famous Players studio to appear with Will Rogers in *Laughing Bill Hyde*, one of the directors he encountered there was his own son, Harry. Like his father, Harry had left the Edison studio in the Bronx in 1915 for greener pastures, taking along with him one of the stenographers, whom he subsequently married. The couple's first child, a daughter, was born in 1916. Dan and Millie got little enjoyment from their first grandchild, however. Hectic work schedules, chilly relations between father and son, and Millie's rapidly declining health made family get-togethers rare.[1]

In the end, however, it was not her heart ailment that doomed Millie, but the influenza pandemic that swept around the world in the months following the end of the First World War. The first flu deaths in Manhattan were reported in September 1918 and by October as many as eight hundred fifty people had died in a single day. Eventually, some thirty-five thousand New Yorkers succumbed, Millicent Page Mason among them. The once popular serio-comic singer and dancer known to variety audiences as Millie La Fonte died of influenza and bronchial pneumonia on February 3, 1919, at the Masons' home in the Bronx. She and Dan Mason had been married for thirty-four years. Millie was buried in the Hackensack, New Jersey, cemetery plot that Dan had purchased years before to accommodate the burials of their two young sons.[2]

In the months immediately following Millie's death, her grieving husband found it impossible to focus his energies and get back to work. Dan did try, briefly, to return to vaudeville with an updated version of *The New Chauffeur* which he renamed *Via the Coal Hole*. He even intimated to reporters that he might return to the legitimate theater for the next season, but his heart wasn't in any of it and after a few weeks of floundering performances in April, he went back to his home in the Bronx. Meanwhile, Dan's agent kept phoning with new offers of movie roles. In September, as the fog around his head slowly began to dissipate, he agreed to make an

7. The Toonerville Trolley

appearance in Theda Bara's final film for Fox, *The Lure of Ambition*, directed by Edmund Lawrence. Portraying the father of a scandalous social climbing vamp provided Mason a light role that helped him regain his footing and ease back into the routine of movie making. A much more challenging part was soon to follow, one that would transform both his professional reputation and his personal life.[3]

Conceived and drawn by ingenious Louisville artist Fontaine Fox (1884–1964), "The Toonerville Trolley That Meets All the Trains" was one of the most popular newspaper cartoons in America in 1919. Syndicated in over three hundred newspapers, it brought the antics of the quaint rural folks of Toonerville to millions of readers every week. The ongoing series was centered on the community's only source of public transportation, a dilapidated old trolley piloted by an equally dilapidated and elderly "Skipper." Fox's characters, a collection of stereotypical and wryly satirical eccentrics, included an irascible old codger (The Skipper), a ubiquitous busybody (Cynthia Snoop), a volatile hot head (The Terrible Tempered Mr. Bangs), and an enormous and dimwitted Swedish housekeeper (The Powerful Katrinka). It was this cast of characters that the Betzwood Film Company, based in the Montgomery County, Pennsylvania, suburbs of Philadelphia, decided to bring to life in live action comedies in 1919.

The Betzwood Film Company operated out of the former flagship motion picture studio that Philadelphia film pioneer, Siegmund Lubin, had established at Betzwood, Pennsylvania, in 1912. About twenty miles northwest of Philadelphia, the production facility was just across the Schuylkill River from the farms and meadows that would one day become Valley Forge National Park. Owned by Wolf Brothers, Inc., of Philadelphia, the Betzwood studio was managed by Lubin's son-in-law, Ira M. Lowry, who also directed most of the films. After a series of feature-length western comedies, the producers hit upon the idea of using Fox's Toonerville characters as the basis for an ongoing series of two-reel live action comedies.[4]

Fontaine Fox was enthusiastic when contacted. He was already exploring numerous other venues for marketing his Toonerville brand. Eponymous toys and games would soon hit the market and, in addition to being potentially lucrative in its own right, a movie series could only enhance his efforts. Fox came to the Betzwood studio and personally supervised the design and construction of a full-scale working replica of his ramshackle cartoon trolley. Precariously balanced on one set of wheels, the whimsical contraption was capable of being pushed and pulled along the tracks of a nearly defunct local trolley line. Fox also sketched out some initial scenarios for the films, storyboarded some ideas, and helped audition and

Part Two: Dan Mason on Screen

choose the cast members who would bring his cartoon characters to life. In early October 1919, the search for an older character actor to play the Skipper brought Fontaine Fox and Ira Lowry to the Manhattan office of Dan Mason's agent.

As a voracious reader of newspapers, Mason needed no introduction to the Toonerville Trolley cartoons when his agent called him about the potential part. Nor did it take much effort for Fontaine Fox and the Betzwood Film Company's general manager, Ira Lowry, to convince Dan to accept the challenge when they subsequently met. Unlike his previous supporting roles in feature films, this was something new, a starring role in a continuing series of two-reel comedies. It not only had the potential to generate steady and significant income for months if not years into the foreseeable future but would as well showcase Dan's talent for character creation in an unprecedented way. It was also an all-consuming project that would provide a welcome distraction from his grief and loneliness. He accepted the part.[5]

A few weeks later, Mason arrived at the Betzwood studio to begin work. It was the farthest he had strayed from home in six years. Though glad to be out of the house where his wife had died, he left with considerable reservations as it meant leaving his recently engaged daughter and her fiancé, Arthur Ryan, alone without any supervision. Nan was only twenty-three and more than a little naïve. As he had previously done with Millie, Dan wrote to Nan every night after work.

Advised that each cast member was responsible for his or her own costume and makeup, Dan began devising a way to evoke the crusty and disheveled old Skipper. Once again crafting a bushy beard one strand at a time, Mason made himself look older than his years. He completed the look with a corncob pipe and a pair of wire-rimmed spectacles perched at the end of his nose. In a rumpled shirt and tie and a pair of filthy overalls, with one leg tucked in and the other perpetually outside of his well-worn boots, Dan's version of the Skipper, slightly bent with age, moved in a rickety, abrupt, and somewhat irritable manner that evoked the character's irascible personality.

During the screen tests, one cast member in particular caught Dan Mason's eye. She was hard to miss. Standing six foot three and weighing at least three hundred pounds, Wilna Hervey was the studio's choice to play the part of Toonerville's resident Amazon, The Powerful Katrinka. Despite her astonishing size, the twenty-five-year-old actress, using the name "Wilna Wilde" to avoid scandalizing her wealthy and socially prominent Long Island parents, was painfully shy and almost childlike in her

7. The Toonerville Trolley

Dan Mason as the Skipper in the Betzwood Film Company's production of the Toonerville Trolley comedy series, c. 1920. For his role as the irascible and unpredictable pilot of the Toonerville Trolley, Dan personally devised every detail of the Skipper's disheveled look. Along with his co-star Wilna Hervey, he raided local thrift shops in search of well-worn vintage clothes for his character.

Part Two: Dan Mason on Screen

demeanor, an odd but endearing combination. After Wilna's awkward screen test, Ira Lowry, who would direct most of the films, introduced Mason to his co-star. As they chatted, the old veteran trouper discovered that this innocent young woman was away from her over-protective parents for the first time, quite homesick and, while she had played a few small walk-on roles in a handful of comedies in New York City, was feeling bewildered and overwhelmed by the expectations now being thrust upon her. Touched by the depth of her inexperience and vulnerability, and in need of companionship to assuage his own deep loneliness, Dan decided to take Wilna under his wing and soothe her anxieties by providing her with emotional support and professional coaching. Since they were staying at the same hotel in the nearby city of Norristown, he escorted her back to the train that afternoon and the next morning met her for breakfast.[6]

As filming got underway in the days and weeks that followed, Dan Mason and Wilna Hervey told each other the stories of their lives and closely bonded. Wilna told Dan about her art studies and her ambition since childhood to become an artist. Dan told stories of his vaudeville days while showing Wilna such practical tips as how to apply her makeup properly and how to take a pratfall without hurting herself. He also became Wilna's protector, making sure that the overly sensitive young woman was shielded from any teasing or practical jokes on the part of other cast members. Their personal chemistry off screen enriched their performances before the camera and the Toonerville films were the better for it.[7]

Winter weather made operating Fontaine Fox's replica Trolley impossible, necessitating a four-month hiatus. When Toonerville production resumed in April 1920, Dan decided to avoid further hotel expenses by purchasing a modest bungalow in the village of Audubon near the studio as an investment. After closing out the rented house in the Bronx and bringing Nan down from New York so he could keep an eye on her, he invited Wilna to live with them. She was happy to accept. The threesome quickly settled into a cozy domestic arrangement with Dan declaring to Wilna that she was like a second daughter to him. The quiet country setting, the addition of pets and a garden, and the girls sitting around at night singing and playing the ukulele gave their time together an almost idyllic quality. Dan took great satisfaction in the way the young actress and his daughter got along. "Like real sisters," he declared. He could not have imagined just how compatible they would turn out to be.[8]

In September 1920, the first film in the series, *The Toonerville Trolley That Meets All the Trains*, was released by the studio's distributors, Associated First National. It was followed by *The Skipper's Narrow Escape*, *The*

7. The Toonerville Trolley

Skipper's Treasure Garden, and *Toonerville's Fire Brigade* in the subsequent months. The new comedies, heralded by full-page ads in several motion picture trade journals, were well received:

> No better proof is needed of the merits of this Toonerville Trolley comedy than the way it was received on the Strand Theatre program.... The house yelled with delight at the novel and uproariously funny adventures of Fontaine Fox's famous one-truck trolley car and its equally noted skipper.[9]

Dan Mason's evocation of the Skipper earned him high praise as well. "Dan Mason ... proved his right to consideration among the screen's leading comedians," *The Reno Gazette Journal* reported. "His impersonation of the skipper of the nondescript trolley is a masterpiece of unique characterization." *The Wichita Beacon* compared Mason's finesse as an actor to that of Lionel Barrymore and commented: "Mason is one of those irresistible

Dan Mason as the Skipper in a scene from one of the Betzwood Film Company's Toonerville Trolley comedies, c. 1920. The Skipper's ongoing quest to enjoy a nip of his homemade "raisin cider" was a running joke in the Toonerville films, which were released only months after Prohibition went into effect. The name of the bemused young man catching the Skipper in the act is unknown.

Part Two: Dan Mason on Screen

chaps who imparts to his character a certain homely comedy that is infectious. He keeps his audience in an uproar from start to finish."[10]

As comedies produced in the first year of Prohibition, the Toonerville films frequently lampooned the unpopular law and the myriad ways it was being flouted. The plot of one surviving film, *The Skipper's Narrow Escape*, follows the attempts of Cynthia Snoop and a federal agent to catch the Skipper making his notorious "Raisin Cider," the likes of which was said to be so potent it could have been weaponized during the recent Great War. In *Toonerville's Boozem Friends*, also extant albeit with some losses of footage, a cache of bootleg is discovered in the trunk of Toonerville citizen Thaddeus Bumstead's car but not before the Terrible Tempered Mr. Bangs gets a snoot full and has to be carried home flung over Powerful Katrinka's shoulder like a sack of potatoes. It is also clear from a surviving production still

As the Skipper and Katrinka, Dan Mason and Wilna Hervey ride the Toonerville Trolley in the Betzwood Film Company comedy *The Skipper's Flirtation* (1921). When a chicken made the unfortunate mistake of sleeping on the tracks, the Skipper took advantage of an opportunity to make some extra cash. Katrinka got a face full of feathers as the Skipper plucked the hen on the way into town.

7. The Toonerville Trolley

that in one unidentified lost film the ladies of Toonerville are scandalized when Mr. Bangs and the Skipper venture out in public, three sheets to the wind. The best Prohibition joke of all, however, was that the Betzwood studio was making more than movies. Somewhere on the vast verdant estate that surrounded the studio was a still, turning out what is said to have been very high quality hooch. How much this resource inspired some of the performances remains unclear.[11]

Sight gags and witty intertitles enhanced the folksy humor of the Toonerville comedies. Katrinka casually tosses around a telephone pole in *The Skipper's Scheme*. In *Toonerville Tactics*, the Skipper goes out to board the trolley in the morning and finds a flock of chickens roosting there. Before he can start out on his day's run, he has to shoo the sleeping hens; they fly off in all directions, leaving behind a cloud of feathers. The intertitles written by Katharine Hilliker, who would later become well known for her work in Hollywood, faithfully captured the "native patois" of Fontaine Fox's country bumpkins. "The idea of my husband leading a double life, when it cost double to lead a single one!" and "It ain't wise to load up with real ammunition when you're nothin' but a cap pistol" were typical of the comments Hilliker imparted to the onscreen characters.

Most location work for the Toonerville comedies was shot in the hamlet of Williams Corner, about five miles west of the studio in nearby rural Chester County, Pennsylvania, where an aging but still functioning trolley line, the Phoenixville, Valley Forge and Strafford Railway, meandered past farms and quaint old houses, providing the perfect setting for the Toonerville tales. Between the runs of the real local trolley, Fox's Trolley trundled along the tracks, discreetly pushed and pulled by poles and wires just out of camera range. As the Skipper, Dan could actually brake the contraption, but had no other means of controlling it. Some of the comical sudden stops that threaten to throw the actor from his platform were not planned. Along with Powerful Katrinka and the Skipper, the Trolley was cast as another featured player in the Toonerville films and several of the releases contained episodes in which the two characters interact with the unpredictable Trolley almost as though it had a life of its own.

Not all encounters with the Toonerville Trolley were the stuff of comedy, however. One August afternoon in 1921, as the production crew pushed the battered old conveyance along the tracks in preparation for a shoot, the trolley pole, normally tethered so that it extended to just a few inches short of the high voltage wire overhead, accidentally came into direct contact with that wire. As Wilna Hervey remembered, "[It was] like a bolt of lightening had come out of the sky and struck the trolley." All of the men were

Part Two: Dan Mason on Screen

instantly knocked flat on their faces, unconscious. One was killed. Standing close by, Robert Maximilian, the actor portraying the Terrible Tempered Mr. Bangs, was badly injured; he walked with a limp for months afterwards. The dead employee left behind a widow and five children with no other means of support. With the Betzwood Film Company's blessing and assistance, Dan Mason and Wilna Hervey led the Toonerville cast and crew in organizing a variety show at a theater in nearby Norristown to benefit the family. One of the highlights of the evening was a revival of Dan's old vaudeville hit *Via the Coal Hole*. It was in fact the last time it would be performed. Altogether, the benefit raised $750, the equivalent of more than ten thousand dollars in today's money. In a macabre irony, the film *Toonerville's "Boozem" Friends*, shot earlier that year, had involved a comic sequence in which all of the passengers on the Trolley suffered a shock under eerily similar circumstances.[12]

With so many scenes requiring outdoor location work, and the

Dan Mason as Dodo, free-spending lounge lizard and friend of all gold diggers, in the Harry Rapf Production of *Why Girls Leave Home* (1921). In devising makeup for this part, Dan was careful to avoid any resemblance to the other old codger he was portraying, the Toonerville Skipper.

7. The Toonerville Trolley

ungainly Trolley hard enough to handle in good weather, the Betzwood studio once again suspended production during the winter months of 1920/1921. Wilna Hervey returned to New York to resume her art lessons until the studio opened again. Her co-star, not inclined to sit idle in his Audubon bungalow no matter how cozy it was, alerted his agent to the fact that he was at liberty for several months. Offers soon followed. Mason spent much of January and February 1921 in Fort Lee, New Jersey. Appearing with Anna Q. Nilsson in the Harry Rapf production of *Why Girls Leave Home*, directed by William Nigh, Dan played an octogenarian lounge lizard surrounded by beautiful gold diggers. Once again he devised a look that made him appear years older than he was, but was careful not to utilize any device that would even remotely resemble the Skipper. *The Washington Times* judged his portrayal of Dodo, the "ancient spender," to be "thoroughly convincing."[13]

With Wilna and Dan away, Nan remained at home in Pennsylvania, making preparations for her upcoming wedding. Tragically, in March, shortly after Dan returned from Fort Lee, Nan's plans were dashed when a telegram arrived informing her that her fiancé, Arthur Ryan, had unexpectedly died of pneumonia while vacationing in Florida. When Wilna Hervey returned a few weeks later as the second season of Toonerville filming got underway, she devoted much of her spare time and energy to consoling Nan, further endearing herself to both of the Masons. As it turned out, Nan's sudden loss would soon be followed by another life-changing misfortune that would affect all three of them.[14]

In the late summer of 1921, the Betzwood Film Company abruptly cancelled all production and closed the studio. Given no prior warning, cast and crew showed up one morning to find that they were unemployed.

Dan Mason as the Toonerville Skipper, 1921. The Skipper was the defining role of Mason's career and the one for which he would be best remembered. The success and popularity of the Toonerville comedies provided Dan with considerable professional credibility when he relocated to California in search of character parts in feature films.

Part Two: Dan Mason on Screen

No explanation was ever provided by Wolf Brothers, Inc., but it is likely that in the face of stiff competition from comedies starring the likes of Charlie Chaplin, Buster Keaton, Harold Lloyd, Roscoe "Fatty" Arbuckle, and many others emerging as comic legends, the slim profit margin the Betzwood investors had tolerated for two years could no longer justify keeping the small studio in operation. Eight as-yet unreleased Toonerville films were slowly parceled out for distribution through Educational Pictures in the seventeen months following the studio's closure. Their continued appearance in theaters every other month or so gave the impression that Toonerville Trolley comedies were still being produced as late as December 1922. By that date, however, Dan Mason and Wilna Hervey were in California working on a completely new series of two-reel comedies about quaint country bumpkins. These new films featured characters remarkably similar to the roles they had played in the Toonerville films. But neither the village of Toonerville nor its venerable Trolley was anywhere to be found.[15]

8

Plum Center

The Toonerville Skipper was the most important character role of Dan Mason's long career and he knew it. No other personality in his decades-long repertoire—not Max Schultz the groceryman, nor Hans Wagner the "Zinzinnati" brewer, nor the horse doctor, Rudolph Dinkelspiel—had brought him such sustained nationwide acclaim as had the irascible old codger from Toonerville. Every week, thousands of moviegoers in the United States and Canada flocked to theaters to see the latest exploits of the Skipper and his nemesis, The Powerful Katrinka. Some theaters even promoted the films by staging Skipper and Katrinka look-alike contests with photos of the winners posted in local newspapers. Riding the crest of this wave of enthusiasm, Dan was not inclined to just let it go. Both he and Wilna Hervey felt that the popular folksy characters they had created had a lot more mileage left in them.[1]

Mason's first reaction when the Betzwood studio closed was to appeal directly to Fontaine Fox for support in finding a way to resume Toonerville productions at another studio. Visiting the cartoonist in September 1921, he found Fox preoccupied with the imminent release of a Toonerville board game and a collection of tin wind-up toys of the Trolley and Katrinka. For the moment at least, he was uninterested in more movies. Without Fox's backing and blessing, producing any comedies using his trademarked Trolley, the name Toonerville, or his specific characters would be impossible. However, Mason, who had written, starred in and produced his own traveling stage shows for decades, and had a long history of reinventing his own farces, saw an opportunity in this minor roadblock. What if a new series of comedies were to embrace the same quaint humor and settings while avoiding any reference to Toonerville? If the endearing and comical characters that he and Wilna impersonated were so popular with the public, might those same characters, looking and acting the same but appearing under different names, continue to delight their fans? Mason had a hunch that they would.

Part Two: Dan Mason on Screen

Thus was born in the mind of Dan Mason the whimsical rural community of Plum Center, a little town much like Toonerville in everything but the name, and populated by a collection of humorous archetypical "rube" characters whose personal foibles would be immediately familiar to any fan of the Toonerville folks. Chief amongst these was the bewhiskered Pop Tuttle, proprietor of a derelict transportation system consisting of a horse-drawn jitney bus, and his enormous and clueless baggage-smashing niece from Sweden, Tillie Olson. Coming up with a detailed concept, plot outlines, and comical new characters presented no real difficulty. Figuring out just how and where such a series would be produced did present a challenge, however.

The closure of the Betzwood production facility was not an isolated event, but part of a pattern of studios going dark on the East Coast. By late 1921 many of the metropolitan New York City studios where Mason had worked only a few years earlier had either gone out of business or relocated west to new and larger studios in Los Angeles. If Mason were to generate interest in his new Plum Center Comedies, his best chance of success was likely to be found in California. For that matter, the same could be said about his own future career in motion pictures. In the late fall of 1921, after scaring up a bit of extra cash with a brief stint in Vaudeville in Philadelphia, Dan Mason headed to California to explore the possibilities.[2]

Putting his Audubon bungalow in mothballs against an uncertain future but leaving his Toonerville-generated savings in a local bank earning interest, Dan Mason relocated himself, his daughter and their pets—two collies, a tomcat, and a parrot—across the continent to Los Angeles. Wilna Hervey, who had gone back to New York to study art when the Toonerville productions ended, was told to stand by; she would be alerted once Dan found support for the new series in which she was to be a featured star. In November, with Nan and the menagerie settled into a rented home near Griffith Park in Los Angeles, Mason made the rounds of the studios in search of some quick income to tide him over while he sought out support for his new comedy series. Finding it "easy to free lance out here," the actor everyone knew as the popular Skipper quickly landed two small character parts in early 1922, first in the James Cruze comedy, *Is Matrimony a Failure?*, at the Famous Players-Lasky studio, and then in *Iron to Gold*, a western directed by Bernard J. Durning for Fox. By the time *Iron to Gold* was in postproduction, Mason had found backing for his Plum Center Comedies.[3]

The producer was to be Harvey C. Weaver, a wealthy Los Angeles entrepreneur who came to the table with more than money and an interest in movies; he had a mission. Weaver, who owed his financial success to oil

8. Plum Center

stocks, had strong opinions about what he viewed as the rampant immorality of the movie industry and felt obliged to bring about some changes. "The public are demanding pictures without sex problems and without suggestions of unclean things," Weaver declared in a public statement in September 1921, only weeks after the Roscoe "Fatty" Arbuckle scandal broke. "They want plots other than those based on ... the defilement of women, or suggestive of immorality. The day of the vamp is finished." Furthermore, Weaver insisted that the first step in reforming Hollywood was to lure film production to a cleaner, purer city, like San Francisco. Just how Dan Mason first encountered Weaver is unknown, but the reason why the Plum Center concept appealed to the investor is easy to see. As in the case of the Toonerville films, which had often been touted as "good clean fun," Mason made a point of promoting his new "rube" comedies as wholesome and innocent entertainment. While Mason's commitment to family friendly entertainment was not quite as ideologically pure as Weaver's, the two men saw eye to eye when it came to producing a series of respectable comedies. The Plum Center films would, in fact, be promoted as "clean, wholesome, and healthy."[4]

With H.C. Weaver's assistance, arrangements were made to film the Plum Center Comedies at the San Francisco studios of Paul Gerson Pictures Corporation, a relatively new concern formed in February 1921, with the backing of one-time actor and director William A. Howell, whose niece, Helen Howell, became an actress at the studio. The fledgling enterprise, an outgrowth of an acting school established by former actor, Paul Gerson, made Weaver the managing director of the studio while his films were being shot there. At Mason's urging, the director recruited for the Plum Center films was Robert Eddy, who had directed several of the Toonerville comedies at the Betzwood studio in 1920. Unlike the phlegmatic Ira Lowry, whom Mason described as "not worth being called a director," Eddy had been willing to accept improvisational suggestions from Mason and others. He was also a man after Dan's own heart. Though a generation younger than the veteran trouper, Eddy was a trouper himself, having spent years in Vaudeville as part of an acrobatic comedy trio; at one point he had performed a high wire act dressed as a clown. Bob Eddy and Dan Mason developed a warm personal relationship that anchored the production of the new comedy series.[5]

In mid–February 1922, Dan Mason and his daughter Nan arrived in San Francisco, accompanied by Wilna Hervey who had been summoned from a vacation in North Carolina. Replicating the domestic arrangements the threesome had enjoyed the year before in the Audubon bungalow, Dan rented a house in Westwood Park where they could live for the duration

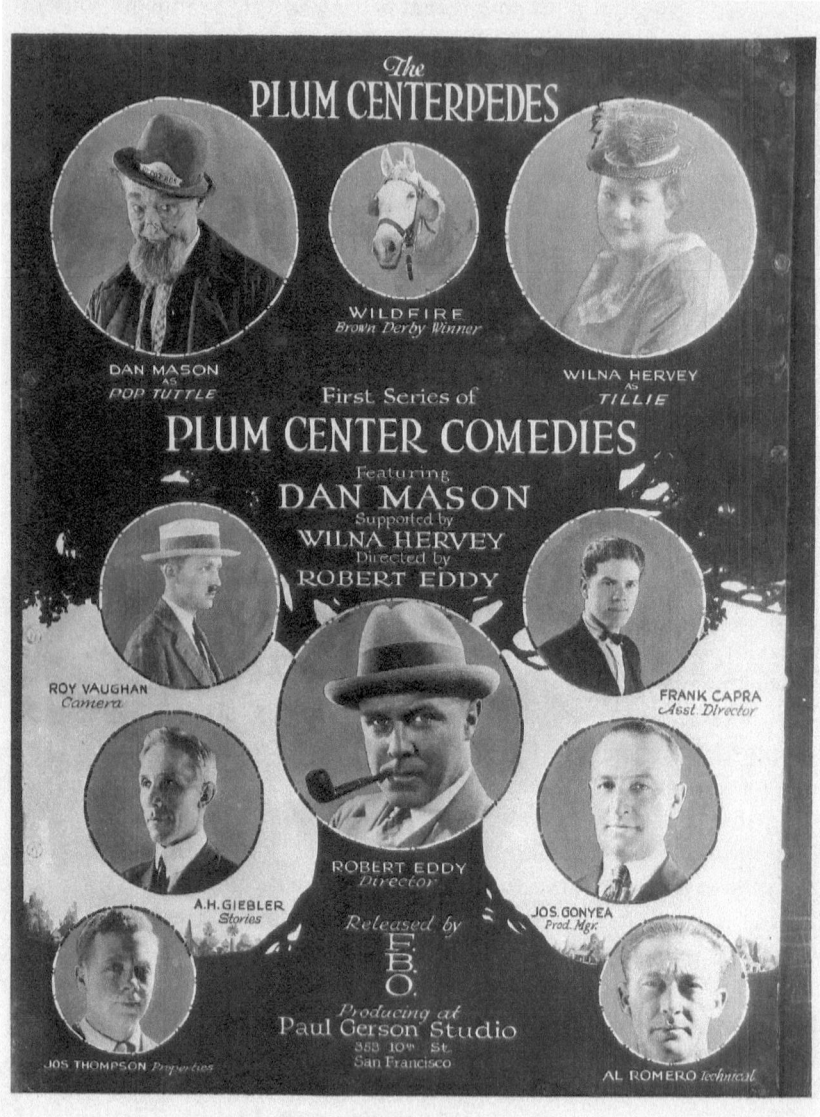

An advertising flyer for the Paul Gerson Studio's production of the Plum Center Comedies (1922). The cast and crew assembled for this series included a young Italian immigrant named Frank Capra, who worked as an assistant director. For the most part, the production team enjoyed a cordial working relationship. Director Robert Eddy told Dan Mason: "You make my work a pleasure and a success."

8. *Plum Center*

Dan Mason and Wilna Hervey, 1922. In this photograph taken by Nan Mason, the two co-stars pose outside their rented house in San Francisco during the filming of the Plum Center Comedies. The two collies, Teddy and Jess, were adopted as puppies the previous year when the Masons and Hervey lived in Audubon, Pennsylvania, near the Betzwood movie studio.

Part Two: Dan Mason on Screen

of their stay in San Francisco. Nan kept house and cooked while her father and Wilna went to the studio or out on location each day. As production got underway, the new film series was announced with a publicity stunt. Having acquired a battered old horse-drawn coach to serve as the Plum Center bus, and an alarmingly emaciated old horse they dubbed "Wildfire" to pull it, the studio arranged for Mason, in costume as Pop Tuttle, to drive the ungainly rig to city hall in search of a license to operate a transit vehicle in the streets of San Francisco. Utilizing vestigial traces of the teamster skills he acquired in his youthful days of traveling with Washburn's Last Sensation, Mason wove his way through the crowded city streets, dodging traffic and attracting lots of attention. Mayor James Rolph, Jr., happy to promote a new filmmaking venture in his city, joined in the fun by supervising the licensing process, as a battery of reporters looked on.[6]

The agreement with the Gerson studio called for twelve two-reel films, which would be distributed by Film Booking Offices of America. With Alfred H. Giebler writing the scripts based on Mason's ideas, the comedies would feature Wilna Hervey as well as Dan Mason. Wilna, now appearing under her own family name, received $150 a week for her efforts, an amount equivalent to approximately $2200 in today's money. Unfortunately, while Wilna's contract has survived, Dan's has not. However, his salary would have been substantially higher than that of his co-star given his status as the creative force behind the whole operation.[7]

Interiors were shot in the Gerson studios. For the village of Plum Center, the production team chose the hamlet of Belmont, about an hour's drive down the peninsula from San Francisco. As Wilna Hervey remembered: "Belmont was unspoiled. It was definitely rural. An old hotel and bar—a few little houses and a real country atmosphere." The hotel became Plum Center's "Palace Hotel" to which location Pop Tuttle delivered both passengers and mail from the train station, and where Tillie Olson welcomed guests. Other structures became the Cloudburst Fire Company, Pop Tuttle's Idle Hour Theater, and the homes and shops of the "Plum Centerpedes."[8]

Unlike the Toonerville comedies, which frequently showcased other Toonerville personalities like Aunt Eppie Hogg or the Terrible Tempered Mr. Bangs, the Plum Center stories revolved exclusively around the antics and personalities of the two main characters, Pop Tuttle and Tillie. Concepts for the films included an amateur Shakespearean theatrical in which a balcony collapses under the weight of a certain large actress, a horse race won by a decrepit old nag, Pop Tuttle's encounter with laughing gas in the dentist chair, and a fire company that takes time out for lunch while fighting a blaze. Three of the twelve Plum Center Comedies films have survived

8. Plum Center

Dan Mason and Wilna Hervey as Pop Tuttle and Tillie Olson in an unidentified Plum Center Comedy, 1922. As can be seen in this Paul Gerson Studio publicity shot, Dan and Wilna's "Centerpede" characters mirrored the appearance and personalities of their former Toonerville roles with great success.

intact to provide insights into the series: *Pop Tuttle's Movie Queen*, *Pop Tuttle, Fire Chief*, and *Pop Tuttle, Detekative*. (A fourth, *Pop Tuttle's Lost Control*, in which Pop Tuttle briefly considers trading his horse-drawn bus for one with a motor, survives on nitrate, condition unknown.)

Part Two: Dan Mason on Screen

A lobby card for *Pop Tuttle's Movie Queen*, 1922, one of the first Plum Center Comedies that Dan Mason filmed at the Paul Gerson Studio in San Francisco. Unable to use anything that resembled the Toonerville Trolley for fear of legal problems with cartoonist Fontaine Fox, Dan and his production crew substituted a rickety old coach pulled by an emaciated horse that they literally rescued from a glue factory. As can be seen here, the unsightly rig sometimes needed a jump-start from Tillie Olson (Wilna Hervey).

Pop Tuttle, Fire Chief revisited two ideas from the Toonerville series; an inept rural fire company and bootlegging. When jettisoned moonshine ends up in the same well from which the water to fight the fire is being drawn, the result is true "fire water," much to the delight of those lucky enough to get a face full. Among the many extras brought in to participate as spectators watching the fire was Nan Mason, who also appeared in several of the other films; no footage of her survives, however. *Fire Chief* also has the distinction of including special effects produced by a very young Frank Capra, whom Robert Eddy hired as an assistant director. The smoke emanating from the house where a stovetop still has caught fire was the result of Capra's efforts.[9] *Pop Tuttle's Movie Queen* finds Tuttle the proprietor of the Idle Hour Theater where he attempts to pass off a

8. Plum Center

young waitress as a visiting Hollywood movie star. He has a packed house thanks to a clumsily crafted poster deployed across the double doors of the theater. When the right-hand section of the door is opened, the remaining portion of the sign seems to read "10 Wild Women Newd," enough to attract a crowd along with the unwelcome attentions of local moral crusaders, "The Society Opposed to Everything." In *Pop Tuttle, Detekative*, the town's self-appointed leading citizen graduates from a correspondence course from Hawkshaw Detective College, and proceeds to sleuth about Plum Center tracking a suspicious character named Nifty Ned, hiding in chicken coops and "disguised" by outrageously large "Russian" whiskers. At one point Tuttle accidentally sets fire to his fake whiskers while "nonchalantly" smoking a cigarette. Corny jokes and puns abound in all three films, with the intertitles mirroring those of the Toonerville films as conduits of folksy wit: "The Idle Hour Theater was on the bathtub circuit. It was only used on Saturday nights." To the extent that these three surviving films are

Dan Mason as Pop Tuttle, 1922. The Idle Hour Theater, where Pop Tuttle was proprietor, impresario, projectionist, star performer, and ticket taker, was the setting for several of the Plum Center Comedies. The converted butcher shop held 98 patrons for Pop's Saturday night "movin' pitcher" shows.

Part Two: Dan Mason on Screen

representative, they suggest that the Plum Center films achieved good production values, were well made and well directed, with coherent story lines. The characters of Pop Tuttle and Tillie seem more three-dimensional than their Toonerville counterparts.

When Film Booking Offices of America previewed the first three Plum Center offerings at a convention of theater managers in July 1922, the films were given such a "generous and spontaneous welcome" that the planned release date was moved up from September to August. As Dan Mason astutely predicted, the fans that he and Wilna Hervey had attracted as the Skipper and Katrinka readily accepted their favorite on-screen personalities under new names. The transfer of affections to the rechristened characters was facilitated by the advance publicity for the films, which made frequent (and often shameless) reference to Toonerville. As a result, many theater owners casually conflated the two series as they advertised the Plum Center films. Tag lines like "The Skipper is back in a new Plum Center comedy" and "Dan Mason returns as Pop Tuttle in a new Toonerville" were common. Since the last lingering Toonerville releases overlapped with the distribution of the first Plum Center films in late summer of 1922, an occasional movie audience had the rare treat of seeing both the Skipper and his alter ego in the same show.[10]

The last of the twelve Plum Center comedies was completed in late January 1923. While another series had been discussed, Robert Eddy and Dan Mason had a disagreement with Paul Gerson over back pay he allegedly owed them. When this disagreement briefly escalated into a lawsuit, any plans for new films were put on hold. Mason subsequently left San Francisco for the East Coast in February, accompanied by his daughter and Wilna Hervey. While all three expected to return for another Pop Tuttle series, Plum Center, like Toonerville, was about to fade into the mists.[11]

9

Hollywood

Leaving San Francisco and heading back east in February 1923, Dan Mason went to check on his shuttered house in Audubon and took Nan to visit their relatives in Syracuse. After visiting her family, Wilna retreated to the Woodstock art colony in New York's Catskill Mountains. Using some of her movie earnings, she built herself a rustic cabin/art studio in the hamlet of Bearsville two miles west of the center of the village of Woodstock. In late May, Dan and his daughter and their pets traveled back to California, this time to Los Angeles, where they rented a house. Before leaving, Dan once again promised Wilna a featured role in a new rural comedy series he hoped to produce; he advised her to be ready to join him on the West Coast. The Masons' arrival in Hollywood coincided with the release of the final Plum Center comedy, *Pop Tuttle's Russian Rumors*, which like the rest of the series was well received and widely booked in theaters throughout the country. As the Plum Center films and even an occasional stray Toonerville comedy continued to play in theaters throughout 1923 and well into 1924, Dan was convinced that the ongoing success of their Skipper/Pop Tuttle and Katrinka/Tillie characters gave him and Wilna Hervey considerable leverage in negotiating another new series. Accordingly he began an aggressive campaign to find support for a new venture in the nation's movie capital.[1]

As he had when the Toonerville series abruptly ended, Mason first approached the distributor of the Plum Center Comedies, Film Booking Offices of America, to gauge their interest in a new series to be produced as Dan Mason Comedies. The terms they were willing to offer were not to his liking, however, and in a sign of his confidence in his new scheme, he turned them down and continued to search elsewhere. Throughout the summer and fall, rumors rose and fell, periodically suggesting that Mason had arranged deals to make another series of rustic comedies. In June, Dan thought he had found a backer and immediately wrote Wilna Hervey with the good news. In short order, he was forced to back track, apologizing to Wilna for getting her hopes up; the backer didn't really have the money

Part Two: Dan Mason on Screen

he claimed. Mason then attempted to form his own production company, Bonnie Brier Productions, named for the hotel where the company's "offices" were supposedly located. Rounding up a disparate group of friends and associates to form a cooperative, he planned to produce a two-reel comedy as a pilot for a series. "Smith's Tavern" was to be directed by veteran actor Frank Norcross. According to the surviving typed and signed contract, the quirky spellings and typos of which clearly indicate it was prepared by Dan Mason himself, the group agreed "to give their services in their different capacities to produce and make and release a 'two-reel comedy intitled [sic] Smiths [sic] Tavern....'" It appears that this venture went no further than the signing of the contract, however, as nothing was ever heard of it again. By December there were multiple reports that Mason was about to appear in comedies produced by Hollywood Pictures Corporation at the Grand-Asher studio. This too did not pan out. In the end, Mason was forced to the reluctant realization that when it came to being a producer in Hollywood, he was in way over his head. While rumors of another new series would persist into the early months of 1924, Dan Mason had, by the end of 1923, come to the end of his decades-long ambition to be his own boss in the world of show business.[2]

Meanwhile, the popular comedian discovered that even if he couldn't find viable support for another comedy series, his talents as a character actor were very much in demand in Hollywood. In mid–July 1923, Mason received multiple offers of character roles. Forced to choose only one, he opted to sign a four-week contract with Warner Brothers to appear in a film with actor Johnny Hines: *Conductor 1492*. This fresh source of income was quite welcome, as Dan was now supporting not only his twenty-seven-year-old daughter, who proved unable to find employment in Los Angeles despite her skills as a stenographer, but his thirty-one-year-old son as well. Divorced and without a job, Harry Mason had followed his father to California seeking his professional advice and assistance. Despite the chronic tension between them, Dan allowed Harry to move in while he looked for employment at one of the studios. Ironically, for a man who spent precious little time with his children when they were young, Dan now found himself in the unwelcome position of supporting both of them as adults. Writing to Wilna Hervey, whom he had come to regard as his most trusted confidante, he lamented: "All these cares and the drain on my pocket should not be at my time of life."[3] However, more cares and more financial burdens occasioned by his adult children—including Wilna—were to follow. In counterpoint to his success as a Hollywood character actor, these vexations would persist for the rest of Dan Mason's life.

9. Hollywood

The plot of *Conductor 1492* was based on a story by F. Scott Fitzgerald, *The Camel's Back*, with the script written by the movie's featured player, Johnny Hines. The star's brother, Charles Hines, was the director. It was a tale of an Irish immigrant, Terry O'Toole, who becomes a trolley car conductor in Loteda, Ohio. As the lad's perpetually pugnacious father, Mike O'Toole, Dan Mason played a pivotal supporting role that was central to the resolution of the plot. The film was a great success, with both Hines and Mason receiving praise for their efforts. Reviews taking note of Mason's performance almost invariably invoked his fame as the Toonerville Skipper. Several advance notices of the film's arrival in theaters even headlined the veteran actor: "Dan Mason, of Toonerville Fame, in 'Conductor 1492.'" One moment in the film illustrates Mason's ability to invent the kind of business that epitomized the character he was playing and endeared him to his costars and directors. Mike O'Toole is seated at a café table beside another man who is obviously quite drunk. When the old Irishman, now living in Prohibition-era America, catches a whiff of whisky on his friend's breath, he pretends to be hard of hearing and urges him to speak closer to his ear, harvesting yet another blast of alcoholic fumes. Then with a look of utter contentment on his face, Mike quickly pours himself a splash of water and downs a chaser. In the wake of his success as the Skipper and Pop Tuttle, Mason's portrayal of Mike O'Toole firmly established the seventy-year-old trouper as a sought-after character actor in Hollywood. In the next five years Dan Mason would appear in at least twenty-nine feature films.[4]

Dan Mason as Mike O'Toole in the Johnny Hines film *Conductor 1492* (1924). Like his son, Terry, Mike had once been a trolley car conductor himself. In the film, this is the photograph that Terry O'Toole (Johnny Hines) keeps as a memento of his father.

Part Two: Dan Mason on Screen

Shortly after the completion of *Conductor 1492*, Wilna Hervey arrived in Los Angeles for what she hoped would be a new start to her movie career. Encouraged by Dan's multiple letters telling her how easy it was for him to get work in Hollywood, and missing her former co-star and his daughter, whom she now considered her second family, Wilna left New York for California in September. Her late summer arrival meant that she was on hand when the last of Dan's quixotic schemes to get them a new comedy series was still being negotiated. Thus, Wilna was as disappointed as he was at the ultimate failure of all these plans. Meanwhile, following her mentor's advice, Wilna looked for character parts at the various studios, but met with limited success. At six foot three and three hundred pounds, Wilna discovered that finding roles that fit her was as difficult as finding clothing. An uncredited bit part in Mary Pickford's film *Rosita* was all she could manage.[5]

After several months of frustration and seeing no chance of another comedy series with Dan, Wilna Hervey decided to give up on making movies once and for all and return to her cottage/art studio in Woodstock, New York, to make a serious attempt at becoming a working artist. This time, however, she invited Nan Mason, with whom she was now romantically involved, to come with her. Thoroughly smitten with Wilna, bored and unemployed in Los Angeles, Nan enthusiastically accepted Wilna's offer. Though sorry to see them go, Dan reluctantly agreed with Wilna's assessment of her career situation and accepted the girls' decision to move to New York. He also accepted and blessed their new relationship, telling them, touchingly: "I am happy when I know you are both happy.... Love is life, without it life is a void." He promised to send Nan a generous allowance each month—$60 (about $800 in today's money) so she could pay her own way.[6]

While Nan and Wilna made plans to move to Woodstock, Dan spent the last month of 1923 away on location in Sonora, California, working on his next film, a William Fox production of *The Plunderer*. Starring Frank Mayo and directed by George Archainbaud, *The Plunderer* was a gritty western melodrama taking place in a gold mining camp, and offered a hearty menu of violence and spectacle, including a mine collapse, a dam burst that floods the town, a spate of shootings, and several all-out bare-knuckle brawls. Mason had the role of Bells Parks, a wizened old mountain man who was once an engineer for a gold mining company. His role this time around was anything but comedy. When Bells Parks enters the saloon and tries to avert a strike by confronting the agitator who is stirring up discontent, an angry mob of miners attack him and beat him to death. "I never went through the rough stuff that I did in this picture," Mason told a

9. Hollywood

reporter afterward. "I saw more fists than I ever saw stars on the bumpety old trolley, believe me."[7]

Just as Mason had long thought nothing of returning to a vaudeville theater with popular prices, just days after starring in a Broadway show, he also never turned down work as an extra after finishing up work on a featured movie role. Even though he was now well fixed financially, with savings piling up in multiple accounts, he insisted on working, even if the income was minimal. Until the next big part came along, any source of income was better than nothing. About the time that *The Plunderer* first appeared in theaters in April 1924, a Hollywood writer reported being on the set of Pola Negri's film *Men* to watch Dmitri Buchowetzski direct the filming of a spectacular fancy dress ball that Negri's character, Cleo, was hosting. In the crowd of extras he spotted "an elderly man with a Vandyke beard dressed in pink tights and little white wings like a Cupid." It was Dan Mason. Only a week later, another reporter spotted Mason, attired and bewhiskered like the Toonerville Skipper, poolside in a wheelchair on the set of Lloyd Hamilton's film *A Self-Made Failure*, directed by William Beaudine. Along with former Essanay comics Vic Potel and Harry Todd, also dressed in their old character costumes as Slippery Slim and Mustang Pete, Dan was playing one of several old men seeking relief from rheumatism at a sanitarium, and the idea of several recognizable vintage comedy characters being among them was apparently intended as an in-joke. This bit part called for more than just lounging by the warm sulfur springs pool, however. When a bevy of bathing beauties show up to officially inaugurate the new pool, their presence invigorates the old men to such an extent that the Skipper and his fellow geriatrics fling themselves into the water, wheelchairs and all.[8]

Dan Mason had barely dried himself off when the Fox studio's casting director, James Ryan, called to offer him a featured role in a farce inspired by public interest in the ongoing sensational Scopes "Monkey Trial." In *Darwin Was Right*, directed by Lewis Seiler, Mason played an elderly professor, Henry Baldwin, who concocts an elixir of youth and tries it on himself and two aging friends. When Baldwin and his friends are then kidnapped and three runaway chimps coincidentally find their way into the professor's study, his family assume the men have been reverted back to their ultimate evolutionary origins. As a publicity stunt, the studio advertised that they had invited the eloquent Scopes trial prosecutor William Jennings Bryan, who argued against evolution at the trial, to attend the premiere. While Bryan had more of a sense of humor than he is often credited with, he didn't accept the invitation.[9]

Part Two: Dan Mason on Screen

While all of the parts Mason played during his Hollywood years were elderly men, a natural consequence of his own advanced years, one of the things that struck both co-stars and directors alike was the vitality and energy of the veteran actor. While he often affected slow or stiff movements of age before the camera, he was in fact remarkably limber and energetic for a man in his seventies and exhibited no reluctance in tackling the physical demands of his scenes. In *Conductor 1492*, Johnny Hines's character, excited to see his old father just arrived from Ireland, jumps halfway down a staircase and lands on top of the elder O'Toole, roughly knocking the old man to the floor. The horrific fight scene in *The Plunderer*, in which the ancient Bells Parks is beaten to death, required considerable endurance and flexibility for hours as it was shot and reshot from multiple angles. For his role as Henry Ward Beecher Payson in the Thomas Ince Corporation's film *Idle*

Mark Hamilton as the bootlegger Bluey Batcheldor (left) and Dan Mason as Henry Ward Beecher Payson in Thomas Ince Corporation's production of *Idle Tongues* (1924). Henry, the salty old Cape Cod handy man, was missing a leg thanks to an accident brought on by his fondness for homemade liquor. Dan's portrayal of Henry provided comic relief in a tale of prejudice and self-righteous gossip.

9. Hollywood

Tongues, Mason performed with his right leg tied back behind his thigh while he balanced on a wooden peg leg, He could only stand with his leg in this position for ten minutes at a time, but stoically persisted for as many scenes and takes as director Lambert Hillyer required. "Mason, despite his age, is able to endure all the rigors and hardships attendant upon motion picture production," one observer commented.[10]

If anyone remarked on his robust health and stamina, and they sometimes did, Dan Mason was more than happy to tell them his "secret." "Right living and right thinking," he would explain: He was a practitioner of Christian Science. "I am never going to allow myself to grow old," he told Wilna Hervey. "Mind is everything. It governs the body. Young mind, young body." Exactly when Mason embraced the teachings of Mary Baker Eddy is unknown. While it is known that his family upbringing was Presbyterian, his two marriages were performed as civil ceremonies, giving no clue as to his religious orientation at those times in his life. Likewise, the surviving paperwork for Millie's funeral gives no indication of a church service. It is possible that Mason came to Christian Science late in life, after moving to Hollywood, where in the twenties the religion had several advocates among movie royalty. In letters to his daughter and Wilna Hervey after they settled in Woodstock, Dan frequently mentions going to the Christian Science church on Sunday and to their Wednesday night meetings, occasionally urging his girls to take up the practices themselves. His enthusiasm gives the impression of a fresh convert. However, Mason's embrace of Christian Science was only one facet of a somewhat eclectic metaphysical outlook that included superstitious practices, like carrying a horse chestnut in his pocket to ward off rheumatism, and beliefs that bordered on Spiritualism. He was convinced, for instance, that the spirit of his late wife, Millie, constantly hovered over him and Nan, actively intervening in their lives to protect and assist them. He once told Wilna that he was sure that Millie was responsible for sending Wilna into his life to fill the emotional void caused by Millie's death. He would continue to attribute all his good fortune to his late wife's direct intercession for the rest of his days.[11]

In the physical realm, Dan Mason now lived in two different worlds. One was the world of Hollywood, the world where he made his home and made his money. The other world was three thousand miles—and several light years—away in the free-wheeling bohemian Woodstock art colony where Nan and Wilna had chosen to live. As he had in the days when he toured in successful shows and was away from his loved ones for as much as a year at a time, Dan wrote letters to his family nearly every night, and sent

Part Two: Dan Mason on Screen

money as well. Nan not only received her promised allowance but supplementary cash for other contingencies as needed. Even though Wilna Hervey had inherited a fortune from her mother in 1922 and was willing to pay for everything, Dan's fatherly pride required that Nan make her own equal contributions to their joint lifestyle. At one point he told his daughter: "I want you to think of what your needs are ... and then tell me. Do as Mama did." In time, his determination to provide for his "Nannie" and make sure he left her a substantial nest egg would become a concern bordering on obsession. It would, in fact, contribute to his final illness.[12]

In Hollywood, the old trouper's lifestyle was quiet and existed far outside the mainstream of moviedom's celebrity culture. There is no evidence that Mason was ever a reveler at any of the spirited parties of Hollywood legend. While he might occasionally have dinner with an old theatrical friend who looked him up when visiting Los Angeles, he otherwise lived simply, venturing out to work each day when he had a job and otherwise remaining close to home, puttering around the house. His only vice, now that his long-standing habit of one beer at night was denied him by Prohibition, was his passion for cigars, which he ordered a thousand at a time direct from the manufacturers to get a discount rate. He shopped for and cooked his own food, not only because it was cheaper than eating out, a major concern for the notoriously frugal old Dutchman, but also because he could make sure of the purity of the foods he ingested.[13]

In September 1924, upon finishing up his part in *Idle Tongues*, and with *The Plunderer*, *A Self Made Failure*, and *Men* all playing in theaters, Dan Mason took the train back east. Along with his usual visit to his family in Syracuse, Dan was eager to see for himself what his girls were up to. They had recently written that they purchased more land in the Woodstock hamlet of Bearsville and were considering going into farming. Dan was accompanied on his visit by the two collies that the girls left behind earlier in the year when they took their cat and parrot to their new home. Much as Dan loved the dogs' company, they had become a burden. Since Harry had moved out again after a disagreement, there was no longer anyone at home to care for them when he went out on location for more than a day. The two dogs would now make their home in Woodstock, with Dan sending them an allowance as well, for their food. In late October, Dan returned to Hollywood, having received a telegram offering him a prominent role in Colleen Moore's next film, *Sally*. Before returning to the West Coast, however, he asked Nan and Wilna to come and stay the winter months with him in California. Eager to avoid another harsh Woodstock winter of the sort they endured the year before, they were only too happy to oblige. By the time

9. Hollywood

production on *Sally* began in mid–December, Dan's girls and the family's entire well-traveled menagerie were all with again him in California.[14]

In the First National pictures film version of *Sally*, adapted by June Mathis from the popular stage musical and directed by Alfred E. Green, Mason played Pops Shendorf, proprietor of the Alley Inn cafe. For once dressed in formal attire instead of miner's overalls, peg legs, or pink tights, Mason played a complicated serio-comic role as a *maître d'* who, as Sally's boss, is a central figure in her world. Shendorf, by turns frazzled, unctuous, and devious, hires the impoverished Sally as a dishwasher. When it turns out that the girl is a talented dancer, he arranges for her to perform in his café. Later, however, when she is poised for success after passing herself off as a famous Russian dancer at a posh party, he exposes her true identity and nearly derails her opportunity to escape from poverty. His appearance in the film was noted as especially welcome as it was a difficult role. The assessment that "the character part of Pops Shendorf, played by Dan Mason, is a masterpiece," was typical of the reception he got for his interpretation of this role.[15]

Dan Mason and Colleen Moore in First National's production of *Sally* (1925). As Pops Shendorf, proprietor of the Alley Inn Café, Mason played a character who was both benefactor and nemesis to the winsome young dancer Sally. It was a difficult role requiring a delicate balance and Dan won accolades for carrying it off.

With his girls in Hollywood for the winter, Dan solicited their help in making some major lifestyle adjustments. In February 1925, he celebrated his 72nd birthday by buying himself a brand-new Durant automobile. Nan and Wilna took turns teaching him to drive, albeit with some reservations about his safety. To assuage their concerns, he promised to go no faster than fifteen miles an hour, even though the Los Angeles traffic typically roared beyond the twenty-mile-per-hour

Part Two: Dan Mason on Screen

Dan Mason's Hollywood home at 724 North Stanley Avenue, Los Angeles. Dan's large bungalow was beautifully furnished and decorated with artistic flair by Nan Mason and Wilna Hervey. Like so many of the homes of the silent movie stars, the vintage Hollywood residence has since been replaced by a larger and more modern home.

limit on the boulevards. Then the family went house shopping. As he had five years earlier when he bought the Audubon bungalow, Dan hoped to avoid throwing money away on rent, preferring instead to own his own home and build equity as an investment. He also quietly hoped, somewhat desperately—and quite unrealistically as it turned out—that a large and well-appointed home would induce Nan and Wilna to give up their Spartan cabin in Woodstock and return to live with him in California. Thus he spared no expense, a lapse of his usual frugality and common sense that he would come to regret. They found the perfect property; a large, recently built Spanish Colonial-style bungalow with a red tiled roof, at 724 North Stanley Avenue in West Hollywood, a neighborhood that had been mostly oil fields only a few years before. The girls helped him buy suites of furniture and decorate the house. They also dug and planted a garden so that Dan could have fresh vegetables and flowers year-round. In April, much to Dan's distress, his girls coaxed the collies into their crates for the trip back east and departed for Woodstock, eager to do their own spring planting and resume their art lessons. Alone again in the silence of his luxurious Hollywood bungalow, Dan Mason decided it was time to get back to work.[16]

10

"Characters, Comic or Otherwise"

The years 1925 and 1926 were Dan Mason's peak years in Hollywood, with more demands for his talents than he had time to satisfy. It was a heady time, the culmination of his long career, and it would pass very quickly. In the nine months that followed the return of Nan and Wilna to Woodstock, he appeared in ten films, with featured roles in five of them and small but credited roles in another three. Two other films provided uncredited bit parts. Though he preferred freelancing for his parts and often crowed in his letters about getting a job without having to pay a commission, Mason did employ the services of at least four Hollywood talent agencies in the mid- to late 1920s. Based on his letters and the rubber stamped information on the backs of his surviving 8 × 10 glossies, Dan was by turns represented by the now-obscure Sherrill, Friedman, Schuessler, Inc. agency for several years, and to a lesser extent by the Edward Small, Andrew Arbuckle, and Hugh S. Jeffrey agencies. The exact dates for these representations are impossible to discern, however. Considering how often the agency stamp marks are carefully covered over with glued strips of white paper or vigorously crossed out, it would seem that the client who handed out his own cards advertising "Characters, Comic and Otherwise" was constantly switching back and forth among them.[1]

In April 1925, Mason took on the role of the American Consul in *American Pluck*, a low budget production by Chadwick Pictures that showcased the physical (as opposed to dramatic) talents of the handsome and athletic George Walsh. Mason and Walsh were well acquainted, having appeared together as father and son in the Fox production of *Jack Spurlock, Prodigal* at Fort Lee seven years earlier. Mason's role as the animated consul in *American Pluck*, while crucial to the final resolution of the story line, was small enough that he was able to shoot his part in only a few days. Thus, he was able to complete his work in time to board a train for a two-day journey up the Pacific coast to the State of Washington for a rendezvous with the

Part Two: Dan Mason on Screen

patron who had bankrolled the Plum Center Comedies in San Francisco, Harvey C. Weaver.[2]

Weaver, who in addition to his appreciation for Dan's talents, had developed a deep affection for the veteran actor, and once told him he loved him like a father, had not given up on his idea of establishing an alternative to Hollywood in some unspoiled northern location. His new choice as a site for the H.C. Weaver Productions studio was Tacoma, Washington. There, Weaver purchased five acres at Titlow Beach with spectacular views of Mount Rainier, and at a cost of $50,000 (about $700,000 in today's money), built a cavernous and well-equipped studio that he opened in December 1924. When Dan Mason and the rest of the cast of Weaver's inaugural Tacoma film, *Hearts and Fists*, arrived in May 1925, they were greeted at the train station by excited crowds of locals eager to see real Hollywood celebrities in the flesh. This warm reception helped to mitigate the actors' chagrin as they discovered that in the far north beyond sunny California it was still snowing. Fortunately, the studio was well heated by two separate furnace systems that Weaver had installed.[3]

Hearts and Fists, starring John Bowers, Bowers' wife, Marguerite De La Motte, and Alan Hale, and directed by Lloyd Ingraham, was a tale of bitter competition in the rugged logging country. Mason played the part of Tacitus Hopper, a faithful old worker elevated to partner in a small lumber company struggling to survive. The fact that Mason's salty character, who provided the only comic relief in an otherwise tense and melodramatic storyline, began nearly every sentence with "Hell!" delighted him; he made sure to enunciate clearly so audiences would be able to read his lips, in case censored intertitles failed to record the utterance. "It's the most expressive word of all," he drolly assured reporters. While cussing a blue streak demanded little exertion, the filming of the thrilling climactic scene put Mason's vaunted physical strength and stamina to the test. To rescue Bowers' character, Dan had to join De La Motte and the director's daughter, Lois, in a hair-raising ride on an aerial cableway usually intended only for transporting huge logs hundreds of feet above the valley floor. The scene was accomplished in one take, partly due to the three players' refusal to do it a second time. When *Hearts and Fists* opened in theaters the following January, it garnered mixed reviews, with some critics praising its thrilling story, realistic fight scenes and dramatic photography, and others pointing out that the film had employed every "thrilling" cliché in the book. One review credited Mason's "excellent character work" for single handedly redeeming what was otherwise a "tiresome and unrealistic affair." For Dan, however, the best review of all came from the producer himself. "Harvey

10. "Characters, Comic or Otherwise"

Weaver writes me that my part in Hearts + Fists ran away with the picture," he wrote to Nan shortly after the premiere. "He will want me in the next picture."[4]

Two weeks after returning home from Tacoma, Mason was recruited by Fox's casting director, James Ryan, to play the role of an old hillbilly, "Pa" MacBirney, in *Thunder Mountain*, a film based on Pearl Franklin's successful Broadway play *Howdy Folks* and directed by Victor Shertzinger. With the Santa Cruz Mountains chosen to stand in for the Kentucky hills, the cast, including Madge Bellamy, Zasu Pitts, and Leslie Fenton, headed north from Hollywood, arriving in Santa Cruz on June 25, 1925, for an extended stay at the Hotel St. George. With the press reporting that a large contingent of Hollywood actors were staying locally, a sizeable crowd of movie fans assembled early on the first day of shooting, hoping to see some of their favorites coming out of the hotel on their way to location. When the cast stepped forth into the morning sunlight in costume and makeup—filthy overalls, torn shirts, old buckskin shoes minus laces, unkempt hair and beard stubble—the locals looked on in stunned silence. Mason's boots were so distressed that they became the subjects of special scrutiny from reporters on the scene. For his impersonation of an old mountain man, the veteran trouper had pulled out of his bottomless trunk a pair of battered boots he had originally purchased for the part of Hubert Peepfogel in *It Happened in Nordland*, twenty years earlier. That the former Toonerville Skipper was among the celebrities visiting Santa Cruz did not go unnoticed. One local theater hastened to arrange a screening of a Toonerville comedy and Mason agreed to make a personal appearance that evening as a way of thanking the city for "the many courtesies being extended to the Fox Film Company."[5]

Filming the tale of an illiterate circus girl who seeks refuge with crude and simple mountain folks was an ordeal for all concerned. "Facilities" were improvised on location, they were on constant lookout for rattlesnakes in the mountains, and at one point someone in the group accidentally touched off a small forest fire which forced all hands to immediately drop what they were doing to put out. After frantically wetting down any cloth available, including the shirts of several of the men, to beat out flames, the cast returned to their hotel that night looking even more bedraggled than when they left in the morning. Long days were followed by long nights, with the daily rushes screened at eleven o'clock in a local theater. Mason played Pa MacBirney as a downtrodden man "who dares not call his house his home" for laughs and got good reviews for his efforts. Unfortunately, for all the cast's exertions, the film itself did not excite much attention.[6]

Returning to Los Angeles in mid-July, Mason took on three small

Part Two: Dan Mason on Screen

parts in rapid succession. For Warner Brothers he appeared as a crooked doctor, one of several would-be thieves trying to rob the same house, in *Seven Sinners*, a comedy marking the directorial debut of Lewis Milestone. This job was followed by an appearance with acrobat turned actor Richard Talmadge in *The New Butler*. Directed by Jack Nelson for the short lived and low budgeted Carlos Productions, this Talmadge film, also released as *The Wall Street Whiz*, earned Mason a few dollars but no credit; he was listed as "John Mason" in press releases. Professionally, the high point of the summer came in a visit to the Metro Goldwyn Mayer (MGM) lot to make a cameo appearance in the epic World War I film *The Big Parade*, directed by King Vidor. Though officially uncredited, Dan's dramatic appearance as a French peasant in a scene with the film's stars, John Gilbert and Renée Adorée, did not go unheralded by the studio. One press release pointed out that the film featured a number of "unbilled stars in minor roles," and noted that "the French orator who recites the poilu's letter from Verdun with so much sabre-charging and intensity of gesture is none other than Dan Mason whom many theater goers will remember as one of the best dialect comedians of the last quarter of a century."[7]

Dan Mason as Mr. Tevis in the Fox production of *Wages for Wives* (1926). The kindly old stationmaster who minded everyone else's business was the key to resolving all the marital disagreements that made up the plot lines of the film. In keeping with the generous spirit of his character, Dan Mason brought a daily bouquet of roses from his garden to each of the women in the cast.

September 1925 brought a featured role in *Wages for Wives*, courtesy once again of Fox's James Ryan, who had become one of Mason's biggest fans. Directed by Frank Borzage, with Creighton Hale and Jacqueline Logan heading up the cast, *Wages for Wives* was based on John Golden's successful stage play *Chickenfeed*, in which three wives go on strike to protest their husbands' management of the family bankrolls. Mason played the part of the "philosophical and quaint" old stationmaster, Mr. Tevis, who

10. "Characters, Comic or Otherwise"

intervenes to reconcile the warring couples. In the spirit of the character he was playing, Dan brought daily bouquets of roses from his garden to the studio for each of the three "wives" in the cast: Jacqueline Logan, Margaret Livingston, and Zasu Pitts. Mason's evocation of Tevis was cited as one of the highlights of the picture: "Dan Mason who took the part of the station master and village gossip supplied a lot of good comedy, by means of which the triple reconciliation was made."[8]

Upon completion of work on *Wages for Wives*, Dan Mason headed east at the request of Johnny Hines who was filming a new comedy at the Tec-Art studio in the Bronx and wanted Dan for a key role. Remembering Mason's work in *Conductor 1492* and the good personal chemistry the two actors had enjoyed on and off screen, Hines specifically requested the old veteran actor be included in the cast of his new picture. As the title

Dan Mason (left) and Johnny Hines in the Johnny Hines production of *Rainbow Riley* (1926). When the naïve cub reporter was sent out to cover a mountain feud, he ended up getting involved in the conflict and making matters much worse. The crafty old doctor/undertaker who befriended him had to rescue him by literally calling in the cavalry. This was Mason's second of three films with Johnny Hines.

Part Two: Dan Mason on Screen

character in *Rainbow Riley*, Hines played a cub reporter who is sent into the Blue Ridge Mountains of Kentucky to cover a feud and ends up triggering a worse one. Among the stereotypical "hillbillies" he encounters is a local doctor, Lem Perkins, who not so coincidentally also doubles as the community's undertaker. This was the part Hines wanted Dan Mason to play.[9]

Substituting the dramatic scenery of Pennsylvania's Delaware Water Gap region for the Blue Ridge Mountains, the Hines company went on location for a couple of weeks in October. While there, Mason learned from his daughter that Wilna Hervey's father had died. Writing her long letters of condolence each evening for the next several days, Dan assured Wilna, as he had before, that he considered her his second daughter: "You and Nannie are my girls.... I have no love for anybody like I have for my two girls." He signed the letter "Dad." Once filming with Hines was finished, Dan hastened to Woodstock to spend more time with his daughters and join Nan in trying to comfort Wilna. During his stay in the Catskills, Dan looked over the latest sketches and paintings the two aspiring artists had produced. They were remarkably good as it turned out, a source of considerable relief since he was now bankrolling Nan's art lessons with several prominent painters. In fact, both budding artists had joined the Woodstock Artists Association and were planning to exhibit their work. Dan also got to see the new barn his girls had recently constructed. He was especially impressed with the huge garden that was already allowing them to sell produce locally. Both Nan and Wilna repeated their previous requests that he retire and come to live with them. Once again, Dan promised he would do so eventually, but pointed out that he needed to make more money "to leave Nannie safe" when he was gone. That Wilna, as her late father's sole child, was about to inherit her second large windfall in the space of five years made Dan even more determined to put aside a large nest egg for Nan so she could be an equal partner in her domestic relationship and avoid becoming dependent on Wilna's largesse. With new parts big and small coming to him on a regular basis, he was in any case not disposed to pull up stakes in Hollywood. There was clearly much more money to be made.[10]

As if to reinforce Mason's determination to keep working, Banner Productions, working out of the Riverdale studio in the Bronx, learned that the popular character actor was on the East Coast and recruited him to play a role in a picture they were about to begin shooting. Dan extended his stay in New York long enough to take on the part of Jim Warren in a low budget production of *A Desperate Moment*, starring Wanda Hawley and Theodore von Eltz, and clobbered together by director Jack Dawn in November. Just what Mason's part in this obscure love and adventure melodrama entailed is

10. "Characters, Comic or Otherwise"

unknown, as he was never mentioned in press releases or in the few reviews that the film received upon its release in January 1926. Since the film was denounced as "silly from the story ... to the direction," he may have been grateful to be ignored. That he got paid, for a part that "bobbed up" unexpectedly, would have sufficed to give the actor sufficient satisfaction. Once the raw footage of *A Desperate Moment* was in the hands of the editors, Dan finally departed for California.[11]

Two more offers were waiting for Mason upon his return to Hollywood; he immediately chose the part that did not require paying a commission. "I seem to be in demand, for which I am thankful," he wrote to his daughter on Christmas Eve, adding his conviction that the spirit of their late lamented Millie had once again intervened on his behalf. That he could declare "I got my salary and no argument" seemed proof of Millie's involvement. Work on his next picture, *Forbidden Waters*, in which he was cast as an old prospector, Nugget Pete, began the week after Christmas. Directed by Alan Hale, with whom Mason had previously worked in *Hearts and Fists*, *Forbidden Waters* was produced at the Metropolitan studio that had recently merged its operations with those of Cecil B. DeMille in Culver City. The film starred Priscilla Dean as an adventurous pistol-packing divorcee who rescues her ex-husband from the clutches of a gold digger.[12]

Though a comedy, *Forbidden Waters* nearly turned tragic when an accident during filming came close to costing Dan Mason his life. While heading out to a small island off the California coast to shoot some scenes, the launch

Dan Mason as Nugget Pete in Metropolitan Pictures' production of *Forbidden Waters* (1926). A boating accident while working on this film tossed the actor and his co-star, Priscilla Dean, into the Pacific. Despite the fact that he nearly drowned, Dan did what troupers do: He put on dry clothes and went on with the day's filming.

Part Two: Dan Mason on Screen

in which the actor and Priscilla Dean were riding encountered the wake of a steamer; a wave swamped their boat and tossed them both into the Pacific. Struggling to keep his head above the waves, Mason quickly became exhausted. Seeing her co-star in distress, Dean, who was a strong swimmer, managed to reach him and hold him up until director Alan Hale and other crew members could turn their launches around and haul them both out of the water. Hale offered to take Mason back to the studio, but he refused, insisting that all he needed was dry clothing. "It certainly is forbidden waters that we're working in" was Mason's only comment on the incident. Dan prudently avoided telling Nan and Wilna about his narrow escape, lest they redouble their efforts to persuade him to retire. Privately, the realization that he had tired so quickly, and might well have drowned but for the quick action of Priscilla Dean, sobered the aging actor. Just shy of his seventy-third birthday, he had to face the fact that his vaunted health and energy were not going to last forever.[13]

While *Forbidden Waters* was in production, Mason received an offer from Warner Brothers that he had to turn down as he was already engaged. He did accept another small part offered by Famous Players-Lasky as it involved only a day's work and thus could be squeezed in. Once free in mid–January, Mason alerted Fox's James Ryan of his availability and was not only offered a part in an upcoming western with Tom Mix but also a raise of $50 a week (about $700 in today's money) beyond what they had previously paid him. In *Hard Boiled*, directed by John G. Blystone, Mason was to play Abner Boyden, owner of a dude ranch and the wealthy uncle of Mix's character, Jeff Boyden.[14]

The location used for the western town and dude ranch in *Hard Boiled* was at Newhall, near Santa Clarita, some twenty-five miles north of Los Angeles, a site used by Mix for his several of his films. Used to sandwiches and coffee for lunch on most movie locations, Mason was delighted to find that the Mix outfit utilized a real western-style chuck wagon that served up fresh-cooked meals. A man of simple tastes, he reveled in the "backed [*sic*] macaroni, beans, peas, stewed corn, veal chops, bread, butter, coffee, canned peaches, marmalade, and cake" he and the rest of the cast and crew feasted upon under the shade of a large tree. As the progress of *Hard Boiled* depended heavily upon shooting Mix's riding and fight scenes, one of which was to take place on the top of a moving train car, the picture was held up by a bad ankle injury the star had suffered doing a stunt in his previous film. This created a dilemma for Mason, who had already signed a contract with Harvey Weaver for another movie scheduled to begin production in Tacoma immediately after Dan was slated to finish with the Mix

10. "Characters, Comic or Otherwise"

Dan Mason (left) and Tom Mix, with Emily Fitzroy (beside Mason) and Helen Chadwick, in a scene from the Fox Film Corporation production of *Hard Boiled* (1926). As Mix's crusty old uncle, Abner Boyden, Dan tried to make his restless nephew settle down by sending him out West to work on his dude ranch. Lots of riding, roping, fighting, and romancing soon followed.

picture. In the end, with *Hard Boiled* weeks behind schedule, the actor was forced to wire his friend and tell him he could not reach Tacoma in time. Though disappointed, he rationalized away this missed opportunity. "The Fox company can give me considerable more work than Weaver can," he explained to Nan and Wilna. As it turned out, however, he had made his last film for Fox. For reasons unknown, after recruiting Dan Mason for eighteen films on two coasts since 1917, James Ryan would never again offer a part to the long time Fox character actor.[15] In retrospect, the end of his nine year association with Fox would be seen as the beginning of a downward spiral that would continue until the end of his career.

Completing work on *Hard Boiled* in mid–March, Mason quickly lined up two more small parts. The first was one day's work at Paramount in an unusual two-reel dramatic film, *The Elegy*, inspired by and meant to

Part Two: Dan Mason on Screen

be accompanied by the music of Jules Massanet. While the nature of Dan's part is unknown, it does not seem to have involved his usual comic relief, though the film about a policeman killing the pet dog of a homeless child could certainly have used some. *The Elegy,* starring Tyrone Power, Sr., and Gladys Brockwell, marked the directorial debut of Andrew Stone. Several days later, Mason found himself at the Warner Brothers studio under the direction of Ernst Lubitsch, playing the role of a rehearsal pianist in *So This Is Paris,* the last of the five pictures the legendary German director made for Warner. The old trouper and the urbane director half his age seem to have made a positive impression on each other. "[I]t was not a long part but just the same was glad of an opportunity to work with him," Dan wrote to his daughter. "When I finished he said he hoped to have me with him again in a longer part."[16]

It was to be another two months before another acting job came along, the longest dry spell he had experienced in quite a while. In the meantime, Dan Mason used his free time to focus on a role he was recruited to play in another drama unfolding three thousand miles away in Woodstock, New York, where Nan and Wilna were rapidly expanding their real estate holdings in Bearsville. Since his last visit there, Dan's girls had decided they wanted to make a major investment on a large farm just across the road from their existing properties, a neglected and allegedly haunted eighteenth century homestead known locally as Treasure Farm. Knowing just how to push his buttons, they persuaded Dan to help them financially by conjuring up a vision of his eventual retirement to a farm where they would grow their own fresh food, sell the surplus at a profit, and all live together in the clean country air. That it was "the kind of place Mama would have loved" served to seal the deal. "I do not hesitate to acquire what she would be pleased with," Dan replied. In the next year, the indulgent father would sink a substantial amount of his scrupulously saved earnings, in three different bank accounts, into this purchase, assuring Nan (and perhaps himself) that any money he had was destined to be hers anyway: "You both know that my desire is to leave Nannie safe and independent." He cautioned that Harry was not to know about the money he was investing in the farm. Dan's prodigal son, who had moved back in once again, had recently asked him for a substantial loan to buy his own movie camera so he could freelance, a request his father refused.[17]

In mid–May, Mason was called to the MGM studios in Culver City to play one of his most physically challenging roles in the melodramatic nine-reel feature *The Fire Brigade,* directed by Dan's former director from Fort Lee, William Nigh. His character was Peg Leg Murphy, an elderly,

10. "Characters, Comic or Otherwise"

battle-scarred fireman kept in uniform out of respect for his former services. Not only did the small part entail wearing a peg leg, with his right leg bent back against itself and his foot "worn in the seat of his pants," but also involved a lengthy makeup session very early each morning. There were several long nights for the climactic fire scenes involving five hundred extras and thirty-two pieces of fire equipment that had to be shot in the dark. On one occasion, when they didn't finish until three in the morning, the aging actor arrived home at dawn, aching and limping, for only a couple hours' sleep before heading back to the studio. Making matters worse, work on the film continued long beyond what anyone had anticipated, leaving Mason waiting for the director to get back to scenes in which he was to appear. At one point, the idle interval was so long that director Nigh took pity on his frustrated player and arranged for MGM to give him a small part in another film to keep him busy while he waited. Thus, Dan appeared as a flamboyant French photographer in *Tin Hats*, a World War I comedy, being directed by Edward Sedgwick at the same time.[18]

Altogether, the *Fire Brigade* ordeal left Dan Mason, who was beginning to feel his age, exhausted and impatient for filming to wrap up. Nevertheless, when the film premiered in Hollywood in December, he was pleased with his part and noted with satisfaction that he was in at least fifteen scenes. When Nan went to see it in a small theater near Woodstock months later, however, she saw her father in only three scenes. "It must be all cut to pieces for the smaller towns," Dan lamented.[19]

The long delays in finishing *The Fire Brigade* interfered with Mason's plans to travel back east to appear in another Johnny Hines film, *Stepping Along*. He finally got underway in early July and after a visit to his family in Syracuse and a tour of the new farm his girls wanted to purchase, he arrived at his bungalow in Audubon in early August. Despite the drop in local real estate values since the Betzwood movie studio closed, with a subsequent loss of local jobs, Dan hoped to sell the property and recoup at least some of the money he had invested in it. While there, airing out the closed-up house and pulling weeds in the oppressive summer heat, he received a telegram from Hines's producer, C.C. Burr, directing him to report to the Jackson Avenue studio in the Bronx for the start of production on the Hines film. Taking a room at the National Vaudeville Artists club in Manhattan, the actor spent most of the next month commuting between the studio in the Bronx and the Selwyn Theater on 42nd Street where many of the George White's Scandals dance routines featured in the film were shot. As the film is lost, the nature of Mason's role as "Mike" is unknown, but while Hines had once again requested Dan's presence in the cast, it appears to

Part Two: Dan Mason on Screen

have been a smaller role than those he had played in his previous Hines comedies. Mason considered it an easy part, but even so work on the film in the summer heat and humidity exhausted him and made him uncharacteristically irritable. Apologizing to Nan after a "mean" exchange of letters, he

Dan Mason as Peg Leg Murphy in MGM's production of *The Fire Brigade* (1926). The old battle-scarred veteran of decades of fire fighting was kept in uniform out of respect for his years of sacrifice and dedication. Playing this role left Dan limping and exhausted from the long nights of shooting the spectacular fire scenes.

10. "Characters, Comic or Otherwise"

added: "I wonder if I will ever get any rest until I follow your Mama.... Am tired, and have to admit it."[20]

Mason's two visits to Woodstock, just before and after his work with Hines, were both destined to be memorable, for very different reasons. When he gave his final approval to the girls' purchase of Treasure Farm and supplied the thousands of dollars needed to clinch the deal in July, he could not have imagined how his free-spirited girls would respond to shouldering this significant new responsibility. When he returned in September, Nan and Wilna cheerfully informed him that they had just finalized plans to go to Europe for six months to further their education as artists by visiting all the great art museums in France and Italy. Wilna, who had just received a substantial inheritance from her late father, some $19,000 (about $270,000 in today's money), planned to bankroll the whole thing; they were traveling first class. When Dan asked his mercurial daughters what they planned to do with all their livestock and pets for the time they would be away, he was told that they would be boarding all the animals—one horse, two cows, a motley flock of chickens, ducks, and geese, a cat, and a half dozen puppies left over from an ill-advised attempt to make money breeding collies—with the neighbors for the duration. Incredulous, yet reluctant to scold them lest he have two hysterically weeping women on his hands (it had happened before), Dan Mason used his best acting skills to cover up his exasperation and opted instead to focus solely on issues of their safety and well being during the trip.[21]

Nan and Wilna departed for their grand tour of Europe in late October 1926. By then, Dan Mason was back in Hollywood, beginning to regret having so much money simultaneously tied up in real estate in Hollywood, Audubon, and now Woodstock, and fretting over the welfare of his girls as they struck out on their European adventure. Fortunately, another small part came along, temporarily allowing him to lose himself in his work. Chosen to play the role of a butler in Columbia Pictures' *The Price of Honor*, directed by Edward H. Griffith, Mason once again provided comic relief in a drama.[22]

Beyond that, however, there was nothing. Dan Mason spent the remaining months of 1926 idle, complaining in a letter to Nan that he was experiencing the "dullest time I've had in over two years." That he had recently raided his savings accounts and now found himself without his accustomed rush of work and steady income stream left him feeling anxious. His lack of employment also left him with more time to ruminate and thus intensified his ongoing concerns about the safety of his naïve and impulsive girls half a world away. The time it took for their letters to travel

Part Two: Dan Mason on Screen

from Europe to California, with many missives getting lost along the way, only compounded his sense of apprehension.

Paris was the first stop on Nan and Wilna's itinerary and the innocents abroad visited all the notable museums, churches, palaces—and restaurants—in search of timeless masterpieces. They also took a two-day packaged tour of the battle-scarred region just outside Paris, where they visited devastated villages and battlefields still littered with unexploded shells from the recent Great War and stared in mournful disbelief at the gutted cathedral at Rheims. Aware that Dan was worried about their safety, they took special pains to reassure their nervous parent that Paris wasn't any more "wild" than Hollywood was rumored to be, and then, without missing a beat, gave him more things to worry about; the water was unfit to drink and they saw two people run over by taxicabs in the street just outside their hotel. After a month in Paris, where several other American tourists recognized "Katrinka," and stopped to chat, Nan and Wilna headed to Switzerland and Germany before descending through the Alps into Italy for visits to Venice, Florence, Sienna, and Rome. All along the way, the girls posted to Hollywood lengthy accounts of their travels, occasionally accompanied by photos and sketches, to keep Dan apprised of their progress through the world of European art, culture, and cuisine.[23]

Not all the letters were travelogues, however, and one particular letter from Wilna sent Dan's blood pressure through the roof. Four years earlier, when they were all in San Francisco making the Plum Center films, Wilna had traveled down the coast to Carmel-by-the-Sea to visit her brother, composer Thomas V. Cator, and liked the little town and its art colony so much that she purchased a couple of lots there with an eye to building herself a house. Since then, however, she had not returned, and it had never occurred to her to pay her property taxes. When she received mail forwarded to her in Germany warning that her parcels were in arrears and about to be seized, she urgently wrote to Dan asking him to intervene to save her investment. She also asked his intervention in another more mundane matter. The multiple collie puppies she and Nan had deposited with a neighbor in Bearsville had rapidly eaten their way through the food budget the girls left behind and the beleaguered woman taking care of them was demanding more money to feed them. Could Dan take care of this, too? In his usual businesslike way, the indulgent father did as he was asked, and wrote Wilna to simultaneously reassure her and issue an obligatory but gentle scolding. It was not to be the last of his sleepless nights brought on by the girls' overseas adventures, however.[24]

Only a month later, in late January 1927, Nan and Wilna decided on

10. "Characters, Comic or Otherwise"

a whim to visit North Africa and set out for Algeria without the benefit of the careful planning and tour guides they had thus far employed. In the legendary oasis of Biskra (the locus of the story in both the popular 1919 novel *The Sheik* and subsequent 1921 Valentino movie), a twelve-hour journey by train deep into the desert, Wilna suddenly collapsed with a massive gall bladder attack and it proved impossible to find an English-speaking doctor. Nan became so frantic that she wrote her father asking him to use his daily Christian Science prayers to focus on curing Wilna. When the letter finally reached Los Angeles two weeks later, Dan went into a tailspin. It would take him nearly a month to learn that Wilna was well on the road to recovery.[25]

Out of work, out of projects to work on around his house and garden, and out of sorts with worry about his girls overseas, Dan Mason badly needed a distraction and began to seek out the company of old friends and colleagues at meetings of The Troupers Club. Founded in December 1925 by veteran actor Robert Dudley, the social organization invited men with at least thirty years' experience on the stage to join their ranks and meet for "rehearsals" as their meetings were called. Finding it helpful in soothing his loneliness and agitation, Dan Mason became one of the most enthusiastic boosters of this new organization, even participating in their revival of an old-fashioned minstrel show. In a letter to *The Vaudeville News* he wrote: "[T]here are so many old friends and members of 'The Troupers' to hobnob with that there is no time for that lonesome feeling.... There is no place in this broad land of ours where the trouper can meet so many familiar faces as in Hollywood...."[26]

However, the bonhomie of Mason's reunion with so many of his old theatrical colleagues was tempered by the sudden death of several elderly thespians during the first year of the Troupers Club's existence, including some with whom Mason had once appeared on stage. Meetings and banquets alternated with funerals. Inspired by the flood of memories this group of vintage entertainers evoked and sobered by the loss of old acquaintances so soon after his reunion with them, Mason decided it was time to preserve his own memories of a half century in show business. Writing in pencil on lined tablet paper, he began a memoir he intended to call "Fifty Years a Trouper." Though he worked on it on and off for the next two years, with portions being sent to Wilna Hervey for her feedback, the project would never advance beyond sketching out some memories of his earliest years. As 1926 came to an end, Mason tallied up his earnings for the year and wrote to Nan and Wilna that he had made significantly less than in the previous two years. Though he didn't cite his earnings for 1925, his total for 1926 was $7725, the equivalent of about $100,000 today.[27]

Part Two: Dan Mason on Screen

In the spring of 1927, after more than four months without a job, Dan Mason finally landed more character work. Universal Studios called him to appear in three films, *The Chinese Parrot*, *Out All Night*, and *A Hero on Horseback*, to be shot sequentially between March and June. While the first two films provided only small, albeit welcome, parts, the third would cast him in one of his best roles in years.

While working on *The Chinese Parrot*, Dan received word that his wandering girls had returned safely to Woodstock. They could now give their full attention to renovating the old farmhouse at Treasure Farm and make it their home. To accompany the checks he sent to cover Nan's share of the indoor plumbing, new kitchen, and new furnace, Dan included liberal quantities of fatherly advice on mundane matters he suspected they were likely to ignore, like taking out insurance on the new property. Perpetually concerned for their welfare and safety, he also advised both girls to bolster their health by taking up Christian Science practices, and pointedly advised Wilna to stop climbing apple trees. Apparently the thought of three-hundred-pound Wilna up in a tree picking fruit conjured up nightmares.[28]

In *The Chinese Parrot*, Paul Leni's film based on the second of Earl Derr Biggers' Charlie Chan mysteries, Mason played William Cherry, a grubby old prospector who witnesses a murder. That his character lived in an abandoned trolley car in the desert was an irony not lost on Dan. It seemed an apt metaphor for his own circumstances. When the completed raw footage of *The Chinese Parrot* went to the cutting room, Mason walked from his sand-swamped trolley across the Universal lot to board a full-size ocean liner sitting on dry land. Built for the filming of William Seiter's *Out All Night*, the S.S. *King George* was complete in every detail, at least in terms of what movie audiences would see of the vessel. Mason's role, as Uncle McDermott, was cited in several reviews as an example of his "usual fine acting," though unfortunately nothing more is known of his part in this lost film.[29]

Unlike his first two roles for Universal that spring, Mason's next part, as Hoot Gibson's sidekick in *A Hero on Horseback*, brought the old veteran considerable attention, with his performance praised as one of his finest. Directed by Del Andrews, *A Hero on Horseback* featured Mason as an old prospector, Jimmie Breeze, who strikes it rich with Gibson's grubstake, joins him in buying a bank, and later nearly gets lynched when the bank's funds are stolen. Quite appreciative of Mason's talents and reputation for enhancing a film with his comic relief, Gibson made sure that "Uncle Dan," as he called him, got lots of screen time in their scenes together. This

10. "Characters, Comic or Otherwise"

generosity on Gibson's part resulted in the sidekick receiving more acclaim than the cowboy himself in some quarters. "Much of the comedy in this picture is supplied by Dan Mason, a veteran stage and screen trouper who is as droll a character as has ever been filmed," one critic opined. Another went so far as to credit Mason with the best acting in the film: "The others just mess about and do no serious harm," he wrote.[30]

At least some of Hoot Gibson's appreciation for Dan Mason's efforts may have stemmed from the old trouper's willingness to continue working despite the pain and temporary disability he suffered as a result of an accident while filming. Though the details are unclear, partly because he took care to downplay the incident in letters to his girls, it appears that Mason fell off a horse and hit his head, suffering a concussion in the process. His face was discolored for weeks, occasional forgetfulness lingered for a month or more, and he still felt wobbly in the legs as late as that fall. Consistent with his Christian Science beliefs, the dazed and bruised actor refused to see the studio's doctors, a decision that possibly made matters worse. "I do nothing dangerous in pictures nor am I asked to," he insisted when Nan and Wilna expressed alarm and renewed their efforts to get him to retire. However, even while attempting to assure his girls that all was well, Dan took this incident as another reminder of his own mortality. He began putting his daughter's name on all of his deeds and accounts to make sure she inherited his entire estate once he was gone. "I don't intend there will be much to dispose of by will," he told Nan.[31]

Dan Mason as the old prospector Jimmie Breeze in Universal's production of *A Hero on Horseback* (1927). As Hoot Gibson's sidekick, Jimmie struck it rich with Gibson's grubstake and split the winnings with his pal. When Gibson bought a bank, Jimmy treated himself to a respectable new suit. Gibson enjoyed "Uncle Dan's" character work so much that he encouraged the veteran actor to upstage him in several scenes.

Part Two: Dan Mason on Screen

When Hoot Gibson vanquished the bad guys and rode off into the sunset with the girl, Mason's three-month rush of near non-stop activity came to an abrupt end in mid– June. Though he needed a rest to recover, he nevertheless fretted over finding himself idle. He soon tired of poking about in his garden and looking for things to fix around the house. With not a hint of another job in the offing, and with the rising summer heat lowering the prices for cross-country rail tickets on the non-air-conditioned trains, Mason opted to travel back east in July. This time, along with his usual family visits to Syracuse and Woodstock, he was intent on unloading his Audubon house once and for all. After packing and shipping all his furniture and personal items off to Woodstock against his eventual residence there, Dan put the bungalow on the market. It would take a year to sell and even then would be on terms not especially favorable to its frustrated owner. Unlike his previous trips back east when the popular actor could often grab a small part or two at one of the eastern studios to supplement his income, this time there were no parts available. However, Mason did accept an offer to appear on the radio, courtesy of station WODA in Paterson, New Jersey, a few miles northwest of Fort Lee. His fifteen minute "Talk by Dan Mason," a humorous monologue, was broadcast on at least three August evenings at eight p.m., sandwiched in between the "Radio Shopper's Guide" and songs by "The Mooney Brothers." This was not Mason's first appearance on the radio; he had made a similar broadcast over San Francisco's station KUO in 1922.[32]

Returning to Hollywood in September, Mason accepted an offer from First National to appear in a minor role as one of five councilmen in Charles Brabin's *The Valley of the Giants*. However, after returning from weeks on location amidst the towering redwoods of northern California's Humboldt County, Mason again faced a total lack of work for the rest of the year. For the four roles he played in 1927, Dan earned a total of only $2180 (about $30,000 in today's money). It was less than one third of what he had made the previous year. To meet his living expenses, pay his mortgages, send Nan her accustomed allowance along with supplemental checks for Treasure Farm upgrades, travel east for a month, and ship his belongings from Audubon to Woodstock, he was forced to take even more money out of his already depleted savings. Discouraged, tired and demoralized, Dan lamented his decision to invest so much money in real estate, when that money could be earning interest in the bank. While careful not to begrudge the girls the funds he had already invested in Treasure Farm, he did peevishly complain to them that the posh Hollywood home he didn't need or want was their fault since he bought it thinking they would come to live

10. "Characters, Comic or Otherwise"

with him there: "I have $12,000 in this place ... $5,500 in Audubon place.... If I had the $17,500 invested with the Warranty Trust Co. who pay 6 percent interest, it would earn one thousand and fifty dollars per year." (The $17,500 and $1050 would equate to some $253,000 and $15,200 in today's dollars.) Such income would have been especially welcome in the face of the financial shortfall occasioned by his lack of work, a realization that kept him awake at night. In desperation in that "worst year in a long time," Dan Mason considered and even announced a return to vaudeville in November. It was, however, only a knee jerk reaction based on years of past practice, and nothing came of it. Instead, he put his Stanley Avenue home on the market, hoping to sell it furnished and resigned to taking a loss on it; he just wanted to be rid of it and recoup at least some of his badly needed funds. However, much as he longed to join the girls in Woodstock, he determined to stay put until the house was sold. "It's really an unsatisfying existence out here," he wrote to Nan. "And here I am doing no good for you or for me."[33]

The scarcity of parts coming Dan Mason's way, after being so much in demand only two years before, can be attributed to several factors. For one thing, he had become a victim of his own success. Having appeared in twenty films in two and a half years, he was beginning to suffer from over exposure, his "comic relief" shtick perilously close to becoming a cliché and thus less appealing to casting directors. As Hollywood flourished and grew, the studios were not exactly suffering from a lack of character actors; the talent agencies had literally dozens of them available in all shapes, sizes and ages. In addition, Mason's once vaunted vitality was noticeably fading and his age was beginning to work against him: "I rather think the[y] look at me as being old or rather to [sic] old for lots of work," he lamented to Nan. Dan's previous healthy salaries were also becoming a liability, especially with Hollywood doing a bit of belt tightening. "Wall Street and bankers who loan money to finance productions have had men out here watching the game," he wrote to his daughter. "Nothing but figures count with the financial interests. There is [sic] a great many actors here in bad shape because of idleness." Aware that he might be pricing himself out of competition in a market with no shortage of talent, he alerted his agent in April 1928 that he was willing to reduce his weekly fee by fifty dollars. When one studio countered this offer with a demand that he reduce his pay by three times that amount, Mason abruptly backed off the notion of demanding less money. "If I did that I would have to do same for all," he wrote to the girls. "[T]he producers keep each other posted."[34]

In April 1928, Dan Mason's financial and employment anxieties were eclipsed by the news that his daughter was suffering from a serious medical condition that required immediate surgery. Though the exact nature of Nan's illness is unknown, the veiled language and extreme delicacy with which the matter is discussed in their letters suggest that her illness involved problems specific to the female anatomy. Frantic to be so far away and frustrated when he didn't receive daily updates, Dan sent multiple emotional telegrams and letters alternately begging for more information and assuring his girls that he would pay all expenses for the surgery and postoperative hospitalization even if he had to empty out what was left of his bank accounts. Long convinced that the backbreaking farm chores they were both performing were dangerous for women and thus a possible contributor to Nan's condition, he also scolded Nan and Wilna for risking their health by doing "man's work" on their farm. Though Nan came through her ordeal to achieve full good health again and Wilna survived shouldering all the farm work singlehandedly for a couple of months, Dan Mason's stress level was slow to recede. Now more than ever, he longed to leave California and be with his girls on their farm. However, his Hollywood home had not yet sold, and now concerned that his girls might need more of his financial help to meet medical expenses, he also felt obliged to stay and make just a little more money first.[35]

11

The Idle List

Dan Mason's trip to New York City in August 1926, to film *Stepping Along* with Johnny Hines, coincided with the Manhattan premiere of Warner Brothers' initial Vitaphone feature, *Don Juan*. As the first film to be released with a soundtrack (orchestral music and sound effects recorded on sixteen-inch diameter disks) the romantic drama starring John Barrymore would be seen in retrospect as a landmark event, albeit one overshadowed a year later by the more popular *The Jazz Singer*. The movie industry's erratic but inexorable transition from silent to sound film had begun. The program at the Warners' air-conditioned theater that season also included several Vitaphone shorts whose soundtracks, unlike that of the feature, showcased the human voice singing and speaking. These eight shorts took the place of what would ordinarily have been live vaudeville acts preceding the evening's main movie event, another foreshadowing of big changes in the American entertainment business soon to come. It is not known whether Mason took advantage of the opportunity to see this novel program, but he cannot have been unaware of it or oblivious to its potential implications.[1]

By the spring of 1928, as Dan Mason struggled to get new parts and fretted over his distance from Woodstock when he felt that his girls clearly needed his assistance, the dramatic changes taking place in Hollywood added another level of uncertainty and stress. Mason had seen the world of entertainment transformed by technology before. Like so many performers, he had looked on with appreciation as hot and flickering gaslights in theaters slowly gave way to electrical lighting systems that illuminated both theater and stage, in the late 1880s and early 1890s. The transition from silent films to sound, however, while equally tentative and unsteady, was at first not as universally welcomed; producers and players alike pondered the future of the movies with misgivings and apprehension.

The year 1928 saw the movie industry make a full shift to sound films in one form or another. In addition to the Vitaphone system, there was also the competing MovieTone sound-on-film system. However, many theaters

Part Two: Dan Mason on Screen

in small towns were not yet adapted to either of the new technologies for reproducing sound. Thus, films were issued in three different formats: (1) silent with intertitles; (2) with a soundtrack, on disk or on film, of orchestral music and sound effects; (3) with a soundtrack of music, sound effects and partial dialogue.[2] The four films Mason appeared in that year reflected all of these formats. In January, the veteran actor was chosen by First National to play a prominent role in Colleen Moore's film, *Lilac Time*.[3] It was a good part and one he embraced with enthusiasm. "My part [is] a Frenchman Grandfather," he wrote to Nan, "a soldier in the Franco-Prussian War of 1870. An irascible fellow who prided himself on his valor as a soldier. Legs paralyzed, moved about in a wheel chair." While he concluded his description of his new role with "Nothing like work to be in a contented frame of mind," his part as Jeanine's *grand-père* would in fact prove to be his last significant performance in a feature film. *Lilac Time* was released in October with a Vitaphone soundtrack of music and sound effects, but with no dialogue. It also went out to unconverted theaters as a purely silent film that required live accompaniment.[4]

Dan Mason's next film, *The Bellamy Trial*, was released to newly equipped theaters as a "part talker," with an estimated seventy-five percent of the story line carried by dialogue recorded via the MovieTone process. Production on *The Bellamy Trial* began in April at MGM, with director Monta Bell holding voice rehearsals for the film's long trial scenes. Mason's voice was not one of those heard, however. He was cast in a small non-speaking part as the court janitor, a role that was apparently intended to provide some comic relief in an otherwise tense and serious story of murder and deceit. While the film itself was well

Dan Mason as the elderly French grandfather in First National's production of *Lilac Time* (1928). As *grand-père* to Colleen Moore's character, Jeanine, Dan's role as a proud disabled veteran of the Franco-Prussian War was the actor's last significant character part in a feature film.

11. The Idle List

received and got lots of attention, Mason was mentioned only in passing on a few occasions and nothing was said about his performance. There followed an uncredited part as an extra in Victor Fleming's *The Awakening*, starring Vilma Banky, in late spring. As the story took place in an Alsatian village before and during the First World War, it may be that Mason was one of the villagers. *The Awakening* was released with a MovieTone soundtrack of music and sound effects; it had no dialogue.[5]

In May 1928, Dan Mason was called in for three days' work at the Los Angeles studio of the brilliant and innovative animator Charles R. ("Charley") Bowers. In a two-reel silent comedy, *Hop Off*, Mason played the role of an eccentric inventor whose bald head is used as a skating rink by two trained fleas from a flea circus. The "fleas" were in fact small models created by Bowers and their movements were achieved by Bowers' trademark stop action photography. In publicity for the film, the fleas were facetiously referenced as though they were genuine insects and even had names—Romeo and Juliet. However, while the supposed "smallest actors in the world" got coverage in the press, Dan Mason did not. The owner of the head upon which the fleas cavorted was never mentioned in connection with this film.[6]

Co-starring with two fleas in a comedy short would prove to be Dan Mason's final performance. Though he was reported in June to have been added to the cast of Paul Leni's *The Last Warning*, he is nowhere to be found in the surviving version of this atmospheric mystery thriller. If he was indeed at one point included in the cast, his efforts ended up on the cutting room floor. It is possible that the report of his inclusion in the cast was simply a rumor or a mistake. It is also possible that a bout of ill health prevented him from following through with the part. In any case, beyond June 1928, after fifteen years in the movies, the veteran actor would land no new parts.[7]

Mason spent his last summer in Hollywood waiting for calls that never came while watching the movie capital rapidly change around him. "Production does not pick up to any extent," he wrote to Nan in July. "Talking pictures is the cry now ... the principle [sic] studios are equipping sound proof stages with an eye to producing them. Whether it is the spurt of a fad or going to be permanent is to be seen." Determined to remain optimistic, he noted that his many years in the theater might work to his advantage: "At any rate they require actors with stage experience and use of voice to get a talking picture over."[8]

As the summer of 1928 waned, so did Dan Mason's health and optimism. By autumn he was experiencing intervals of significant physical ailments that worried him, though not enough for him to violate his Christian

Part Two: Dan Mason on Screen

Out of work and out of projects at home, Dan Mason adopted a stray cat and let it live in his garage as a sanctuary from the neighborhood dogs. He once told Wilna Hervey: "I do not think anyone is human who does not feel love for animals."

Science principles and actually consult a doctor. In addition to arthritis, which had gotten noticeably worse, there was a persistent cough, along with headaches, fevers, chills and fatigue. At one point Mason was forced to retreat to his bed as the only way of keeping warm on a cold rainy day. Alarmed by his reports of ill health and the fact that he was once more living alone, Harry having now decamped for Las Vegas, Nevada, in pursuit of a job as a cameraman, Nan and Wilna decided to escape the impending harsh Catskills winter and travel west that fall to see for themselves just what Dan's circumstances were. What they found was a stubborn old trouper in near complete denial in the face of his fading abilities. Determined to bring in more money, Mason had recently completed a voice test to appear in a talking film and had his agent trying to find him a speaking part. Meanwhile, he was contemplating going back on the stage and hoped to tour the R-K-O circuit in a stage version of *The Bad Man* with a group of other film actors. Neither preparing for the future nor resurrecting the past

11. The Idle List

was a viable option, however. Given his state of health, he could not have fulfilled any new commitment no matter how minor or how hard he tried. As the December holidays approached, Dan's girls succeeded in convincing him to leave Hollywood for an extended vacation at the home of his brother Fred Grassman in Syracuse, in the hope of lifting his spirits and recovering his health. That he acquiesced rather than resist suggests that Mason was beginning to understand that his condition was serious. The trio traveled east just in time for Christmas.[9]

The family holidays and kind ministrations of Fred Grassman and the extended Grassman family did not prove therapeutic, however. As Dan observed his seventy-sixth birthday in February 1929, his condition continued to deteriorate. By spring, he was so weak that he struggled to write his daughter even a short letter. "I do not gain in strength," he wrote in April. "A few minutes on my feet is all I can stand.... I surely am an invalid." Prompted by this alarming note, Nan and Wilna drove to Syracuse and brought Dan back to Woodstock so they could personally supervise his care. In a final blow to the ailing actor's morale, however, it proved impossible for Dan to live with his girls at Treasure Farm, the bucolic acreage he had largely paid for himself and hoped would be his final refuge. The steep stairs in the old farmhouse proved an insurmountable burden, denying him access to the home's only bathroom. Dan Mason was forced to spend his final days in one of the "studio" cottages that Wilna had built for artist rentals. In the face of debilitating illness, the devoted Christian Scientist finally consented to a visit from a doctor who determined that Dan was suffering from kidney failure and tuberculosis; there was no realistic hope of his recovery. A nurse was brought in to see to Dan's daily care as his girls went about their farm chores. As warmer weather approached, Dan briefly seemed to rally. Nan reported to her uncle Fred that his brother had actually gotten out of bed and gone outside in a bathrobe to take in the fresh air and sunshine. He soon took a turn for the worse, however. Realizing that her father was sinking fast, Nan sent her brother an urgent telegram. Living unemployed in Las Vegas, Nevada, three thousand miles away, Harry was unable to make it to his father's bedside. To the very end, Dan Mason kept his wits about him, even showing occasional flashes of ironic humor as he gave his girls his parting advice. At eight in the morning on July 6, 1929, with Nan and Wilna by his side, the veteran of fifty-seven years on stage and screen breathed his last.[10]

The following day, the pastor of Woodstock's Dutch Reformed Church, a friend of Nan and Wilna, conducted a simple funeral service in the bungalow where Dan Mason had died. His remains were then transported to

Part Two: Dan Mason on Screen

the Hackensack, New Jersey, cemetery where, on July 8, 1929, he was buried next to his beloved Millie and their two young sons.[11]

When Nan Mason telephoned her uncle to inform him of her father's death, Fred Grassman alerted the Syracuse newspapers that one of the city's celebrated native sons had passed away. Within hours, the Associated Press picked up the news and issued a brief death notice nationwide. Appearing in dozens of newspapers, the notification soon inspired longer tributes published in papers all over the country. With no reporters old enough to recall Dan Mason's early career in variety, memories of his decades in the theater began with recollections of his appearances in shows like *Peck's Bad Boy* and *Rudolph and Adolph*, his tours in his own vehicles like *The New Chauffeur*, and his several appearances on Broadway. His associations with Tony Pastor and David Belasco were noted as well, as were the countless comic roles he played at movie studios on both coasts. In particular, however, the veteran trouper was remembered as the Skipper who piloted the ramshackle Toonerville Trolley. More than any memory of his more recent character work in Hollywood feature films, it was the image of the bewhiskered old codger of Toonerville that still lingered in the popular imagination. Photos of Dan as the Skipper illustrated many of his obituaries.[12]

One of Dan Mason's publicity photographs from the mid-1920s. His normal appearance without makeup was so different from any of the characters he played that fans sometimes passed him on the street without recognizing him. He was never without his signature cigar.

Over a career that spanned fifty-seven years, from the day he stumbled onto a lantern-lit stage in 1872, to the day he heard a Hollywood director shout "cut" for the last time in 1928, Dan Mason concocted the facial expressions, mannerisms, costumes, and makeup of over one hundred fifty unique and colorful characters. Whether his personifications enlivened variety afterpieces, strode the stage as

11. The Idle List

leading figures in Broadway musicals, or flickered onscreen in short comedies and feature films, Dan Mason's ready supply of eccentric personalities delighted three generations of audiences seeking a respite of good-natured amusement in a theater.

No stone or monument marks the final resting place of Dan Mason. Frugal to the end, the old Dutchman felt that grave markers were a waste of good money that could be invested elsewhere more profitably. Had he been willing to pay for a tombstone, however, a simple memorial tribute offered by an old Syracuse friend, one who still remembered young Dannie Grassman performing in the neighborhood barn during the Civil War, might have served as a fitting epitaph: "His talent for fun on the stage found him out. And he never quit."[13]

APPENDIX A

Afterpieces, Plays and Scenarios by Dan Mason

Key:	
Extant, Complete*	Extant, Fragments**
[A] Afterpiece	[P] Play
[MC] Musical Comedy	[S] Scenario

1878

The Rival Tradesmen (aka *The Rivals*) [A]
The Dutch Agency [A]
The Dutch Shoemaker [A]

1880

Our Uncles (with Dan Sully) [A]
Hop Scotch, the duke, the dowager, the Fenian, the German ambassador, the two maids of honor, and the Rajah of Singapore (with Dan Sully) [P]

1881

** *The Crowded Hotel* (with Dan Sully) [A]
***Unneighborly Neighbors* (with Dan Sully) [A]
**All Fools' Day* [A]

1882

Dinkle and Maginty's Racket [A]
The Krouse Family [A]

1883

Ganzmier's Blunders [A]
The Ladies' Archery Club [A]

1883

Errors [A]

1884

Krousmeyer's Elevation (rewrite of *The Ladies' Archery Club*) [A]
Two Pills in a Box [P]
Two Widowers [P]

Appendix A

1885

The Tigers (rewrite of *Two Widowers*) [MC]
Crazy Quilt (with John T. Kelly) [P]

1887

Sideshow by the Seaside [P]
A Boy Wanted [P]

1888

In a Fix (aka *Winkle's Fix*) [A]
**Keintz's visit to O'Harra* [A]
Rudolph Keints [A]
A Clean Sweep (formerly *Two Widowers/The Tigers*) [MC]

1891

An American Boy [MC]

1895

A Day in June/(aka *A Bachelor's Wives*) [P]

1909

Winning a Widow [S]
Our German Uncle [S]
The Crowded Hotel [S]

1910

The New Chauffeur [A]

1914

The Janitor's Quiet Life [S]
The Janitor's Flirtation [S]
**Dinkelspiel's Baby* [S]

1915

An All Fools Day Affair (based on *All Fool's Day*, 1881) [S]

1919

**Via the Coal Hole* (rewrite of *The New Chauffeur*, 1910) [A]

Appendix B

The Crowded Hotel
by Dan Mason and Dan Sully

Surviving sections of Dan Mason and Dan Sully's popular 1880 vaudeville afterpiece *The Crowded Hotel* demonstrate the challenges that cast members encountered in presenting the play. With the recently invented typewriter still largely unavailable except in upscale offices, Mason was compelled to write everything out by hand, and he opted to save time and energy wherever he could. As can be seen in the following sample pages of the individual scripts, each actor had only his own part before him, with his cues indicated by the last three words of the line he was supposed to respond to. There is little punctuation, and on occasion the cue lines given don't exactly match the lines the actor would hopefully hear from the other players. Quick wits and a keen ability to improvise were required for success. The cursory nature of these handwritten scripts makes it all the more remarkable that the sketch was allegedly plagiarized to such an extent that the authors felt obliged to post copyright warnings in *The New York Clipper*.

By combining these particular four scripts (and cleaning up the spelling and punctuation), it is possible to reconstruct a brief sample episode from scene one—the entrance of the belligerent John Brady, a feisty Irishman spoiling for a fight. Brady's pugnacious demeanor becomes the source of much of the play's humor when he and a visiting "Dutchman," Gottlieb Schoffer, are forced to share not only a room but also the room's one small bed. Unfortunately, aside from his spoken cues, most of the Schoffer script has been lost, making a full reconstruction of *The Crowded Hotel* impossible.

The Crowded Hotel, Scene One

In order of appearance:
Winslow Slopover, a returning Hotel guest
Pete, the Colored Porter
Hotel Landlord
John Brady, an Irishman

In the lobby, where the scene is already in progress:

SLOPOVER: (*Enter Center Door, when Pete is going out*) Hello Pete.
(**GIVES SATCHEL TO HIM**)
PETE: How do you do, Mr. Slopover. (*Takes satchel*)

Appendix B

LANDLORD: Why, Mr. Slopover, how do you do? Glad to see you.
SLOPOVER: How'd do, Landlord. How's business with you?
LANDLORD: Oh, rushing. Never had the house so full in my life. Races here this week. How's business with you?
SLOPOVER: Very good, can't complain. But what's the prospect of getting my old room?
LANDLORD: Well, sorry to say, your old room is taken. I didn't know you were coming, you know. I've got two rooms left on the top floor. I'll give you the best one of them.
SLOPOVER: Top floor, I couldn't think of climbing up stairs.
LANDLORD: But Mr. Slopover, since you were here last I've put an elevator in.
SLOPOVER: Oh then, if that's the case, I'll try and put up with it for tonight. I go away in the morning.
LANDLORD: Very good, I'll try and make you as comfortable as possible.
SLOPOVER: Oh by the way (*takes off duster*) have you got some ice water? I'm very thirsty. It's very dusty traveling.
LANDLORD: Yes, you'll find some right there. (*Points. Business*)
BRADY: (*Enter Center Door, when Slopover goes to water tank. Business to Pete as Pete tries to take satchel*) What are you trying to do, steal my carpetsack?
PETE: No I ain't. You are going to stop here, ain't you?
BRADY: How do you know I am?
PETE: Well, I guessed so.
BRADY: Well, you guessed wrong. How do you know this hotel is high toned enough for me?

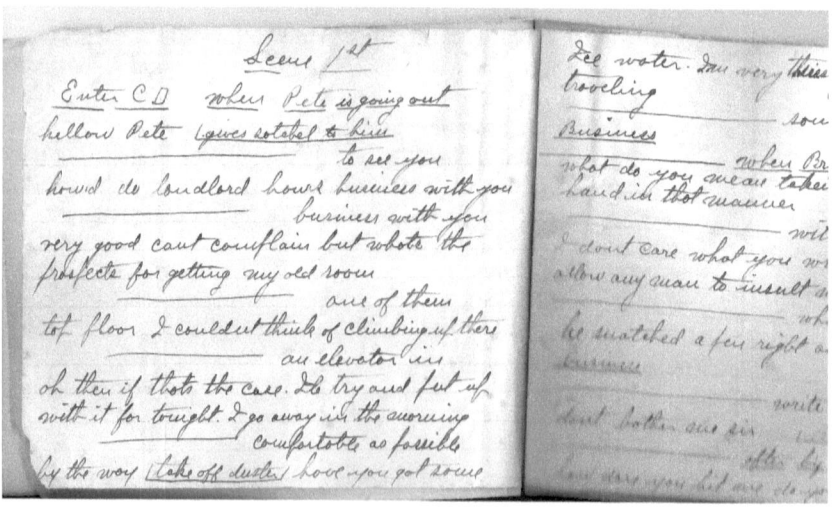

The Crowded Hotel (1881): The script for Winslow Slopover, a returning hotel guest. Obviously written out in haste, Mason's individual scripts are riddled with misspellings and have only minimal punctuation for clarity.

The Crowded Hotel *by Dan Mason and Dan Sully*

The Crowded Hotel (1881): The script for the Hotel Landlord. All of the individual scripts were written on lined tablet paper, then cut and pinned together into 6 × 7.5 inch booklets by Mason. He labeled each script with his own name to make sure they were returned to him.

The Crowded Hotel (1881): The script for Pete, identified by Mason as the "Colored Porter." Most likely performed by a white actor in blackface, the part of Pete, with his humorous observations about the hotel guests, may be a distant echo of Mason's one-time appearances in minstrel shows.

Appendix B

The Crowded Hotel (1881): The script for John Brady, an Irish businessman. Mason likely intended the comment "What ales your porter" to register with the audience as a pun.

> **Pete:** I don't know anything about the tone, but you'll find it high enough if you take one of those rooms on the roof.
> **Brady:** Well, I'm not going on the roof. If I don't have a room with a piano and a fire escape in it, I'll not have any.
> **Pete:** Well, I guess you won't have any then.
> **Brady:** Here, don't give me any of your back talk, for I'm a hard crowd.
> **Pete:** You look like it.
> **Brady:** Do you know who I am? I'm the worst son-of-a-gun in seven states.
> **Landlord** (*comes down*): Well sir, what is the matter?
> **Brady:** Who is that fellow?
> **Landlord:** Why, that's my porter.
> **Brady:** Well, what ails your porter?
> **Landlord:** Nothing ails him, he only wants to take your grip, that's all.
> **Brady:** Wants to get a grip on this, does he? Well, he'll not.
> **Landlord:** You don't understand. He wants to put in in a place of safety.
> **Brady:** Will he give it back to me again?
> **Pete:** Of course I will. (*business*)
> **Brady:** Shut your jaw, I'm not talking to you.
> **Landlord:** Certainly, you'll get it whenever you want it….

Appendix C

Dan Mason, Raconteur

Dan Mason was much appreciated as a raconteur whose gently humorous stories were often repeated by newspaper reporters assigned to cover his appearances in local theaters. On occasion, without waiting for journalists to contact him, Mason wrote up anecdotal press releases for his agents to forward to newspapers ahead of his arrival in town. He also wrote up a series of his anecdotes for inclusion in his planned memoir. In addition to providing glimpses of Mason's many years of life on the road, these collected stories reflect some of the core elements of the veteran comedian's approach to humor; the bone-dry wit, the pithy one-liner, and a deep appreciation for the quaint, simple, and sometimes unintentional, humor of ordinary folks he met along the way. In each example below, the original wording, spelling and punctuation have been preserved.

The Can-Can Dancers

"While Dan was at the National Theater, in Cincinnati, he had a funny experience. Wood's Theater was displaying the can-can dance, and in the spirit of opposition the management of the National put on a tame affair of a like nature. One night, during the middle of the week, Wood's was raided upon by the police, and the entire company was escorted to the station house. Rumors got afloat that the National was to share the same fate the following night, and the management, becoming frightened, substituted men for the female can-can dancers. A rehearsal was held and Dan Mason, Niblo, the French Clown, Charley Shaffer, and one of the stock actors appeared as exponents of the great *Jardin Mabille* dance.

According to the program, the can-can finished the show and just before the moment for ringing up the curtain for it, the police made their appearance. The word was instantly passed among the boys, and the four hurriedly donned their scanty skirts and "went on." A more disgusted set of officers was never beheld. They found they were badly beaten, for a more uncouth, raw, and laughable burlesque was never seen. The audience howled with delight, and the police left."

—Dan Mason Scrapbook, unattributed clipping,
c. 1880, Gelfand Collection

The Elks Lodge

"Dan Mason ... played at Natchez, Miss, last season, and was invited to a meeting of the 'Elks.' During the afternoon, after strolling about the town, he remarked that

Appendix C

Natchez looked like a little 'village'.... This aroused the home spirit of the 'Natchez Elks' and they decided that they would prove to Mr. Dan Mason's utmost satisfaction, that the city was, rather than slow, decidedly rapid. During the lodge meeting at night at Elk Hall, two of the members became involved in a realistic altercation. One called the other a very dreadful name, and the other replied with violent emphasis, while they both drew revolvers. The exalted ruler endeavored to interfere, but before they could be stopped, one had fired point blank at the other, and every man in the hall, except Mason, drew a gun. Then by preconcerted arrangement, the lights were turned out and a hundred blank shots were fired. The lights were quickly turned on again, and Mason, with a worried look, was found under the piano, in an attitude of prayer, and it was only after he had bought several kegs of liquid exhilaration, and promised that he would never again say that Natchez was 'slow' that he was allowed to resume a standing position."

—*Daily Capital Journal* (Salem, Oregon),
26 October 1901.

(N.B. Dan Mason was a life long member of the Benevolent and Protective Order of Elks, and often participated in theatrical benefit programs they staged as fundraisers. One of his short plays, *Krousmeyer's Elevation or The Ladies' Archery Club*, was written for just such an occasion in Providence, Rhode Island, in 1882.)

The Rube Opera House Manager

"To reduce a long railroad trip last fall, the company played one night in a rather small town. Ever since that memorable visit ... the play and the players were the one topic of conversation—the standard of comparison. Songs, dances, funny characters and incidents of the last minstrel show, the opera company, Uncle Tom's Cabin and other attractions were all weighed ... and found wanting in the balance, so when a new musical production appeared in a nearby city, the manager was importuned to write for a 'special return engagement.'

Mason promptly replied, giving the cast, and referring to the new specialties, musical numbers, addition of a dozen or more really pretty girls, attractively gowned, and an unusual amount of horse play; incidentally remarking that he (Dan) played the horse doctor.

The astute purveyor of theatrical amusements penned the following:

_____, Maine Aug. 11, 02.

Mister Dan Mason.

Dear Sir: Yours received and I am sorry we can't play you. The hoss play O. K., but we are on the third floor, and as there is no elevator I don't see how you could get your hosses up 3 flites of stairs even if you are the hoss doctor.

Yours,
James Hurd,
Mgr. Opera House."

—*Reading Times* (Reading, Pennsylvania),
25 August 1902.

Dan Mason, Raconteur

The Small Town Barber

"They are telling a good story with the honors to Dan Mason, of 'Rudolph and Adolph' fame. It is about a barber.

Mason had gone into the most convenient shop, soliciting a shave, and the cordial knight of the scissors and razor promptly 'sized him up as an actor.'

'You're with the show, ain't you,' he observed, to introduce a conversation.

'Yes,' said Mason briefly.

'Never been here before, have you,' he pursued.

'Yes,' said Mason—'Got shaved here before.'

'Is that so,'—the barber displayed a lively interest. 'Why, I don't remember your face.'

'Perhaps not,' acquiesced Mason—'It's all healed up now.'"

—*Vancouver Daily World*, Vancouver, Canada, 29 November 1902, p. 11.

The Night Cap

"Before leaving St. Joseph, Mo., Dan Mason was presented with a bottle of 'five year old' ... as they were about to leave for an all night trip. Dan produced the bottle in the sleeper and gave a nip to one or two present. Charles Mason [Dan's co-star in *Rudolph and Adolph*] was in the smoking car and when he returned, Dan had gone to bed. Someone told Charles of the fine liquor and he at once asked what berth Dan had. 'Lower seven,' replied one of the company at hazard. Charles went to the number directed, peeped in, and dimly saw a bottle lying on the cover. 'Ah ha, Dan's going to take a night cap all by his lonesome,' said Charles. He jerked aside the curtain, grabbed the bottle with a 'Here, you have had enough,' and made off. Just then an infant set up a howl and a woman's voice cried 'What do you mean, sir?' Charles glanced at the bottle. It was half full of milk and had a rubber attachment. He threw it into the berth on the opposite side of the aisle, made a dash for another car, and kept quiet for the balance of the trip."

—*The Richmond Item* (Richmond, Indiana), 12 March 1903

The Hotel Landlord

"During my early days in theatricals,' said Dan Mason, 'I was with a company playing New England. The landlord of a hotel where the company stopped was a long, lean individual, who looked as if a good square meal would do him good. It was a rainy day and he was much concerned over it. In those days the Manager paid all hotel bills, and the entire company were put up at the same hotel. A rainy night meant bad business for the traveling company, and sometimes our landlord had found it a hard matter to collect his bill when it rained. He sized us up to see if we were prosperous, and watched weather conditions all day. Along about four in the afternoon it began to clear off and the sun to peep out. Several of the company were sitting on the hotel porch. The landlord joined us, looked at the sky, and with the first smile he had allowed to appear upon

Appendix C

his face that day, said to us, 'Well, boys, I'm afraid you're going to have a good night after all.' He hinted about usually getting a pass for himself and his wife. He attended the theatre on the pass which he got. After the performance I said to him, 'Did you take in the show?' He replied, 'Oh yes, fust rate; fust rate.' I said, then, 'You liked it, did you?' 'Liked it?' says he. 'Well I guess yes. It was all I could do to keep from laughing.'"

—Dan Mason & Company, "Press Matter,"
c. 1905. Gelfand Collection.

The Irishman

"Dan Mason, in relating some of his experiences, says, 'In a Pennsylvania town I stopped, with others of the company I was with, at a hotel run by a good natured Irishman by the name of Tom Foley. After registering I said to Foley, who was behind the office counter, 'Is your hotel American or European plan?' Foley replies, 'Oh, tis nayther. We put it all on the table, an' ye can go at it an' help yerselves.'"

—Dan Mason & Company, "Press Matter,"
c. 1905. Gelfand Collection.

The Talented Pointer Dog

"Dan Mason ... owns a pointer dog which is either well trained or has the pointing instinct born in him. Mason walked down Eighth Avenue yesterday when his dog suddenly came to a point.

Mason looked around but could see no birds, so he ordered the dog to follow him. The animal never budged, and the actor observed that he was 'pointing' a young man, smooth faced, dark eyed, teeth gilded, and a good looking woman. Dan shouted at his dog, even pushed it, but he pointed and pointed and nothing else.

Mason walked up to the couple. 'Are you hypnotists?' he asked. 'Do you see how my dog points you?'

'Yes, we see,' said the man. 'What's the matter with him?'

'He's pointing,' said Mason. 'Will you kindly tell me who you are? I'd like to know who has such influence over my dog.'

The young man handed Mason his and the young woman's cards. Mason read: 'Eddie Pigeon and Hattie Partridge. Pigeon and Partridge, eh? The dog's all right: He knows why he pointed.'"

—*The Morning Telegraph* (New York City), 29 January 1906.

(N.B. Eddie Pidgeon [correct spelling] was an actual theatrical agent who worked for the William Morris Agency in Manhattan in the first three decades of the twentieth century. Whether or not he actually had a female companion named Hattie Partridge is another matter.)

Mistaken for a Cab Driver

"A firm belief has been implanted in Dan Mason's mind that through some peculiar psychological twist of mind, the best of friends will accept the worst impression that might be gathered from a situation.

Dan Mason, Raconteur

It all happened in Providence, R. I., where Mr. Mason was filling his part [in a movie]. As per scenario, Dan, in typical cabdriver style, drove his vehicle to the railroad station. Just as he was helping the heroine into the cab, three men passed who had formerly known him well.

'Poor Dan,' one was heard to commiserate. 'He was once a good actor. Now he's a hack driver.' And shaking his head sadly, the friend passed right on."

—*The Hutchinson News* (Hutchinson, Kansas),
9 February 1917.

Rain at Half Past Seven

"When we were playing Ware, Mass, I said to the local manager, 'The advance sale doesn't look good.' His reply was, 'Oh, don't go by that. The door sale is always big. If we have good weather tonight, the house will be O.K.' I said 'It has all the earmarks of a good weather night.' He came back with 'Yes, if it don't rain.' It was an ideal night, but the expected door sale was not there. I said to him afterwards, 'How do you account for it?' 'Well,' says he, 'I'll tell you. The night was too good. If it had rained about half past seven it would have drove them in.' I asked if it was necessary to have weather made to order for his town. He said, 'No, but a little rain at the right time would have helped!' I have heard many excuses for poor business while trouping, among them the old standbys of 'Mrs. So-and-So has a dance on at her house, everybody is there,' and—'if you only had a band,' and—'If you had only got here on pay day,' but it was the first time I had heard, 'If it had only rained at seven-thirty!'"

—Dan Mason, Memoir Notes, c. 1927

How to Get a Full House

"While touring in A Clean Sweep I played Rochester, Minn. Before the Overture I peered out through a peep-hole in the curtain. The house was about one-third full. I asked the house stage carpenter who stood near by what attractions had played there and their business. He took a peep and says 'Oh, about like the house tonight.' I said, 'Don't you ever get a full house here?' He answered, 'Oh yes, you ought to see it when we have free lectures!'"

—Dan Mason, Memoir Notes, c. 1927

Filmography

Key:	
D: Director	C: Cast
* Written by Dan Mason	** Extant
AFC: Astra Film Corporation	BCC: Bowers Comedy Corporation
BFC: Betzwood Film Company	BP: Banner Productions
C/C: Colonial Motion Picture Corporation (Cameo Films)	CCB: C.C. Burr Productions
CKY: Clara Kimball Young Film Corporation	CP: Columbia Pictures
CPC: Chadwick Pictures Corporation	EMC: Edison Manufacturing Company
EFC: Eastern Film Corporation (made in 1915, released in 1917/1918 as Jaxon or Sparkle comedies)	FNP: First National Pictures
FPL: Famous Players-Lasky Corporation	FOX: Fox Film Corporation
GPC: Goldwyn Pictures Corporation	HCW: H.C. Weaver Productions
HRP: Harry Rapf Productions	JGB: J.G. Blystone Productions
JKM: J.K. McDonald Productions	MPC: Metropolitan Pictures Corporation
MGM: Metro-Goldwyn-Mayer	PGP: Paul Gerson Pictures Corporation
PP: Paramount Pictures	RBP: Rex Beach Pictures Company
RPI: Radin Pictures, Inc.	RTP: Richard Talmadge Productions
SGC: Samuel Goldwyn Company	SPC: Selig Polyscope Company, Chicago
THI: Thomas H. Ince Corporation	UP: Universal Pictures
WB: Warner Brothers	

Filmography

All dates given are release dates. Where official release dates were not available, the date cited is the month when the film first appeared in theaters. Some lists of cast members have been supplemented with information from the International Movie Data Base: https://www.imdb.com

Winning a Widow.* (SPC, 30 August 1909) Split Reel, 450 ft. D: Dan Mason. C: Dan Mason.
  Synopsis: A young man and his girl are frustrated by their respective uncles, who object to their marriage. Since both uncles are attempting to woo the same widow, the youngsters intervene, offering innuendoes that threaten to ruin the uncles' good names and creating humorous complications. In the end, the uncles relent and approve their plans.

Our German Cousin.* (SPC, 31 January 1910) Split Reel, 285 ft. D: Dan Mason. C: Dan Mason.
  Synopsis: A newly arrived German immigrant encounters much in America that baffles him.

A Crowded Hotel.* (SPC, 14 March 1910) Split Reel, 370 ft. D: Dan Mason. C: Dan Mason.
  Synopsis: With a convention in town, the hotel is so crowded that several delegates are packed into the same room, a circumstance they consider unworthy of them. The newly married couple in the next room take exception to the noise they make and file a complaint. The result is a riot that nearly wrecks the hotel.

Professor William Nutt. (EMC, 2 June 1913) 1 reel. D: C.J. Williams. C: Dan Mason, Madeline Adair, William Wadsworth, Mrs. C.J. Williams, Maggie Weston, Alice Washburn.
  Synopsis: When Mr. Hastings invites Professor William Nutt (Mason), an ardent vegetarian, to dinner, Mrs. Hastings is horrified, as she is unprepared. She and her husband quickly ask the neighbors for help and assemble a wonderful meal. But when they sit down to eat, the Professor refuses everything and starts pulling his own dinner out of his pockets: walnuts, peanuts, prunes and a carrot.

How Did it Finish? (EMC, 25 June 1913) 1 reel. D: Ashley Miller. C: Dan Mason, Alice Washburn, Elsie MacLeod, Benj. F. Wilson, Gertrude McCoy, Herbert Prior, Beatrice Mable.
  Synopsis: Father (Mason) finds his daughter reading a sensational novel and takes it away. Before destroying it, however, he decides to read a bit to see how low his child has sunk. He get hooked on the book, but when he gets to the climax of the story—with the hero speeding to the rescue of the heroine—he finds the last page missing. It turns out his wife has it in her hair, using it as a curling paper, and she refuses to give it up.

All Account of a Portrait. (EMC, 2 July 1913) 1 reel. D: C.J. Williams. C: Dan Mason, Mary Fuller, Benjamin F. Wilson, Frank A. Lyons, Yale Boss, Gertrude McCoy, Richard Neill, Mrs. C.J. Williams, Harry Linson.
  Synopsis: Jessie and John are sweethearts but have a falling out over John's dislike of a noted pianist's long hair. Jessie breaks off their romance and gives back all his gifts and he does the same. However, both end up at a wedding, standing before the minister (Mason) as bridesmaid and best man for their friends. When both are invited to the home of the young couple, they are mistaken for the newly weds by the neighbors and realize that they want to resume their romance.

The Signal. (EMC, 5 July 1913) 1 reel. D: George Lessey. C: May Abbey, Richard Tucker, Mrs. William Bechtel, Julian Reed, Dan Mason, Charles Sutton.
  Synopsis: The royalist Count, St. Pierre, hides in the cottage of an old family servant (Mason) and evades the republican forces looking for him. He plans to escape to England and sends the servant with a message to his paramour, the Countess d'Avroi. However the servant is intercepted and

Filmography

the plot is discovered by Citizen Bompard, who then attempts to romance the countess while he waits to apprehend St. Pierre. When the countess tricks Bompard's men into shooting him by mistake, she and St. Pierre make their escape.

A Pair of Foils. (EMC, 14 July 1913) 1 reel. D: C.J. Williams. C: William Wadsworth, Alice Washburn, Richard Neill, George Conway, Robert Lett, Dan Mason, Edward, O'Connor, Robert Milash.

Synopsis: An actor dreams he has wandered into a palace where he hides behind the throne. When he is discovered by one of the councilors (Mason), the queen, who has just dismissed several potential husbands, falls madly in love with him. The palace is attacked by the rejected suitors and the hero fights them off and wins the hand of the queen. The actor then awakes.

As the Tooth Came Out. (EMC, 30 July 1913) Split Reel, 600 ft. D: C.J. Williams. C: Dan Mason, William Wadsworth, Mrs. C.J. Williams, Patrick Walshe, Alice Washburn.

Synopsis: Mr. T. Aik has a toothache and goes to see Dr. Pullem (Mason). Because of the patient's fears, the Doctor administers laughing gas. Mr. Aik hallucinates that the Dr. has turned into a demon and when he extracts the tooth, it grows to an enormous size and chases Mr. Aik down the street. When he awakes from the gas, he sees the tiny tooth and the Dr. assures him all is well.

The Awakening of a Man. (EMC, 5 September 1913) 2000 ft. D: George Lessey. C: Benjamin F. Wilson, Charles Ogle, Dan Mason, William West, Richard Tucker, Robert Brower, May Abbey.

Synopsis: The Company of Wentworth and Son is in financial decline. Richard Wentworth turns to his fiancée's father for help, causing the young woman to break off their engagement. When Richard contemplates suicide, he is inspired by the bravery of the ancestors whose portraits surround him. An elderly family servant (Mason) reacts with delight to see his young master thus emboldened and ready to fight for his future.

The Comedian's Downfall. (EMC, 17 September 1913) Split Reel, 600 ft. D: Charles H. France. C: Dan Mason, Alice Washburn.

Synopsis: Bob Buster (Mason), a comedian, copies the outfit worn by Semolina, an ardent suffragette, for his comedy act, but both he and Semolina confuse their venues, Holburn Hall and Holburn Club, and go to the wrong locations. Bob is greeted by wildly excited women and Semolina finds herself lecturing men who hoot and holler. When each of them causes a riot, they end up in the same jail cell.

Why Girls Leave Home. ** (EMC, 3 October 1913) 2 reels. D: C.J. Williams. C: Dan Mason, Bessie Learn, Edward Boulden, Alice Washburn, Gladys Hulette, Edwin Clarke, William Wadsworth, Mabel Trunnelle, Herbert Prior, William Bechtel, Mrs. William Bechtel, Charles Morgan, William West, Phillip Tannura, Mrs. C.J. Williams.

Synopsis: A minister (Mason) receives a flyer for a play, "Why Girls Leave Home," and is sure it poses a threat to the moral well-being of his flock. However, in order to preach against it effectively, he decides he must see the play himself and plans to secretly attend. Unfortunately, his daughter, secretary, and cook all attend as well, with their respective young men. When they all arrive home at the same time, the minister tries to avoid telling where he has been, until the usher arrives to bring him the coat he forgot.

A Short Life and a Merry One. (EMC, 6 October 1913) Split Reel, 700 ft. D: Charles H. France. C: Frank A. Lyons, Dan Mason, William West, Gertrude Ryan, Bessie Learn, Marion Weeks, Edwin Clarke.

Synopsis: A tramp falls asleep in a cornfield beside a scarecrow, and a mischievous imp sets him up in place of the scarecrow, which he turns into a real man. He gives the enlivened scarecrow a magic wand, warning him that the wand must never leave his hand. The scarecrow sets out for the city, using the wand to bring another scarecrow (Mason) to life along the way. Once in town, the duo attempt to romance two female store window dummies unsuccessfully and decide to stop for a beer. When

Filmography

the first scarecrow puts down the wand to pick up the beer, he finds himself back in the cornfield, dressed in rags again.

His First Performance. (EMC, 22 October 1913) Split Reel, 600 ft. D: Charles France. C: Edward O'Connor, Jessie Stevens, Edward Boulden, Carlton King, Mrs. C. Jay Williams, William Sadler, Herbert Prior, Frank A. Lyon, Dan Mason.

Synopsis: Tommy McGuire has the leading role in a melodrama and invites his parents to attend his performance. When they arrive, they have an argument with the stage doorkeeper (Mason). During the play, they assume their son is in actual danger and make such a fuss that they have to be repeatedly restrained by the ushers. In the end, Mr. McGuire, who has been taking nips from his flask, ends up charging the stage and succeeds in knocking out both the villain and his son.

The Horrible Example. (EMC, 29 October 1913) 1 reel. D: Charles M. Seay. C: Dan Mason, Edna Flugrath, Edward Boulden, Edward Mack, Jessie Stevens, Marian De Forest, Martin Mann.

Synopsis: Mr. Joe Drywun (Mason) is a staunch prohibitionist. He has a lovely daughter, Kathleen, who in is love with a traveling cork salesman. Since corks are used in liquor bottles, Drywun doesn't like his daughter's beau. Drywun and his neighbor, Mr. Waters, decide to help with a prohibitionist political campaign in a nearby city. Meanwhile, an out of work actor, Reginald Barrystone, gets a job in that campaign, acting as a "horrible example" of the effects of drink. Just before the election, a Mr. Gritt comes to town, meets Kathleen, but is scolded by Drywun for paying too much attention to his beautiful daughter. To get revenge, he arranges to take on the role of "horrible example" himself and secretly switches Drywun's throat tonic for something stronger. When Drywun suddenly becomes benevolent and promises Mr. Gritt he will grant him any wish, he asks for Kathleen's hand in marriage, and gets it.

Porgy's Bouquet. (EMC, 3 November 1913) Split Reel, 650 ft. D: C. Jay Williams. C: William Wadsworth, Alice Washburn, Dan Mason, Mrs. C. Jay Williams, Arthur Housman, Andrew J. Clark.

Synopsis: Georgy Porgy buys a bouquet of flowers for his lady friend, Gerty, who lives across the street, and has them delivered to his home. When he shows her the flowers at his window and gestures they are for her, Mrs. Smith, who lives in the apartment just below Gerty, thinks he is flirting with her. Meanwhile, Mrs. Smith is trying to keep a secret from Mr. Smith (Mason) regarding an anniversary present, and he wonders what is going on. His suspicions are aroused by Georgy's "flirting" at the window and it gets worse when Georgy's flowers are delivered to Mrs. Smith by mistake. When Georgy comes to their flat looking for the missing flowers, pandemonium ensues.

Getting a Patient. (EMC, 15 November 1913) 1 reel. D: Charles H. France. C: Yale Benner, Robert Brower, Dan Mason, Edna Flugrath.

Dr. John Maxwell is new in town and tries to drum up customers by putting up a notice that he has been called away. He then races through town in his carriage to smoke his pipe in the woods before returning home. On one of his "missions" he meets Marian, a young woman, and they begin to see much of each other. Marian's father has the gout and is very unhappy with his current doctor (Mason). Marian convinces him to engage John, and all is well.

Enoch and Ezra's First Smoke (EMC, 24 November 1913) Split Reel, 500 ft. D: Charles H. France. C: Yale Boss, Andrew J. Clark, Dan Mason, Jessie Stevens.

Synopsis: Two young boys, Enoch and Ezra, are on their way to the fishing hole when they encounter a camp of gypsies. Seeing the men sitting around smoking pipes, they decide this is something they would like to try. They throw down their fishing rods and race home to retrieve their father's pipe. Hiding behind the woodshed, they puff away. It doesn't take long before both of them are quite ill. Meanwhile, their father (Mason) is looking for them. When he finds two gypsies fishing with their rods, he assumes the worse. However, the boys are soon discovered behind the woodshed

Filmography

where they have been cured of any desire to become gypsies.

Wanted, A Burglar (EMC, 1 December 1913) Split Reel, 550 ft. D: Charles H. France. C: Dan Mason, Marion Weeks, Carlton King.

Synopsis: Thad Rowly, a printer in a newspaper office, falls in love with Helen, the daughter of the editor, Mr. Penrose (Mason), and she with him. The editor is furious as he thinks Rowly isn't worthy of his Helen. One morning Penrose discovers that someone has entered his office during the night and stolen his cigars. He places an ad in the paper suggesting that he has money in the safe and dares anyone to try and take it. Then he sits in his office with two pistols, waiting to catch the burglar, but soon falls asleep. So he misses a slight boyish figure who creeps through the window and quickly uses the right combination to open the safe and take the money. When Penrose wakes up and discovers his loss, he calls the police. Just then, Rowly dashes in with an offer to find the thief, himself. If he does, will Penrose let him marry Helen? Penrose agrees and is soon presented with the burglar, Helen in disguise.

The Thrifty Janitor. (EMC, 3 December 1913) 1 reel. D: Charles M. Seay. C: Dan Mason, Richard Neill, May Abbey, Alice Washburn, Harry Eytinge, Marion De Forest, Arthur Housman.

Synopsis: When Mr. and Mrs. Blythe disagree over where to spend their vacation, he goes off to stay at his club and she goes home to mother. Meanwhile, the janitor (Mason), seeing that they are not at home, assumes they have gone away on their scheduled two-month vacation. He decides to make some quick cash and rent the apartment in the interim. A young couple on their honeymoon soon move in. However, the Blythes, convinced by friends and family they are making a mistake, decide to forgive each other and return home. Mrs. Blythe gets there first and discovers a woman's hat on the table. When her husband comes in, she confronts him. The husband soon discovers another man in the apartment and tries to apprehend him. The frightened groom barricades himself in the bedroom and calls out from the window for the police. When the authorities arrive, the janitor explains the reason for all the fuss.

Peg o' the Movies. (EMC, 12 December 1913) 2 reels. D: George Lessey. C: Gertrude McCoy, Benjamin F. Wilson, Harry Eytinge, Mrs. Wm. Bechtel, Richard Tucker, Bigalow Cooper, Yale Benner, Kathleen Coughlin, Darel Goodwin, Robert Brower, Dan Mason, Carlton King.

Synopsis: Peg and Stephen are sweethearts, but Peg refuses his proposal since she must care for her siblings and their drunken father. When Peg gets a new job at a movie studio, Stephen takes a job with a bridge building company and moves out west. Peg ends up being recruited as an actress and is a big success. She is sent out west with a company on location. Stephen has by now seen her in a film, and keeps going back to see it again, a fact noticed by the theater manager (Mason). On his way to the movies, Stephen comes across Peg and her company filming an Indian uprising. He is recruited to play a role but after rescuing the heroine, he rides off with his sweetheart clasped in his arms.

The Janitor's Quiet Life. (EMC, 24 December 1913) Split Reel, 415 ft. D: Charles M. Seay. C: Dan Mason, Yale Boss, Andrew Clark.

Synopsis: The janitor (Mason) prides himself on the air of respectability he cultivates at his apartment house. So, when a group of boys and their pet goats raise a ruckus out front, he chases them away. Not easily discouraged, the boys decide to stage a circus in one of the empty flats. When the tenants in the apartment directly under the circus alert the janitor, he grudgingly goes to investigate. However, the boys have now moved on to another location and now another complaint is lodged. When the janitor finally finds them, he encounters an enraged goat, with predictable results.

Mary's New Hat. (EMC, 24 December 1913) Split Reel, 585 ft. D: Charles H. France. C: Elsie MacLeod, Edward Boulden, William Wadsworth, Bliss Milford, Dan Mason.

Synopsis: Mary wants an expensive new hat, but her husband says no, and Mary complains to her father. Though he agrees with the husband, father pretends to be outraged and storms off to thrash Mary's spouse. To convince Mary he has been thrashed, the husband paints a fake black ring around one eye. When Mary sees this, she scolds her father for being a brute, and dabs at the supposedly injured eye with her handkerchief. Unfortunately, some of the black paint comes off and when Mary dabs her own weeping eyes and looks in the mirror, the whole ruse is revealed. To teach the two men a lesson, Mary hastens to the constable (Mason) who arrests father and husband for disorderly conduct. When the two men try to bribe the constable, he gives the money to Mary so she can buy her hat.

The Sherlock Holmes Girl. (EMC, 7 January 1914) Split Reel, 600 ft. D: Charles H. France. C: Bliss Milford, Frank Lyon, Dan Mason, Horace Newman, Cora Williams.

Synopsis: Sally is a dull maid at the Palace Hotel, run by Mr. Jones (Mason). When a guest leaves behind a book on detective work, Sally reads it to do some sleuthing on her own. Since a jewel robbery has occurred nearby, Sally suspects the next guest to be the thief. She shadows him and peers over the transom, catching him removing jewels from his suitcase. Letting herself into the room and pretending to have a gun, she apprehends the thief and ends up collecting the reward money.

The Witness to the Will. (EMC, 9 January 1914) 2 reels. D: George Lessey. C: William West, Gertrude McCoy, Harry Beaumont, Richard Neill, Jessie Stevens, Dan Mason, Benjamin F. Wilson.

Synopsis: Just before he dies, Major Thorndyke has his attorney (Mason) make out a will leaving everything to his niece, Margaret. But his worthless son, Beldon, steals the will and lays claim to the entire estate. Margaret goes into the city to try and earn her own living, nearly starving in the attempt. She is rescued by her neighbor, Terrence, the late Major's former groom. Since he had witnessed the will, he suspects Beldon of treachery and confronts him. Beldon pushes Terrence off a cliff, thinking he has killed him. However, Terrence is rescued by Lieutenant Preble, and the two men go to confront Beldon again. When Terrence reappears, battered but alive, Beldon loses his nerve and hands over the will. Margaret gets the estate, and gets Lieutenant Preble in the bargain.

Deacon Billington's Downfall. (EMC, 16 January 1914) 2 reels. D: Charles H. France. C: Dan Mason, Darel Goodwin, Martin Faust, Frank Lyon, Cora Williams, Edward Boulden, Mrs. Ida Ward, Elizabeth Miller, William West, Jessie Stevens, Harry Linson, Mrs. William Bechtel, May Abbey.

Synopsis: Deacon Billington (Mason) is a mean spirited tightwad and a hypocritical prohibitionist. He forbids his daughter, Millie, to see her boyfriend, George, but the youngsters ignore him. He doesn't notice because he is busy trying to woo the widow Divine. His romance is made difficult by the widow's other suitor, Si Higgins. The widow likes to listen in on the telephone party line and overhears George and Millie planning to elope. She tells the Deacon and he tries to prevent the marriage. However, when he follows them to the parsonage, he finds them already married. He also finds that the widow Divine has just married Si Higgins.

The Janitor's Flirtation. * (EMC, 19 January 1914) Split Reel, 600 ft. D: Charles M. Seay. C: Dan Mason, Jessie Stevens, Yale Boss, Gladys Hulette, Mrs. William Bechtel, William Bechtel, Frank Lyons.

Synopsis: As a prank, young Jimmie dresses up like a girl and flirts with the janitor (Mason). Jimmie and his friend make sure the janitor's wife, a woman of considerable size, knows about it. When she starts after the janitor and his flirtatious female admirer, they flee down the stairs. But the wife trips and falls on them, pinning them down so completely that the police and fire departments are forced to perform a rescue.

Love's Young Dream. (EMC, 25 February 1914) Split Reel, 500 ft. D: Charles H. France. C: Frank Lyons, Dan Mason, Jessie Stevens, Marjorie Ellison.

Synopsis: Mr. Watkins and his girlfriend, Miss Brown, are both rather stout. Mr. Marker (Mason) and his ladylove, Miss Whitcomb, are both quite slender. But when the two couples meet on the streetcar, both men find themselves attracted to the other's companion, and in fact, they soon marry them. Unfortunately, in due course, Watkins and Marker find themselves unbearably henpecked and decide to teach their wives a lesson. They write up fake suicide notes and leave their clothes side by side on the riverbank. Their ruse works, and when they finally reveal themselves to their distraught wives, safe and sound, all is well.

Mr. Sniffkin's Widow. (EMC, 2 March 1914) 1 reel. D: Charles M. Seay. C: Elizabeth Miller, Bliss Milford, Cora Williams, Nellie Grant, Jessie Stevens, Edna Hammel, Frank Lyons, Edward O'Connor, Dan Mason, Harry Eytinge.

Synopsis: Even though Mr. Sniffkin has been dead for five years, his widow refuses all offers of marriage and prefers to extol the virtues of her late husband. Following her example, several other marriageable ladies frustrate their suitors (Mason as one suitor). When an attractive young single schoolteacher arrives in town, the frustrated beaux turn their attention to her. When the teacher's fiancé shows up, the men go back to their former objects of desire, who are now much more receptive. Even the widow Sniffkin now relents and agrees to marry Hiram Brown, but he first insists she get rid of a hideous photo of her late husband hanging in her parlor.

Dinkelspiel's Baby. * (EMC, 23 March 1914) 1 reel. D: Charles M. Seay. C: Dan Mason, Jessie Stevens, Gertrude Braun, Nellie Grant.

Synopsis: Mr. Dinkelspiel (Mason) and his wife have no children and Mrs. D. treats the family dog like a baby, even seating him at the table. One day, while sitting in the park, Dinkelspiel witnesses a desperate woman abandon her baby with a note explaining that she can't support it. He decides to take the child home, but fears his wife might object. So he purchases a basket, leaves the baby in the basket on his own doorstep and waits for his wife to discover it. Mrs. Dinkelspiel's heart melts, and when her husband arrives, she pleads with him to let her keep the baby. Dinkelspiel pretends to protest at first, then "relents" and they adopt the child. The dog is returned to his own doghouse in the yard.

A Night Out. (EMC, 25 March 1914) 1 reel. D: Charles H. France. C: Dan Mason, May Abbey, Edward O'Connor, Cora Williams.

Synopsis: Mr. Vincent (Mason) and Mr. Jessup both buy identical overcoats on the same day while out running errands for their wives. Mr. Vincent has to exchange a baby bottle while Mr. Jessup has a pink slipper to be repaired. As it turned out, both men eat lunch at the same restaurant where a prankster sets a small fire as a joke, and both men are drenched by a fire extinguisher. As they rush out the door, each man grabs the other's coat by mistake. When they see the prankster and attempt to punish him for their inconvenience, they get arrested and spend the night in jail. By the next morning their wives are frantic, but neither man wants to admit to being in jail. When Mrs. Vincent finds the pink slipper, Mr. Vincent is in serious trouble. The same is true for Mr. Jessup when his wife finds a baby bottle. The confusion is resolved when it turns out that neither man fits into the coat he brought home.

Mrs. Romana's Scenario. (EMC, 1 April 1914) Split Reel, 460 ft. D: Uncredited. C: Dan Mason.

Synopsis: Mrs. Romana sees an ad promising untold wealth and fame for writing scenarios and decides to try her hand at it. Awakening in the night with a great idea, she scribbles her thoughts on the first thing she finds, her husband's shirt. Her notes include words like "$5000," "death," and "blackhand," but Mr. Romana doesn't notice any of it when he hastily dresses in the morning. When he later does notice what he thinks is dirt, he sends the shirt to be laundered, only to have a detective see it and take it to the police. The "evidence" is traced back to Mr. Romana who is hard pressed to explain until his wife solves the mystery.

A Weekend at Happyhurst. (EMC, 4 May 1914) 1 reel. D: Charles M. Seay. C: Edward Boulden, Dan Mason, Jessie Stevens, Frank Lyons.

Synopsis: Mr. Lowe (Mason) invites Mr. Glink out to Happyhurst for the weekend, but his outing turns into a nightmare. He has to walk in deep snow from the train station to the mansion where he is obliged to shovel snow, carry coal, and chop wood. It turns out food is in short supply, so dinner consists of cold beans. Then he is compelled to give up his bed for the children because chicken pox has broken out in the house. Finally, after getting injured while sledding, and getting drenched by a broken pipe, Glink sneaks out and goes back to town, to a restaurant for something to eat.

Seraphina's Love Affair. (EMC, 20 May 1914) Split Reel, 600 ft. D: Charles M. Seay. C: May Abbey, Augustus Phillips, Dan Mason, Jessie Stevens, Edwin Clark.

Synopsis: The wealthy Ezra Haskins (Mason) runs a boarding house with his adopted daughter, Seraphina. When a handsome young stranger, Sport MacSweeny, takes a room, Seraphina falls madly in love. Sport takes advantage of her crush and enlists her help in robbing her father, who keeps his money under his pillow. He proposes they elope and "borrow" some of Haskin's cash. But once Sport gets his hands on the money, he runs off without Seraphina. She pursues him, finds him unconscious from being thrown from his horse, and retrieves the money. Back home, she confesses her misdeed and goes back to her work.

A Tight Squeeze, Part Eight of Dolly of the Dailies. (EMC, 23 May 1914) 1 reel. D: Walter Edwin. C: Mary Fuller, Charles Ogle, Edward Earle, Yale Boss, Warren Cook, Julian Reed, Dan Mason, Arnold Prisco, Harry Semels.

Synopsis: When Mr. Montenegro is murdered, the intrepid reporter, Dolly Desmond wants the assignment, but the editor gives it to a new reporter, Hillary Graham. Dolly is assigned to cover a Salvation Army wedding. When Hillary is foolish enough to enter a dingy bar and tell the landlord (Mason) he is looking to solve the murder, he ends up unconscious in the coal cellar. Meanwhile, Dolly, who has donned a Salvation Army uniform and followed their band into town looking for more material, enters the bar and finds Hillary's necktie on the floor. When she sneaks into the cellar and finds Hillary, she is nearly crushed by a load of coal being delivered. Outside, a boy hears her cry and stops the delivery and rescues her. When they run to the police, the officers raid the bar and arrest everyone, discovering the murderer in the process. Back at the newspaper office, Hillary proposes, but Dolly isn't ready for marriage just yet.

The Tango in Tuckerville. (EMC, 8 June 1914) 1 reel. D: Charles M. Seay. C: Frank A. Lyons, May Abbey, Dan Mason, Nellie Grant, William West, Ida Ward, Bliss Milford, Marie La Manna, Miriam Nesbitt.

Synopsis: Three lovely young manicurists arrive in Tuckerville and turn a lot of heads when they walk down the street. When they open their shop, Mr. Jenkins (Mason), Mr. Henshaw, and Mr. Simkins are first in line to get their manicures. Meanwhile, Mrs. Henshaw has taken her son Willie, with her to her sewing circle, across the street from the manicure shop. Willie has a toy telescope and sees a young lady holding his father's hand and tells his mother. Realizing from her reaction that he's made a mistake, he warns his father, so when the enraged Mrs. Henshaw and her friends storm the shop, their husbands are gone. To get even with their husbands, Mrs. Henshaw and her circle start a Tango class to which they admit only young men. The manicurists react by opening a Turkey Trot Temple to which only young women are admitted. But the outraged wives start a new dance club, ostracizing the manicurists, and ruling that husbands may only dance with their wives.

The Mysterious Package. (EMC, 24 June 1914) Split Reel, 700 ft. D: Charles M. Seay. C: Edith Peters, Elizabeth Miller, Frank Lyons, Nellie Grant, Edward Boulden, Edward O'Connor, Cora Williams, Andrew J. Clark, Richard Peer, Julian Reed, Dan Mason.

Synopsis: After several thefts and other crimes, the town of Pohonkasville decides to do something about tramps. Led by their constable (Mason), the villagers gather and venture out to drive them away. They run right past three tramps who wonder what the fuss is all about and join the chase. When they are discovered, they are turned out of town. However, when the triumphant villagers return to the village store, they find a mysterious package that they are sure is a bomb sent by the tramps. They throw it in a bucket of water and run from the store, expecting an explosion. As they wait for the blast, two boys enter the store and retrieve the package. Finding that it contains fudge, they proceed to eat the "bomb."

An Up to Date Courtship. (EMC, 15 July 1914) Split Reel, 500 ft. D: Charles M. Seay. C: Dan Mason, Cora Williams, Harry Mason, Helen Bauer.

Synopsis: Abe Perkins (Mason) and Si Prime are rivals for the hand of the widow Gray, but she is reluctant to make a choice. When Si sees the widow going for a ride in Abe's buggy, he buys a motorcycle and succeeds in luring the widow into taking a ride. Seeing this, Abe decides to buy an automobile and chases after the motorcycle. Meanwhile, the widow is terrified by her motorcycle ride and gladly accepts a ride back home with Abe in his car. However, as they arrive at her door, the car blows up, and the widow decides she will never speak to either of the two men again.

His Wife's Burglar. (EMC, 22 July 1914) Split Reel, 500 ft. D: Charles M. Seay. C: Dan Mason, Jessie Stevens, Gertrude Braun.

Synopsis: Mr. Smith (Mason) is annoyed when he comes home early one afternoon and his wife isn't there to greet him. Since she is always out gadding about, Mr. Smith decides to teach her a lesson. He fabricates a dummy from pillows, an old suit and some shoes, and makes it look like someone is under her bed. He hides in the closet to wait. When Mrs. Smith sees the dummy, she runs screaming from the house and tells a patrolman that there is a burglar in her room. Meanwhile, Mr. Smith dismantles the dummy and is looking for his glasses on the floor when the policeman finds him and hauls him to the station. No one believes his story until Mrs. Smith comes in to explain.

A Tango Spree. (EMC, 3 August 1914) 1 reel. D: Charles M. Seay. C: Dan Mason, Jessie Stevens, Elsie MacCleod, May Abbey, Edward Earle, Cora Williams, Yale Benner, Bliss Milford.

Synopsis: Mr. Sparks (Mason) is the only man in town who disapproves of the Tango. He won't even sell shoes to girls unless they promise not to use them for dancing the Tango. About the time that Sparks' mother comes to visit, some townsfolk rent a hall Sparks owns for a party. But when Sparks learns they will be dancing the Tango, he refuses to let them use it. However, a "burglar" with a fake gun obtains the key to the hall from Sparks, who becomes suspicious and goes off to investigate. When he finds both his wife and his mother dancing the Tango, he gives up his protests and joins in the fun.

Faint Heart Ne'er Won Fair Lady. (EMC, 5 August 1914) Split Reel, 550 ft. D: Charles M. Seay. C: Edward Boulden, Dan Mason, Jessie Stevens, Bessie Learn, Richard Neill, Andrew J. Clark.

Synopsis: Billie is in love with Nellie, but Nellie's father, Mr. Bailey (Mason), is Billie's employer. He is so indignant at Billie's request for Nellie's hand in marriage that he fires him. Billie then sends him a telegram expressing his love for Nellie. Billie also waits outside the office to press his case, only to be pushed down the elevator shaft by the outraged Mr. Bailey. Undaunted, Billie is waiting at the foot of the stairs when the astonished Mr. Bailey gets there. Mr. Bailey flees, with Billie in hot pursuit, but both are hit by an automobile. They are taken to the hospital where Billie continues to plead for Nellie's hand. That evening, when Mr. Bailey, in his bandages, comes down to dinner, there is Billie in his bandages sitting at the dinner table. He finally gives the young couple his blessing.

A Village Scandal. (EMC, 2 September 1914) 1 reel. D: Charles M. Seay. C: Dan Mason, Jessie Stevens, May Abbey, Gladys Hulette, Edward O'Connor, Anne Clifford, Arthur Housman.

Synopsis: Wiggles, the adopted daughter of Farmer Haskins (Mason) likes Shrimp but is intrigued by the male boarders who come up to the farm from the city. In response, Shrimp pays extra attention to the girls who also came up from the city. Meanwhile, Old Jim, the village drunkard neglects his daughter, and when her parents refuse to intervene, Wiggles rescues the child and hides her in the Haskins barn. When the child is reported missing,

Filmography

everyone suspects the worst and the sheriff arrests Old Jim. But one of the boarders reveals the little girl's whereabouts and another offers to take the child. Old Jim relinquishes his role as a parent and everyone is happy. Wiggles is seen as a heroine and she and Shrimp are reconciled.

Post No Bills. (EMC, 23 September 1914) 1 reel. D: C. Jay Williams. C: Arthur Housman, Harry Gripp, Gladys Hulette, Mrs. C. Jay Williams, Edward O'Connor, Dan Mason, Gertrude Braun, William Wadsworth.

Synopsis: Will Stark, the bill poster, and Nellie Primm are in love, but Nellie's Aunt Susan works hard to keep them apart. So they decide to elope. Meanwhile, Stark's assistant is posting a poster of a ballet dancer when Aunt Susan sees him and loudly expresses her disapproval. In response, he posts a more scandalous poster on her barn, much to the amusement of her field hands, Cy and Job (Mason). The poster is positioned so that when Aunt Susan opens a barn window to look out, her head replaces the figure's head. When she does so, her photo is taken by the local "Kodak Fiend." Stark and Nellie now return, newly married, and Aunt Susan gives them a hot reception. But when she is shown the photo of herself posing with the naughty poster, she relents and accepts their marriage.

Twins and Trouble. (EMC, 26 September 1914) 1 reel. D: Charles M. Seay. C: Herbert Prior, Bliss Milford, Frank Lyons, Dan Mason, Jessie Stevens, Ida Ward.

Synopsis: Betty and Bob have twins and the two sets of grandparents are in hot competition to spend time with the children. It gets so bad that Betty leaves with her parents, the Colonel (Mason) and his wife, and Bob leaves with his parents, the Major and his wife. The parents each take one twin with them. When the families employ two nursemaids to take the twins out for some air, the two girls get involved in a quarrel over a faithless boy friend and briefly leave the babies unattended in the park. The children are retrieved by a passing washerwoman, and when the nursemaids return to duty, they find their charges missing. Meanwhile, the Major and the Colonel have taken their quarrel to the police station. They are there when the washerwoman appears with the children. They take the children home to their parents and all is resolved.

In a Prohibition Town. (EMC, 30 September 1914) Split Reel, 500 ft. D: Charles M. Seay. C: Dan Mason, Elsie Mac Cleod, Edward Earle, Yale Boss, Allen Crolius, Edward O'Connor.

Synopsis: The Storekeeper (Mason) is annoyed with Zeke, who loves his daughter, Lizzie, and throws Zeke out. To make matters worse, a slick salesman comes to town and Lizzie pays him too much attention. Jake, the delivery boy, dislikes the salesman and finds an opportunity to paint the word "whiskey" on the salesman's sample case. Zeke seizes the case, hoping to get his rival in trouble by taking it to the constable. Meanwhile, a tramp, who had been considering stealing the sample case, pursues Zeke, hoping to turn him in as a thief and reap a reward. The Storekeeper, Nellie, Jake, and the salesman, all join the chase. When the tramp catches Zeke, they fight and get entangled in the flypaper contained in the sample case.

George Washington Jones. (EMC, 12 October 1914) Split Reel, 500 ft. D: Charles H. France. C: Yale Benner, Curtis Cooksey, William Fables, James Harris, Gladys Hulette, Carlton S. King, Edward Mack, Dan Mason, Jessie Stevens.

Synopsis: George Washington Jones goes to a Spiritualist, and joins in a séance with other men (Mason) hoping to learn his future, but is so frightened of the ghosts that appear that he flees the house. On the street, he encounters a butcher dressed in white, and a bride, both of whom he assumes are ghosts. When he flees into a bakery, he struggles with the baker, who is also dressed in white. The baker throws him into a flour bin and goes to find a policeman. Jones runs out of the bakery and heads home where he finds his wife dressed in her white nightgown and cap and assumes she, too, is a ghost. The final blow comes when Jones looks in mirror and sees his own ghostly white face covered in flour.

Jenks and the Janitor. (EMC, 4 November 1914) Split Reel, 500 ft. D: Charles M.

Filmography

Seay. C: Dan Mason, Edward O'Connor, Helen Strickland, May Abbey.

Synopsis: Mr. Jenks decides to dispose of his loud new suit since his sister-in-law Liza, doesn't like it, and sells it cheap to Mike the Janitor (Mason). Mike wears his new suit to call on Maggie, the maid. As they embrace, Liza sees them and assumes it is Jenks who is romancing the maid. She intervenes with a broom and chases Mike out of the house. Jenks comes into the kitchen to see what the fuss is just in time to catch Maggie as she faints. But Mrs. Jenks arrives just in time to see her husband with the maid in his arms and beats him with her parasol. Fortunately, Maggie soon revives and explains the situation.

A Millinery Mix-up. ** (EMC, 18 November 1914) Split Reel, 600 ft. D: Charles M. Seay. C: Dan Mason, Carol Cushman, Gladys Hulette, Andrew Clark, Mathilde Maring, Marie La Manna.

Synopsis: Mr. Tightwad (Mason) refuses to let his wife buy a new hat at an upcoming sale and she belabors the matter relentlessly. At his office, Tightwad admires the new hat of his young stenographer, Tillie. Meanwhile, Mrs. Tightwad decides to attend the hat sale anyway and stops at the office on the way. When she sees her husband admiring Tillie's hat, she assumes he has bought it for the girl and tears it to pieces. Tightwad is obliged to replace Tillie's hat and goes to the sale to find one. As he comes out with a hatbox, his wife sees him and seizes the box. Tightwad has to go back in and buy another hat, for Tillie.

Buster Brown and the German Band. (EMC, 18 November 1914) Split Reel, 400 ft. D: Charles H. France. C: Norris Millington, Helen Millington, Helen Bauer, James Harris, William Fables, Elsie Mac Cleod, Dan Mason, May Abbey, Anne Leonard, Frank Lyons, Harry Eytinge, John Sturgeon, Dan Baker.

Synopsis: Buster and his friends hear a German band (Mason) down the street and decide to bring it home to serenade Mrs. Brown and her guests. The band makes so much noise that Buster's pet goat is awakened and annoyed. He tries to get loose from his tether but at first doesn't succeed. Mrs. Brown and her ladies try in vain to stop the noise. When the goat finally gets free, everyone, including the band, scatters.

A Double Elopement. ** (EMC, 2 December 1914) 1 reel. D: Charles M. Seay. C: Dan Mason, Helen Strickland, Gladys Hulette, Cora Williams, Edward Boulden.

Synopsis: Jack Smalley, a widower (Mason), moves to a new town and the neighbor, Mrs. Downs, comes over to visit. Jack is immediately interested in Mrs. Downs, a widow herself, and the interest is mutual. But both parties try to hide from the other the fact that they have grown children. Meanwhile, the children, May Smalley, and Charlie Downs, are attending the same school and have fallen in love. When a fire at the school brings the children home unexpectedly, Jack mistakes Charlie for a rival and hastily proposes to the widow Brown, who accepts. They decide to elope, but when they reach the train station, they meet Charlie and May, who have decided to do the same thing.

The Colonel of the Red Huzzars. (EMC, 18 December 1914) 3 reels. D: Richard Ridgley. C: Robert Conness, Bigalow Cooper, Miriam Nesbitt, Marc Mac Dermott, Herbert Prior, Sally Crute, Nellie Grant, Dan Mason.

Synopsis: Major Dalberg tries to avoid Marion Spencer, the widow of his late friend, but she insists on a visit before he goes overseas. Her Butler (Mason) shows him in and it becomes clear that she has a romantic interest in him. Later, in the kingdom of Valaria, Dalberg encounters Princess Dehra. They fall in love and her father, the King, bestows a grand-dukeship upon him. This news reaches Marion Spencer, who travels to Valaria and plots with the Archduke Lotzen, heir to the throne, to pose as Dalberg's wife, using a fake wedding certificate. All attempts to foil Mrs. Spencer fail until she and the Archduke are discovered scheming together at a masked ball and their plot is revealed.

Uncle Crusty. (EMC, 2 January 1915) 1 reel. D: Charles M. Seay. C: Dan Mason, Dan Baker, Bessie Learn, Leel Stuart.

Synopsis: On account of his dislike of everything, especially children, Edward

Filmography

Van Nest (Mason), a lifelong bachelor, has earned the name "Uncle Crusty." But when his widowed brother in Belgium asks to send his young son to America because of the war, Crusty reluctantly agrees. Willie arrives, and Crusty finds it impossible to give him love and attention, so the boy wanders off. A kindergarten teacher, Miss Burton, finds Willie wandering and takes him to her class where he enjoys playing with the other children. When Crusty discovers Willie is missing, he realizes that he does have a soft spot in his heart for the child and goes looking for him. He ends up melting further in the company of Miss Burton and soon finds himself surrounded by children and writing out checks to support St. Mary's Free Kindergarten.

Lena. (EMC, 15 January 1915) 2 reels. D: Charles M. Seay. C: Miriam Nesbitt, Dan Mason, Mrs. William Bechtel, Augusta Phillips, Viola Dana, Edward Earle, Julian Reed, Marie La Manna, Jessie Stevens, Dan Baker, Mathilde Baring, Yale Benner.

Synopsis: Mr. Miggles (Mason) and his wife can't find a good maid despite several trips to the employment agency, until they meet "Lena." Unbeknownst to them, however, "Lena" is actually Janet Brewster, President of the Society for Improving the Conditions of Domestic Servants, in disguise and doing research. Once in the Miggles household, "Lena" attracts quite a bit of attention from the Miggles' son, Jack. When Mrs. Miggles misplaces a valuable pin, she suspects "Lena" and accuses her, only to find during a reception that her young daughter is wearing the pin. The next day, Mrs. Miggles is invited to speak before the Society for Improving the Conditions of Domestic Servants and is delighted to accept. When she arrives to address the Society, however, she soon learns the true identity of her maid, "Lena." She rushes home and has the maid's room refurbished before "Lena" comes home. When Jack and "Lena" admit that they have fallen in love, an engagement is announced.

A Weighty Matter for a Detective. (EMC, 20 January 1915) Split Reel, 600 ft. D: Charles M. Seay. C: Jessie Stevens, Arthur Housman, Andrew J. Clark, Marjorie Ellison, Dan Mason, Cora Williams, Frank Lyons, Mrs. Wallace Erskine, Marie La Manna, Gladys Hulette, Julian Reed.

Synopsis: When the very plump young girl, Skinny, sees Mr. Short, Mr. Splits, and Mr. Pitkin (Mason) sneaking off into the woods with a jug, she wonders what they are up to, especially since their wives belong to the Women's Christian Temperance Union. She follows them, but when her boyfriend, Shrimp, can't find her, he worries that she has been kidnapped and goes off in search of his beloved. When he finds Skinny, it turns out that she has fallen and rolled down a hill into the midst of the three men she was looking for.

Joey and His Trombone. (EMC, 25 January 1915) 1 reel. D: James W. Castle. C: Edward Boulden, Gladys Hulette, Dan Mason, Jessie Stevens.

Synopsis: Ezra Perkins (Dan Mason) is losing customers because his employee, Joey, is driving them away by playing his trombone. So he fires Joey, who then goes into the city and joins a German band. Ezra's daughter, Tillie, also moves to the city to be near Joey. When Joey loses his job in the band, he and Tillie go to a movie studio and are hired for their comedy potential. But Joey is insulted by the parts he gets, and when a movie villain makes stage-love to Tillie, a ruckus ensues. Joey and Tillie and the trombone soon make their way back home.

A Thorn Among Roses. (EMC, 3 February 1915) Split Reel, 500 ft. D: Charles M. Seay. C: Dan Mason, Harry Linson, Gladys Hulette, Harry Beaumont, Edward Boulden, Viola Dana, William West, Cora Williams, Andrew J. Clark.

Synopsis: Dr. Berry (Mason) is a miserly old man who is made guardian of May Hope by her father's will. Berry hopes to get his hands on some of her considerable wealth by arranging a marriage between May and his son, Sam. May, however, is in love with Sam Rodney. Sam Berry acknowledges May's preference graciously and even helps her to go out with Rodney without Dr. Berry knowing about it. He also helps the pair get married by disguising Sam Rodney with a fake beard to look like Sam

Filmography

Berry and "misplacing" Dr. Berry's glasses. While the wedding is taking place, the real Sam Berry is marrying his sweetheart, Ellen Lucre. When the truth is discovered, Dr. Berry is furious, until he learns that Ellen Lucre is worth even more than May Hope.

That Heavenly Cook. (EMC, 3 March 1915) 1 reel. D: Charles M. Seay. C: Harry Beaumont, Bessie Learn, Dan Mason, Lou Gorey.

Synopsis: Gladys Rich resents the attitude of her cook, Bridget, and has her husband fire her. Gladys then volunteers to cook, herself. But when she serves dinner to her husband and her father (Mason), they are so disgusted that they throw everything out the window when she's not looking. When the gardener brings the biscuits back into the house for fear they'll kill the birds, Gladys is insulted. So she decides to play a trick on her husband and her father. She gets Bridget back again, has her cook a meal, and pretends to have cooked it herself. However, when Bridget hears them say that the meal was better than she, Bridget, could have done, the outraged cook bursts into the kitchen from her hiding place and reveals the truth. In the end, Bridget is hired again, at a higher salary than before.

Can a Man Fool His Wife? (C/C, 29 April 1915) 1 reel. D: Charles H. France. C: Harry Kelley, Dan Mason, Edward Boulden, May Abbey, Millicent Evans.

Synopsis: Uncle Dudley pretends to be called away on a big business deal so he can frolic at a nearby hotel with an old chum. However, his friend (Mason) is so late arriving that by the time he gets there, Dudley's wife has followed him and is in the next room spying on him. He tries to escape but gets dragged home by his ear.

Can Love Grown Cold Be Revived? (C/C, 9 May 1915) 1 reel. D: Charles H. France. C: Harry Kelley, Dan Mason, Edward Boulden, May Abbey, Millicent Evans.

Uncle Dudley is a doctor who has invented a "love pill" which induces an unquenchable desire to kiss. But his remedy goes awry and Dudley ends up being the object of desire of the maid, the cook, the secretary, and the dog. Mrs. Dudley is furious, but she is "cured" by the administration of the love pill. (Mason's role is unknown)

Where Can I Find a Wife? (C/C, 16 May 1915) 1 reel. D: Charles H. France. C: Harry Kelley, Dan Mason, Edward Boulden, Harry Fisher.

Synopsis: Jim Haskell is the son of a rich father (Mason) who promises, while vacationing abroad, to triple Jim's generous allowance if he marries by a certain date. Jim tricks his father by claiming that he has, in fact, married. When he learns that his father is en route back to America, he needs to find a wife fast. He proposes to his ladylove, but she wants time to consider. In desperation, Jim turns to Uncle Dudley, who dons women's clothing just in time to greet Jim's father as his "bride." The father is impressed, but when Jim's real sweetheart comes by to visit, she takes a dim view of the proceedings. Whisking away Dudley's skirt, she reveals the ruse.

The Scarlet Letter. (FOX, 12 February 1917) 5 reels. D: Carl Harbaugh. C: Mary Martin, Stuart Holmes, Dan Mason, Kittens Reichert, Edward N. Hoyt, Robert Vivian, Florence Ashbrook.

Synopsis: Hester Prynne has been forced to wear a scarlet "A" to mark her shame as an unwed mother. Arthur Dimmesdale, the respected minister of the little Puritan colony is the guilty man, but Hester refuses to implicate him. Roger Chillingworth (Mason), Hester's evil husband, discovers the secret and, as Dimmesdale's physician, makes the minister's life miserable. Dimmesdale is about to go mad with his secret when a pirate captain captures Chillingworth, who is later forced to walk the plank. When Dimmesdale rescues Hester from being burned at the stake, he opens his own shirt to reveal a branded "A" burned into his own flesh. They will bear their guilt together.

The Derelict. (FOX, 16 April 1917) 5 reels. D: Carl Harbaugh. C: Stuart Holmes, Mary Martin, June Daye, Carl Eckstrom, Dan Mason, Wanda Petit, Olive Trevor.

Synopsis: Teddy Brandt, a man about town, marries Rose Hare, a debutante, but after their daughter is born, he reverts to his old ways and returns to his old friends. When he falls in love with Claire, Rose tries to win him back but finally bars him from her home. Teddy loses his job, becomes a human derelict, and takes up with a scoundrel, Walt Collins (Mason). To free his wife, Teddy stages a fake suicide after which his wife marries Victor, an old friend of Teddy. Fifteen years later, Teddy sleeps in a train station where he sees a young girl being lured away by an older man. When he finds her purse he realizes she is his daughter, Helen. He follows them and kills the man. Helen is arrested for the murder, but is freed when Teddy goes to the police and confesses. He finally kills himself in his jail cell.

The Slave. (FOX, 3 June 1917) 5 reels. D: William Nigh. C: Valeska Suratt, Violet Palmer, Eric Mayne, Herbert Heyes, Edward Burns, Edwin Rosenman, Dan Mason, Tom Brooke, Martin Faust, Martin Hunt.

Synopsis: Caroline, an attractive young woman with a good job in a hair solon, tires of her boring existence and is tempted to marry a rich but dissipated old man (Mason) who has thrown his money bags at her feet. But before she makes this fatal mistake, she has a lurid dream in which she sees what life would be like, trapped in a mansion with a wealthy but fiendish old husband. Her dream ends with a murder, which is enough to wake her up. She realizes that she is better off working in the hair salon.

The Broadway Sport. (FOX, 10 June 1917) 5 reels. D: Carl Harbaugh. C: Stuart Holmes, Wanda Petit, Dan Mason, Mabel Rutter, W.B. Green, Jay Sullivan, Mario Majeroni, Jay Wilson.

Synopsis: Hezekiah Dill works as a clerk in the flourmill run by the wealthy local businessman, Hector Sweet (Mason). Dill is in love with Sadie, the boss's daughter, a hopeless proposition considering Dill's looks and social skills. While at work one day, two thieves break in and try to rob the safe. Acting quickly and more boldly than usual, Dill slams the vault door, locks them in and calls his boss. In the process, he sees a roll of money they intended to take, and picks it up. Dill's mind begins to reel with thoughts of what a different life he could have with lots of money. He envisions himself inheriting even more money from an elderly childless benefactor, and attempting to marry Sadie. He is still in mid-reverie when his boss, Sadie and the constable appear. Sadie hails him as a hero while her father heaps praises upon his formerly undistinguished clerk.

Wife Number Two. (FOX, 30 July 1917) 5 reels. D: William Nigh. C: Valeska Suratt, Erin Mayne, Bertha Brundage, John Goldsworthy, Martin J. Faust, T.J. Lawler, Peter Lang, Dan Mason, William Burton, Dan Sullivan.

Synopsis: Emma Rolfe is married off by her father to Dr. Bovar, an old widower who has little interest in her. Emma amuses herself in the company of several young men, especially the wealthy Rudolf, who knew her before her marriage and is a special favorite. She lives lavishly and expects the young men to shower her with gifts, but they do not. In time the young men lose interest in her and Emma finds herself in hopeless debt. She contemplates suicide and goes to the riverbank with the intent of drinking a vial of acid she has taken from her husband's satchel. At the last minute, she regains her courage to live and determines to face her husband and confess everything, but the riverbank collapses under her feet and she is drowned. When her body is brought home, her husband is left to defend the honor of the wife he had made so unhappy. (Mason played the role of an old soldier in this film.)

Every Girl's Dream. (FOX, 26 August 1917) 6 reels. D: Harry Millarde. C: June Caprice, Kittens Reichert, Harry Hilliard, Margaret Fielding, Marcia Harris, Dan Mason.

Synopsis: Gretchen, an orphan, loves Carl, a woodcutter, but Hulda is jealous and tries to steal him away. Mynher de Haas (Mason), an old man, wants to marry Gretchen but she puts him off despite the urgings of her stepmother, whose house is mortgaged to Mynher. One day Carl is kidnapped. The next day, royal messengers arrive and order all orphaned girls in the village to search their possessions for a certain locket. The owner of this locket is in fact a princess. Hulda looks in Gretchen's trunk and finds the locket. She is placed on a throne to await her prince. But when an old man approaches, she thinks he is the prince and flees. She confesses to stealing the locket from Gretchen. Now Gretchen is enthroned and the old man announces the arrival of the prince. It is Carl who is, as it turns out, the prince. As the villagers celebrate Gretchen's good fortune, news comes of the king's death. Carl is now king.

Hearts and Harpoons. (EFC/Sparkle, September 1917) 1 reel. D: Unknown. C: Dan Mason, George Bunny.

Synopsis: retired sea captains, Peters and Hankins (Mason), are old cronies, but when an attractive widow comes to town, they both fall in love with her. As one tries to impress her, the other sabotages his plans. They finally agree to a duel; harpoons at twenty paces. But just as the duel is about to begin, another man who has long been courting the widow rushes in and takes her away.

Toodles. (EFC/Sparkle, September 1917) 1 reel. D: Unknown. C: Dan Mason

The plot of this film is unknown.

Bangs Renigs. (EFC/Sparkle, September 1917) 1 reel. D: Unknown. C: Dan Mason

The plot of this film is unknown.

Thou Shalt Not Steal. (FOX, 14 October 1917) 5 reels. D: William Nigh. C: Virginia Pearson, Claire Whitney, Erin Mayne, Bertha Brundage, John Goldsworthy, Martin J. Faust, Robert Elliot, Lem F. Kennedy, Danny Sullivan, Dan Mason.

Synopsis: Mary Bruce loves Roger Benton, but is being pursued by Lord Haverford, who presses his proposal with a loan of $100,000 to Mary's father, a banker who is in dire need of cash. Unwilling to allow herself to be sold off in marriage, Mary attempts to steal the money from the safe, only to be overpowered by a thief whose wrist she bites in the struggle. Mary, Benton, and Mary's father are now under suspicion in the theft. Dr. Steele, the detective assigned to the case, is convinced that Lord Haverford is an imposter, and is able to prove he was the thief when the bite marks on his wrist are revealed. Steele then reveals that he is the real Lord Haverford, and the real culprit is arrested. (Dan Mason's role is this film is unknown.)

Unknown 274. (FOX, 16 December 1917) 5 reels. D: Harry F. Millarde. C: June Caprice, Kittens Reichert, Florence Ashbrook, Inez Marcel, Dan Mason, Richard Neill, Tom Burroughs, Jean Armour, William Burns, Alex Shannon.

Synopsis: Placed in an orphanage by her distraught mother who commits suicide, young Dora Belton grows up with no knowledge of her parents, aside from the shawl and violin left with her when she was abandoned. As a young woman she is discovered by an unscrupulous couple who intend to dress her well and auction her off to a wealthy man in marriage. Instead, she wins the love of a rich young man who appreciates her, She is eventually reunited with her wrongly imprisoned father by means of her violin playing. (Dan Mason played Professor Jim in this film.)

Shirley Kaye. (CKY, 29 December 1917) 5 reels. D: Joseph Kaufman. C: Clara Kimball Young, Corliss Giles, George Fawcett, George Backus, Claire Whitney, Nellie Lindrich, John Sutherland, Mrs. F.O. Winthrop, Frank Otto, Dan Mason.

Synopsis: Shirley Kaye is the beautiful and outgoing daughter of Egerton Kaye, president of a railroad founded by his ancestor, "Pirate" Kaye. The Kayes' neighbor on Long Island, T.J. Magen, and his younger associate, John Rowson, buy a controlling interest in the railroad and try to oust Shirley's father from his position. Shirley uses her charms to manipulate Magen into allying with her and her father's interests by welcoming Magen's daughter, Daisy, into the social set she so much desires to be a part of. When Rowson quits the venture in disgust and heads west, Shirley goes after him and wins his heart. (Dan Mason's role in this film is unknown.)

Over the Hill. (AFC, 30 December 1917) 5 reels. D: William Parke. C: Gladys Hulette, J. H. Gilmour, Dan Mason, William Parke, Jr., Chester Barnett, Richard Thornton,

Filmography

Joyce Fair, Paul Clerget, Tula Belle, Inda Palmer, John Carr, William Sullivan.

Synopsis: When the Rev. Timothy Neal (Mason) is forced to retire because of his age, he and his granddaughter, Esther, move to Columbia where Neal hopes to make a living selling books. He is not successful, despite Esther's efforts to help him, and their small savings dwindle away. When Neal passes away, Esther is on her own. Meanwhile, Allen Stone, one of Esther's acquaintances, is the business manager of the local newspaper. Allen struggles with Roy Winthrop, the son of the newspaper's owner. Roy wants to publish sensational stories to boost sales. When he attempts to publish a scandalous story about the supposed elopement of the department store owner's daughter, Esther intervenes and burns the entire edition. Roy Winthrop is sent packing, and the paper gets a lucrative advertising deal with the department store. For her efforts, Esther receives a proposal from Allen Stone.

Sherman Was Right. (EFC/Jaxon, January 1918) 1 reel. D: Unknown. C: Dan Mason.

The plot of this film is unknown.

Jack Spurlock, Prodigal. (FOX, 10 February 1918) 5 reels. D: Carl Harbaugh. C: George Walsh, Dan Mason, Ruth Taylor, Robert Vivian, Mike Donlin, Jack Goodwin.

Synopsis: Jack Spurlock is expelled from college for bringing a bear to class, and his father (Mason) puts him to work in his grocery business as a purchasing agent. Jack buys a large supply of onions, unaware that his father already has more than enough. He gets fired and goes to work for a physical culture specialist. As a result he meets Col. Jackson, who sells a patent medicine. Jackson tells him that he has received a significant order for his medicine but can't fill the order because of a shortage of the main ingredient—onions. Jack solves Jackson's problem, and his father's at the same time. His sweetheart, who has been annoyed with Jack's escapades, forgives him.

Brave and Bold. (FOX, 5 May 1918) 5 reels. D: Carl Harbaugh. C: George Walsh, Francis X. Conlon, Dan Mason, Mabel Bunvea, Regina Quinn, A.B. Conkwright, Mike Donlin.

Synopsis: Robert Booth works for Colonel Wilson (Mason), who sends him to negotiate a billion dollar war contract with a foreign prince who is staying at a hotel in Pittsburgh. As Booth is scheduled to marry his fiancée, Ruth Hunnywell, that same day, he wires her to meet him at the hotel. But Booth is kidnapped by agents of a rival businessman, Chester Firkins, and taken to a prison. He exchanges clothes with his cellmate and escapes, returning to the hotel. There he discovers that Ruth has been kidnapped as well, and taken away in a motorcar. Booth gives pursuit, rescues Ruth, and returns again to the hotel just in time to prevent his rivals from sealing the deal. He gets the contract and marries Ruth.

The Yellow Ticket. (AFC, 26 May 1918) 5 reels. D: William Parke. C: Fannie Ward, Milton Sills, Warner Oland, Armand Kaliz, J.H. Gilmour, Helen Chadwick, Leon Bary, Anna Lehr, Dan Mason, Nicholas Dunaew, Edward Elkas, Charles Jackson, Richard Thornton.

Synopsis: Anna Mirrel, a beautiful Jewish girl in Czarist Russia, is refused a passport to visit her injured father (Mason) in St. Petersburg, but is offered a "yellow ticket" instead. She accepts this badge of prostitution in desperation, but arrives in St. Petersburg to find that her father is dead. When her father's caretaker is killed by a bomb, Anna takes the woman's papers and impersonates her. As Marya Varenka, she gets a job as a governess, and meets a young American newspaperman. But the chief of police, Baron Andrey, is on her trail and finally exposes her, causing her to leave her employment. The American remains her only friend. When the Baron lures her to his apartment, she ends up killing him in self-defense. After turning herself in to the police, she is to be sent to Siberia. The American, who has fallen in love with her, saves Anna by threatening to expose the corrupt methods of the police. Anna is freed and looks forward to a future with her American sweetheart.

All Woman. (GPC, 9 June 1918) 6 reels. D: Hobart Henley. C: Mae Marsh, Jere Austin, Arthur Housman, John St. Polis, John

Filmography

T. Dillon, Joe Henaway, Dan Mason, Hazel Alden, Lois Alexander, Jules Cowles, Alvina Alstadt, Clifford Williams. Madelyn Clare, Elsie Sothern.

Synopsis: Susan Sweeney inherits a hotel in the Adirondacks and sets out with two girlfriends to take possession, assuming it to be a palace. When the cab driver (Mason) takes her to her destination, she finds a decrepit building housing a bar filled with derelict people. A young lawyer, Austin Strong, urges her to just sell the place and take the money. But she stays and manages to renovate the building, close down the bar, and change the lives of some of the unfortunate children living in the community. She also supports Austin's political ambitions and they fall in love.

An All-Fools' Day Affair.* (EFC/Jaxon, August 1918) 1 reel. D: Dan Mason? C: Dan Mason.

Synopsis: The landlady of a boarding house has a niece who gets bored and plays a prank on the guests, signing names to notes requesting meetings in the parlor and implying love interests that don't exist. Thanks to the mix-up of notes and identities, and a misplaced baby, the father of the baby is accused of infidelity and of "making love" to a widow while a hapless German guest (Mason) is accused of having a wife and child, much to the distress of the widow he is courting. The truth is sorted out in the end with the niece telling them everyone that it's All Fools' Day and they're all fools.

On the Quiet. (FPL, 25 August 1918) 5 reels. D: Chester Withey. C: John Barrymore, Lois Meredith, Frank Belcher, Frank Losee, Jack W. Johnston, Alfred Hickman, Dan Mason, Helen Greene, Cyril Chadwick, Nan Christy, Dell Boone, Frank Hilton, Otto Okuga, Louise Lee.

Synopsis: Robert Ridgeway is in love with Agnes Colt, who is to receive twenty million dollars, if and when she marries with the consent of her brother, Horace, the executor of their father's will. Horace plans a brilliant marriage to a nobleman for Anna, but she secretly marries Robert. They must keep their marriage quiet to avoid the loss of her fortune, and go into hiding from the family. In the end, they cleverly trick Agnes's brother into consenting to their marriage. (Dan Mason plays a clerk in this film.)

Bonnie Annie Laurie. (FOX, 1 September 1918) 5 reels. D: Harry Millarde. C: Peggy Hyland, Henry Hallam, William Bailey, Sydney Mason, Dan Mason, Marion Singer.

Synopsis: Old Sandy Laurie wants his daughter, Annie, to marry Donald McGregor, and they are engaged before Donald leaves to fight the Germans in France. Later, Annie finds Lieutenant Hathaway washed up on the shore and nurses him back to health. She also falls in love with him. When Hathaway recovers and goes to fight in France, he and Donald become friends. Both men are wounded in an attack, and Annie, who has volunteered as a nurse, ends up caring for both. Forced to make a choice between them, she honors her pledge to marry Donald. (Dan Mason's role in this film is unknown.)

Laughing Bill Hyde. (RBP, 22 September 1918) 6 reels. D: Hobart Henley. C: Will Rogers, Anna Lehr, Robert Conville, Dan Mason, John St. Polis, Mabel Ballin, Clarence Oliver, Joseph Herbert.

Synopsis: Bill Hyde breaks out of prison and frees his pal, Denny Dorgan (Mason), as well. When Dorgan is injured in a fall, Bill takes him to a doctor in secret, but he dies. Bill goes to Alaska where, some time later, he meets the same doctor, now trying to strike it rich so he can marry his sweetheart. They become close friends. When Bill rescues an Indian, Ponotah, from an assault, he finds she is half owner of a valuable mine, but is being cheated by Slayforth, the man in charge. Bill seeks employment at the mine, finds the gold that Slayforth has stolen and uses some of it to salt a worthless claim. He then tricks Slayforth into buying the claim and turns the money over to the doctor who weds his sweetheart. Bill then gives Ponotah the gold Slayforth had stolen, and she gives Bill her heart and her hand in marriage.

Marriages Are Made. (FOX, 13 October 1918) 5 reels. D: Carl Harbaugh. C: Peggy Hyland, Edwin Stanley, Dan Mason, George Clarke, Al Lee, George Halpin, Ellen Cassidy, William "Stage" Boyd, Ed Begley.

Filmography

Synopsis: Cyrus Baird (Mason) is a retired financier who wants his daughter, Susan, to marry Ethelbert Granger, a wealthy but effeminate young man. When James Morton, nephew of Cyrus's bitter enemy, saves Susan from drowning, it is love at first sight. Ethelbert invites the Bairds to cruise in the houseboat, which unbeknownst to him, is owned by a secret German spy who plans to lay mines to destroy an American ship. Morton swims to the houseboat, and discovers the mines. The spy releases the mines and forces Susan into a speedboat and flees. Morton pursues them and rescues Susan just before the speedboat hits one of the mines and blows up.

The Lure of Ambition. (FOX, 19 November 1919) 5 reels. D: Edmund Lawrence. C: Theda Bara, Thurlow Bergen, William B. Davidson, Dan Mason, Ida Waterman, Amelia Gardner, Robert Paton Gibbs, Dorothy Drake, Peggy Parr, Tammany Young.

Synopsis: Olga Dolan works at a posh New York hotel but lives in poverty with her father, Sylvester Dolan (Mason). When she attracts the attention of Cyril Ralston, he installs her in a suite of rooms in the hotel and promises to marry her. When he returns to England, Olga vows revenge and follows him by taking a job as secretary to Lady Bromley, Ralson's mother. In England, she discovers that Ralston is married. When she meets the Duke of Rutledge, she becomes his secretary and proves to be resourceful and useful to him. When she saves the Duke from being murdered by his insane wife, he falls in love with her. Upon the death of his wife, the Duke marries Olga.

The Toonerville Trolley That Meets All Trains. (BFC, 27 September 1920) 2 reels. D: Ira Lowry. C: Dan Mason, Wilna Hervey (as Wilna Wilde), Helen Gerould Rose, William Randall, Irma Irving.

Synopsis: Everyone is waiting for the Trolley to go to the picnic, but it's late as usual, and the Terrible Tempered Mr. Bangs grows impatient. Once everyone is on board, they are delayed further when the Skipper stops to pull a tooth from one of his fares, using the Trolley rope to do so. When they finally reach the picnic grove, they find Powerful Katrinka cooling her feet in the drinking water. At the picnic, a mother is plotting to marry her daughter off to a rich man, but the girl runs off with her real sweetheart and tries to take the Trolley to escape. Her parents pursue them in their jalopy. The Trolley makes good time until it encounters a section of missing track. Powerful Katrinka has seen a snake and ripped up several pieces of track to kill the varmint. Then the Skipper reveals he is a Justice of the Peace and performs the wedding himself.

Skinning Skinners. (RPI, October 1920) 5 reels. D: William Nigh. C: Johnny Dooley, Maurine Powers, Lillian Hall, Dan Mason.

The plot of this film is unknown.

The Skipper's Narrow Escape.** (BFC, December 1920) 2 reels. D: Ira Lowry. C: Dan Mason, Wilna Hervey (as Wilna Wilde), Helen Gerould, Noah Reynolds.

Synopsis: Everyone knows that the Skipper is flouting the Prohibition laws with his notorious "Raisin Cider," but Cynthia Snoop is determined to catch him red handed. She hires a detective and trails the Skipper. Meanwhile, Powerful Katrinka, who works for Mr. and Mrs. Spriggins, accidentally busts a water pipe and floods the cellar. When the plumber fails to arrive, Katrinka fixes the broken pipe herself with her bare hands. When Snoop and the detective find the Skipper's still, they sample the "evidence" themselves, and get so tipsy that the Skipper is able to haul them into town and turn them over to the Constable.

The Skipper's Treasure Garden.** (BFC, December 1920) 2 reels. D: Robert Eddy. C: Dan Mason, Wilna Hervey (as Wilna Wilde), William Randall, Helen Gerould, Irma Irving.

Synopsis: The Skipper doesn't look forward to digging up his whole garden and opts to have it done for him for free. He plants an anonymous note at the local pool parlor alleging that there is a pot of gold buried in the garden. One by one, the neighbors pitch in and till the garden nicely as they search for the treasure. Meanwhile, Powerful Katrinka arrives by train and takes the Trolley into Toonerville where she gets a job with the household of Mr. Bangs. Her devotion to her housework nearly destroys the Bangs' house and yard. Then Katrinka learns about the rumored pot of gold. She performs her own search with a scoop steam shovel and leaves behind an empty pit where there was once a garden.

*Toonerville's Fire Brigade.*** (BFC, January 1921) 2 reels. D: Ira Lowry. C: Dan Mason, Wilna Hervey (as Wilna Wilde).

Synopsis: The Skipper is appointed fire chief and goes about his new job with the same attention to detail that he bestows on the Trolley. There is great excitement and pride when he leads the company through town in a parade. But then a real fire breaks out. The Skipper gets out the rule book and makes sure that everything is done properly, while the house burns down. The men are unable to work the hand pump hard enough to get the water to reach the flames until Katrinka gives a hand and then everyone gets drenched.

The Skipper's Scheme. (BFC, 6 February 1921) 2 reels. D: Ira M. Lowry. C: Dan Mason, Wilna Hervey (as Wilna Wilde), Helen Gerould, Noah Reynolds.

Synopsis: The Skipper advertises an auction to take place at the general store, tacking up posters at every possible location on his route and annoying his passengers with the constant stops. Thanks to a rumor, spread by the Skipper, that the old worthless furniture contains hidden treasure, bidding is lively, and the junk goes for high prices. When a mattress that sold for twenty-five cents is found to actually contain a wad of cash, the Skipper is furious.

*Toonerville Follies.*** (BFC, March 1921) 2 reels D: Ira M. Lowry. C: Dan Mason, Wilna Hervey (as Wilna Wilde), Helen Gerould, Jule Bernard, Emma Wilcox, Robert Maximillian.

Synopsis: The meeting with the new pastor goes well until some folks realize that their valuables are missing. But spirits are lifted by plans for a Toonerville talent show to raise money for the church. Follies night arrives with many of Toonerville's citizens participating in the fun. Then screams are heard from the ladies' dressing room where the pastor is trying to steal the receipts from the church treasurer. The Skipper shows up with a gun to save the day. He had recognized the new pastor as a notorious crook named "Parson" Kirby.

*The Skipper's Flirtation.*** (BFC, April 1921) 2 reels. D: Ira M. Lowry. C: Dan Mason, Wilna Hervey (as Wilna Wilde), Helen Gerould, Emma Wilcox, Betty Bovee, Noah Reynolds.

Synopsis: Aunt Eppie Hogg goes for a ride on her special flat car pulled by the Toonerville Trolley, but gets a cinder in her eye. While bending over her trying to extract the speck, the Skipper's actions are mistaken for romance by Cynthia Snoop, watching from a distance. She reports the scandal to the Skipper's wife. Matilda doesn't believe Snoop until Aunt Eppie's missing necklace turns up tangled in the Skipper's beard. Matilda is crushed until Tomboy Taylor shows up to tell her what really happened.

*Toonerville's "Boozem" Friends.*** (BFC, 2 May 1921) 2 reels. D: Ira M. Lowry. C: Dan Mason, Wilna Hervey (as Wilna Wilde), Betty Bovee, Jack McClean, Robert Maximillian, Fred O'Beck, Jule Bernard, Helen Gerould, Emma Wilcox.

Synopsis: The Toonerville Trolley stops at the only restaurant in town, and everyone goes in for lunch. Mr. Bangs, the owner, has his lovely daughter Julia working the cash register. Katrinka is in the kitchen. Unknown to Julia, her father has agreed she will marry Louis Lush, who has loaned Bangs a great deal of money. But Julia only has eyes for Jack Dare and flirts with him as he sits at the counter. Meanwhile, Bangs takes a little nip of something stronger than tea, courtesy of the hollow nightstick carried by the local policeman. When it kicks in, Katrinka has to come out of the kitchen to carry her boss home to recover. Later, when Cynthia Snoop catches Julia and Jack by the river, she alerts Bangs to the scandal. Bangs discovers the couple together but before he can intervene, he is told that they were secretly married a few weeks before. Then the restaurant waiter, Boob McNutt, who seemed such a simple soul, turns out to be a federal agent and arrests Louis Lush as a bootlegger. Cynthia Snoop, with more

Filmography

gossip than she can handle, rushes back to inform the village.

The Skipper Has His Fling. (BFC, 1 June 1921) 2 reels. D: Ira M. Lowry. C: Dan Mason, Wilna Hervey (as Wilna Wilde).

Synopsis: The champion horseshoe flinger has his eye on Marjorie, who runs the beauty parlor next door to the barber shop owned by her father, Jeremiah. But Marjorie prefers the Skipper's nephew, Henry, who arrives in town the day of the flinging championship. When the champ challenges Henry to a horseshoe match, the Skipper urges his nephew to accept because he has an idea. The afternoon of the match, Katrinka hides in a tunnel under the field. Every time the champ throws a shoe, the peg disappears and every time Henry pitches, a peg appears in the middle of his shoe. Henry wins the match and the girl.

Toonerville Tactics. ** (BFC, 4 July 1921) 2 reels. D: Ira M. Lowry. C: Dan Mason, Wilna Hervey (as Wilna Wilde), Robert Maximillian, Betty Bovee.

Synopsis: The Skipper's nephew, Adam Bibber, is an efficiency expert and Mr. Bangs promises him any thing he wants if he can find any waste in Bang's counterpane factory. Adam finds that the corners being cut from the counterpanes to fit the bedposts are being sold to the ragman. But the corners are the exact size and shape of babies' bibs, and thus can be sold for a good price. Adam is rewarded with permission to marry Bang's lovely daughter. For good measure Adam sets up Bang's excellent cook, Katrinka, with her own brand of pancake flour, with her picture on the package.

The Skipper Strikes It Rich. (BFC, 1 August 1921) 2 reels. D: Ira M. Lowry. C: Dan Mason, Wilna Hervey (as Wilna Wilde).

Synopsis: The Skipper has a streak of amazingly good luck and it seems as if all his problems are solved. However, his wealth, and his new-found status in Toonerville society, are short lived.

Why Girls Leave Home. (HRP, 4 September 1921) 8 reels. D: William Nigh. C: Anna Q. Nilson, Maurine Powers, Julia Swayne Gordon, Corinne Barker, Katherine Perry (as Mrs. Owen Moore), Kate Blanke, Claude King, Coit Albertson, George Lessey, Jack O'Brien, Dan Mason, Arthur Gordini.

Synopsis: Two young women leave their respective homes, unhappy with the actions of their parents. Lured to the big city with all of its temptations, they endure shattered romances and disappointments. Their paths cross in a cabaret frequented by wealth and dissipated older men, among them the octogenarian lounge lizard, Dodo (Mason). In the end each girl is forced to see the errors of her ways as well as those of their parents, to whom they are reconciled.

The Toonerville Tangle. (BFC, October 1921) 2 reels. D: Ira M. Lowry. C: Dan Mason, Wilna Hervey (as Wilna Wilde), Helen Gerould.

Synopsis: When the Skipper's nephew arrives in town, he attracts the notice of the wealthy bank owner's daughter. The bank cashier, who admires the girl himself, is jealous and determines to frame the lad. He takes money from the bank and hides it in a tree under which the young couple plan to meet later that day. He intends to have him arrested for theft. But a tramp sees him putting the money in the tree and takes it. When the cashier and the police arrive at the tree, they can't find the money but the nephew is arrested anyway. On the day of the trial, a stranger appears and introduces himself as the president of the federation of banks. He reveals that the nephew is the manager of the federation. Then the tramp enters with the money and tells how it got in the tree. The cashier is arrested and put behind bars.

The Skipper's Last Resort. (BFC, 25 February 1922) 2 reels. D: Ira M. Lowry. C: Dan Mason, Wilna Hervey (as Wilna Wilde).

Synopsis: The Skipper heads up a committee that visits an amusement park with an eye to building one just like it in Toonerville. However, the abundance of pretty girls at the park proves too much of a distraction for the gentleman. They forget their original mission until the Skipper's wife and Mrs. Bangs show up to set them straight.

Iron to Gold. (FOX, 12 March 1922) 5 reels. D: Bernard J. Durning. C: Dustin

Filmography

Farnum, Marguerite Marsh, William Conklin, William Elmer, Lionel Belmore, Glen Cavender, Robert Perry, Dan Mason.

Synopsis: Tom Curtis is robbed of a valuable mining claim by his partner, George Kirby, and forced to become an outlaw. Years later, he rescues a woman, Anne Kirby, from two highwaymen. When Tom discovers that Anne is George's wife, he decides to get revenge by holding her captive in his cabin. But Tom was wounded while rescuing Anne and even when he tells her she is free to go, Anne stays in his cabin to care for him. When her husband finds her there, he is outraged and hires Bat Piper to kill Tom. Piper fails in his attempt on Tom's life, and in the end, both he and George Kirby are themselves killed. Anne leaves to go back east and Tom soon follows. (Dan Mason played the part of Lem Baldwin, a hotel keeper.)

The Skipper's Policy. (BFC, 19 March 1922) 2 reels. D: Ira M. Lowry. C: Dan Mason, Wilna Hervey (as Wilna Wilde), Fred O'Beck, Helen Gerould.

Synopsis: The Skipper tries to get elected mayor of Toonerville, but insurance agents frame him with a bogus accident to sabotage his campaign. In turn, the Skipper stages a fake hold-up to collect on his insurance policy. But a real hold-up man appears on the scene and the Skipper's bravery makes him a hero.

Is Matrimony a Failure? (FPL, 16 April 1922) 6 reels. D: James Cruze. C: T. Roy Barnes, Lila Lee, Lois Wilson, Walter Hiers, Zasu Pitts, Arthur Hoyt, Lillian Leighton, Tully Marshall, Adolphe Menjou, Sylvia Ashton, Charles Ogle, Ethel Wales, Sidney Bracey, William Gonder, Lottie Williams, Dan Mason, William Brown, Robert Brower, Philippe De Lacy, Johnny Fox, Newton Hall, Mary Jane Irving.

Synopsis: Four middle aged couples discover that due to a clerical error, they have never really been legally married. The husbands, all of them henpecked and unhappy, enjoy their supposed freedom for a while before returning to their marriages, making sure they're legal this time, only to become unhappy again. Meanwhile, the daughter of one couple wants to marry her sweetheart, but her fiancé is forced to listen to her father and his friends tell him how awful marriage is. (Dan Mason played the part of one of the four husbands, Silas Spencer.)

Toonerville Trials. (BFC, 7 May 1922) 2 reels. D: Ira M. Lowry. C: Dan Mason, Wilna Hervey (as Wilna Wilde), Robert Maximilian.

The plot of this film is unknown.

Toonerville Blues. (BFC, 4 June 1922) 2 reels. D: Ira M. Lowry. C: Dan Mason, Wilna Hervey (as Wilna Wilde), Fred O'Beck, Robert Maximillian.

Synopsis: The local softball team, the Toonerville Blues, are a motley crew to be sure, but enthusiastic about the game. Katrinka is formidable at the bat. Meanwhile, a crooked lawyer has designs on the pretty ingénue, but she is saved by the hero, who also discovers oil in the outfield of the local baseball diamond where the Blues play their games.

Toonerville Topics. (BFC, 10 September 1922) 2 reels. D: Ira M. Lowry. C: Dan Mason, Betty Bovee, Jack McClean.

The plot of this film is unknown.

Pop Tuttle's Movie Queen. ** (PGP, September 1922) 2 reels. D: Robert Eddy. C: Dan Mason, Wilna Hervey, Charles Gerson, Jamie Gray.

Synopsis: Pop Tuttle transports an attractive young woman to Plum Center from the train station in his jitney and hatches a scheme. Though she intends to work as a waitress, he tries to pass her off at his Idle Hour Theater as a visiting Hollywood movie queen. Though his attempts to teach her a few dance steps don't exactly work out, he puts her on stage anyway. Meanwhile, his advertising arouses the suspicion of the local Society Opposed to Everything and they attend the event as well. Pop's handling of the slide and movie projector leaves something to be desired and the event ends in chaos.

Pop Tuttle's Clever Catch. (PGP, October 1922) 2 reels. D: Robert Eddy. C: Dan Mason, Wilna Hervey.

The plot of this film is unknown.

Filmography

The Skipper's Sermon. (BFC, 14 October 1922) 2 reels. D: Ira M. Lowry. C: Dan Mason, Wilna Hervey (as Wilna Wilde).

Synopsis: The Skipper is called upon to substitute for the regular minister. He takes to the pulpit and delivers a scorching sermon that sets all the wicked sinners of Toonerville pondering the evil of their ways.

Pop Tuttle, Fire Chief. ** (PGP, November 1922) 2 reels. D: Robert Eddy. C: Dan Mason, Wilna Hervey.

Synopsis: Nosey Nichols leaves a small moonshine still unattended on his stove and it catches fire. As smoke pours out of his house, Plum Center's Cloudburst Fire Company is summoned but have no idea where the fire is. Tillie Olsen hoists fire chief, Pop Tuttle, up on a ladder so he can locate the smoke. Meanwhile, Nosey Nichols throws all his moonshine down the well in his yard, but falls in himself. Since it is the same well from which the water is pumped to put out the fire, the fire is now being fought with firewater, much to the delight of Pop Tuttle who gets a face full. Tillie works the hand pump so vigorously that it catches fire, too. When the Helping Hand Girls arrive with sandwiches, the fire fighters take a five-minute break. In the end, Tillie discovers that the small still has been the source of all the smoke, and simply carries it from the house. Nosey Nichols is retrieved from the well, and Pop Tuttle enjoys a nice glass of especially good well water.

Pop Tuttle's Grass Widow. (PGP, December 1922) 2 reels. D: Robert Eddy. C: Dan Mason, Wilna Hervey.

Synopsis: Pop Tuttle transports an attractive blond from the station and she flirts with him, telling him she is a grass widow in town doing research for a novel. At the hotel she also flirts with Clem Bodfish, who decides to throw a dance in her honor. With music provided by Homer Skagg's banjo and Tillie Olsen's mouthorgan and bass drum, the dance proves a great success. Then Pop Tuttle overhears the grass widow's conversation and realizes that she and her incognito husband, who has accompanied her to Plum Center, are up to no good. When the couple go outside for a conspiratorial conversation, Pop sends Clem out to offer the widow some ice cream, and Clem gets shot at in return. He escapes by jumping into the hotel through the window but he lands on Tillie's bass drum and destroys it. The grass widow and her husband beat a hasty retreat.

Pop Tuttle's Long Shot. (PGP, January 1923) 2 reels. D: Robert Eddy. C: Dan Mason, Wilna Hervey.

Synopsis: Pop Tuttle enters his sulky in the Plunkett County Handicap race, hoping his aging and decrepit horse, Wildfire, can win the prize. As a precaution, Pop arranges to reinforce Wildfire's energy level with a dose of a special tonic made from rabbit glands. But Tillie accidentally gives the dose to the wrong horse. Pop, who has already bet heavily on his own horse, realizes that there is only one other thing that will make Wildfire run fast enough to win. After years of meeting trains at the station, Wildfire always runs fastest when he hears a train whistle. So Tillie is sent out to put a cow on the tracks in hopes of coaxing a toot from an approaching train. She drags a jersey out of Walt Peter's pasture and pushes it into the path of an oncoming train, where it remains just long enough to provoke the desired blast from the engineer. Wildfire hears the whistle and beats all the competition to win the race.

Pop Tuttle, Deteckative. ** (PGP, February 1923) 2 reels. D: Robert Eddy. C: Dan Mason, Wilna Hervey.

Synopsis: When Pop Tuttle takes a correspondence course in detective work, he receives, in addition to his diploma, a special kit containing handcuffs, six sets of false whiskers, a magnifying glass, and a badge. Since the instruction book said to pay close attention to strangers, he is immediately suspicious of Nifty Ned loafing around the train depot. He decides to secretly follow him, wearing heavy whiskers as a disguise. Despite setting fire to the whiskers while pretending to smoke a cigarette, and getting temporarily locked in the chicken coop he commandeers as a spy station, he persists and catches Nifty Ned in the act of robbing the express office. With

Filmography

the help of his niece, Tillie, he hauls the crook off to the calaboose in handcuffs.

Pop Tuttle's Pole Cat Plot. (PGP, February 1923) 2 reels. D: Robert Eddy. C: Dan Mason, Wilna Hervey.

Synopsis: Nosey Nichols starts his own bus service to rival Pop Tuttle. They try to resolve the matter with a fistfight but that solves nothing. So the manager of the Palace Hotel decides that the man who brings the most guests to the hotel from the next train will become the official driver for the hotel. The competition is intense, with Nosey Nichols scoring the first points by dumping a rain barrel so that a puddle forms just under the steps of his rival's bus. Pop responds by putting an attractive young woman in his front seat so that all the young men get off Nosey's bus and onto his. Nosey then loosens one of the back wheels on Pop's bus and it falls off. Pop retaliates by paying a boy who has captured a polecat to put the critter on Nosey's bus. Everyone flees. Then Tillie supports the missing wheel of Pop's bus with her wheelbarrow and together they get their load of passengers to the hotel.

Pop Tuttle's Lost Control. ** (PGP, March 1923) 2 reels. D: Robert Eddy. C: Dan Mason, Wilna Hervey.

Synopsis: Pop Tuttle decides to get an automobile but finds it gives him more trouble than his old horse, Wildfire.

Pop Tuttle's Lost Nerve. (PGP, April 1923) 2 reels. D: Robert Eddy. C: Dan Mason, Wilna Hervey, Oliver J. Eckhardt.

Synopsis: A so-called painless dentist comes to Plum Center and sets up shop. As a promotion, he invites locals to come and have their teeth pulled free of charge. Despite using laughing gas, he is accompanied by a two-piece band that plays loudly enough to drown out the screams. When Pop Tuttle becomes one of the victims, his niece Tillie puts an end to the doctor's business, and all his equipment.

Pop Tuttle's Russian Rumors. (PGP, May 1923) 2 reels. D: Robert Eddy. C: Dan Mason, Wilna Hervey.

Synopsis: Pop Tuttle has taken over the Palace Hotel and drums up business by letting it be known that a Russian count, who died there recently, hid his fortune in his room. Reservations increase dramatically as folks try to get in to start their own search. Meanwhile, Tillie Olsen has been enjoying a romance with a traveling salesman. When he turns out to be untrue, she unsuccessfully attempts suicide, wrecking the hotel in the process. In the upheaval, money is found in a mattress. Pop Tuttle thinks he has struck it rich, until the money turns out to be rubles.

Pop Tuttle's One Horse Play. (PGP, June 1923) 2 reels. D: Robert Eddy. C: Dan Mason, Wilna Hervey.

Synopsis: Pop Tuttle attempts to improve the cultural life of Plum Center by staging a play by Shakespeare. Combining elements of Romeo and Juliet with Richard the Third, Pop casts his niece, Tillie, as Juliet, while he plays the King, himself. A derelict actor is recruited to play Romeo. During Tillie's romantic scene with Romeo, the balcony collapses under her weight, causing Romeo to flee the scene. The audience is not impressed.

Pop Tuttle's Tac Tics. (PGP, 15 July 1923) 2 reels. D: Robert Eddy. C: Dan Mason, Wilna Hervey.

Synopsis: Pop Tuttle tries his hand at prize fighting, with Tillie as his trainer.

Conductor 1492. ** (WB, 12 January 1924) 7 reels. D: Charles Hines, Frank Griffin. C: Johnny Hines, Doris May, Dan Mason, Ruth Renick, Robert Cain, Fred Esmelton, Byron Sage, Michael Dark, Dorothy Vernon (Burns).

Synopsis: When Irish immigrant Terry O'Toole, rescues a young boy who has fallen in front of his trolley, the child's attractive older sister, Edna, invites the motorman home to dinner. He finds himself in the home of his employer, Denman Connelly, president of the Loteda Traction Company. Denman is the father of Edna and the boy. Terry and Edna quickly fall in love, a fact they try to hide from her disapproving father. Meanwhile, Connelly's hold on his company is threatened with a hostile takeover by businessmen trying to put together a controlling share of the company's stock. When Terry's pugilistic father, Mike O'Toole (Mason) arrives

Filmography

from Ireland, it turns out that he has two shares of the stock, which he bought years before when he himself worked for the traction company. He hid the shares inside an old Irish doll he gave to Terry for good luck. The doll is nearly destroyed in a fire, but is rescued by Terry, giving Connelly the advantage he needs to keep his company. In exchange for the stock, Terry gets permission to marry Edna.

The Plunderer. (FOX, 30 March 1924) 6 reels. D: George Archainbaud. C: Frank Mayo, Evelyn Brent, Tom Santschi, James Mason, Peggy Shaw, Edward Phillips, Dan Mason.

Synopsis: A young easterner, Richard Townsend, goes with his friend, Bill Matthews, to visit a supposedly abandoned western mine he has inherited. He finds that a secret tunnel has been cut into his mine by Bill Presbey, owner of the adjoining mine, and his gold is being plundered. When Richard falls in love with Presbey's daughter, Joan, things get complicated. Bill Matthews tries to act as mediator, hoping that his young friend can win the girl and recover his gold as well. His efforts are complicated by a miners strike, a fire, a treacherous dynamiting of a dam that floods the town, and a mine cave-in. In the end, it is Bill's fists that convince Presbey to yield and make restitution. Townsend marries Joan and Matthews marries the saloon girl, Lily. (Dan Mason played an old miner, Bells Parks, in this film.)

Men. (PP, 4 May 1924) 7 reels. D: Dmitri Buchowetski. C: Pola Negri, Robert Frazer, Robert Edeson, Josef Swickard, Monte Collins, Gino Corrado, Edgar Norton, Dan Mason (uncredited).

Synopsis: Cleo is a young girl of Marseilles who starts off life living in poverty. She rises from working in a wine shop to success and fame as a dancer in Paris. She then finds herself surrounded by men who compete to win her favors by any means, fair or foul. Her solution to this dilemma is to offer herself up for auction, promising her favors to the highest bidder. A brisk competition ensues, with huge fortunes being waged against each other for the hand of Cleo. But even as Cleo sells herself to a wealthy admirer, she realizes that she loves another. From the final struggle between the man who cares for her and the man who has purchased her, Cleo emerges with love at last. (Dan Mason played a guest at a costume party in this picture.)

A Self Made Failure. (JKM, 29 June 1924) 8 reels. D: William Beaudine. C: Lloyd Hamilton, Ben Alexander, Matt Moore, Patsy Ruth Miller, Mary Carr, Sam De Grasse, Charles Reisner, Victor Potel, Dan Mason, Harry Todd, Alta Allen, Doris Duane, Priscilla Moran, Joe McGray.

Synopsis: A dying father leaves his child, Sonny, with an old pal, Breezy, whom he mistakenly thinks is a successful businessman. Breezy is a tramp, however, and he and the boy wander the countryside. When they drop off a train one day in Sulfur Springs, Breezy is mistaken for the professor who was expected to take over the massage parlor at Cruikshank's Hotel, used by guests taking the local sulfur water cure. When the pair find lodgings with Grandma Neal, they discover that the hotel had been stolen from her. They work to restore the property to Grandma and Breezy decides to leave Sonny with her when he goes wandering again. However, Grandma and Sonny persuade him to stay, as he has finally found a home where he is wanted. (Dan Mason played a guest at the Sulfur Springs resort.)

Darwin Was Right. (FOX, 26 October 1924) 5 reels. D: Lewis Seller. C: Nell Brantley, George O'Hara, Stanley Blystone, Dan Mason, Lon Poff, Bud Jamison, Mertle Sterling, Nora Cecil, David Kirby.

Synopsis: Professor Henry Baldwin (Mason) invents an elixir that he believes will restore youth to the aged. His footman and his butler, both old men, agree to join the professor in taking the liquid. Before they can do so, however, they are kidnapped by thugs hired by Courtney Lawson, a lawyer in love with the professor's niece, Alice. Meanwhile, three apes escape from a local zoo and somehow find their way into the professor's study. When Alice finds the beasts, she fears that the elixir has in fact caused her uncle and his servants to revert back to their evolutionary origins. She calls in her fiancé who tries to solve the mystery.

Once Lawson has locked up the professor, he returns to take over the house. But the professor escapes, with the unexpected help of one of the apes, and Lawson's evil scheme is thwarted.

Idle Tongues. (THI, 21 December 1924) 6 reels. D: Lambert Hillyer. C: Percy Marmont, Doris Kenyon, Claude Gillingwater, Lucille Ricksen, David Torrence, Malcolm McGregor, Vivia Ogden, Marguerite Clayton, Ruby Lafayette, Dan Mason, Mark Hamilton.

Synopsis: Dr. Nye, a physician in a New England village, serves a term in prison to protect the reputation of his late wife, who had stolen church funds. When he returns, he is shunned by most and confines his practice to the poor. Only a few old friends, like Henry Ward Beecher Payson (Mason), his cook and housekeeper, remain loyal. His former brother-in-law, Judge Copeland, considers him a disgrace and becomes his worst enemy. However, when the Judge's daughter, Faith, wrecks her car on Nye's property, she must not be moved and convalesces in Nye's home. The doctor becomes protective of the girl and of her forbidden romance with Tom, the son of another of the Judge's enemies. Meanwhile, Nye traces a typhoid epidemic to a pond owned by Copeland, and campaigns against the water's use for town consumption. When a highly regarded local widow joins him in this crusade, she legitimizes his work and they fall in love. Ultimately, to convince the self-righteous judge to permit his daughter's romance, Nye tells the judge that it was his own sister who forged the check that sent the doctor to prison.

Sally. (FNP, 15 March 1925) 9 reels. D: Alfred E. Green. C: Colleen Moore, Lloyd Hughes, Leon Erol, Dan Mason, John T. Murray, Eva Novak, Ray Hallor, Carlo Schipa, Myrtle Stedman, E.H. Calvert, Louise Beaudet.

Synopsis: Sally is an orphan adopted by Mrs. Du Fay, who operates a dance studio. Due to a run of bad luck, Du Fay has to close her studio and loses her students. Sally seeks employment from Pops Shendorf (Mason), who runs the Alley Inn Café, and goes to work for him as a dishwasher. At the café, Sally meets the Duke of Checkergovinia, who works as a waiter. When Shendorf give her a chance to dance at the café, she is a big hit. She hires an agent who advises her to bill herself as a famous Russian dancer. While performing at a reception, using her new persona, she is applauded by all, until Shendorf arrives and exposes her as his dishwasher. However, one of those present at the reception is Florenz Ziegfeld, who hires her for his follies. She becomes a star and finds romance with young Blair, whom she had first met at the café.

The New Butler (The Wall Street Whiz).** (RTP, 29 September 1925) 5 reels. D: Jack Nelson. C: Richard Talmadge, Marceline Day, Lillian Langdon, Carl Miller, Billie Bennett, Dan Mason.

Synopsis: Going into hiding after being suspected of a crime, Richard Butler, a young Wall Street banker, masquerades as a butler in the household of millionaire, Mr. McCooey (Mason). He discovers a plot to ruin McCooey, and falls in love with his daughter, Peggy. To save McCooey's finances, Butler must shuttle between the serving table and his own Wall Street offices, while avoiding anyone who knows him along the way, especially when they attend parties at the McCooey residence. His reward for saving McCooey's fortune is the hand of Peggy McCooey.

Thunder Mountain. (FOX, 11 October 1925) 5 reels. D: Victor Schertzinger. C: Madge Bellamy, Leslie Fenton, Alec B. Francis, Paul Panzer, Arthur Housman, Zasu Pitts, Emily Fitzroy, Dan Mason, Otis Harlan, Russell Simpson, Natalie Warfield.

Synopsis: Azalea, an orphan girl, runs away from Morgan, the cruel owner of small circus that has been her home, and seeks refuge amidst mountain folks. She meets Sam Martin, a young mountain lad who rescues her and fights off Morgan. Sam takes her to the home of Ma and Pa MacBirney (Mason) who are suspicious of her but allow her to stay. Meanwhile, Sam has been inspired by an old itinerant preacher to better himself, and wants to start a school to lift his people out of their ignorance. When he actually begins to build a school, however, he meets opposition to the whole idea

Filmography

of "larnin'" among the righteous mountain folk. Azalea tries to help Sam with his school, but after a disagreement with him, she threatens to elope with Sam's worst enemy. In the end, Sam is falsely accused of murder, and it is Azalea who rescues him and they are reconciled.

American Pluck. ** (CPC, 15 October 1925) 6 reels. D: Richard Stanton. C: George Walsh, Wanda Hawley, Sidney De Grey, Frank Leigh, Tom Wilson, Leo White, Dan Mason.

Synopsis: After being expelled from college, Blaze Derringer is sent out into the world by his millionaire father with orders not to return until he proves he can earn five thousand dollars. He teams up with some hobos and gets into a bar fight which attracts the attention of a fight promoter who recruits him as a ringer against a champ. But he unexpectedly knocks out the champ, and fearing that he may have killed him, flees. Along the way, he saves a young woman from being arrested in a speakeasy. She turns out to be princess Alicia of Bargonia, who is on her way back home to be crowned queen. When they fall in love, Blaze decides to accompany the princess back to her native country. There he discovers that Count Verensky is determined to marry the princess and take power for himself. With the help of the American Consul (Mason), Blaze thwarts the plot and gives Verensky a sound beating in the process. The princess takes the throne and she and Blaze are married.

Seven Sinners. ** (WB, 7 November 1925) 7 reels. D: Lewis Milestone. C: Marie Prevost, Clive Brook, John Patrick, Charles Conklin, Claude Gillingwater, Mathilde Brundage, Dan Mason, Fred Kelsey.

Synopsis: The Vickers mansion on Long Island is broken into by two crooks, Molly and Joe, who proceed to empty the safe of its jewels. But they are caught in the act by another crook, Jerry, who relieves them of their loot. When Pious Joe and his wife Mamie suddenly arrive, they identify themselves as friends of the Vickers, but they are also crooks and after the same prize. The first three crooks claim to be household staff of the Vickers. Then a doctor (Mason) arrives with his sick patient. He is also a crook and puts the house under quarantine as a ruse to cover up his own designs on the Vicker's jewelry. During the quarantine, Molly and Jerry fall in love and decide to give up their criminal ways. When the police arrive, they escape, marry, and make a living selling burglar alarms.

The Big Parade. ** (MGM, 5 November 1925) 13 reels. D: King Vidor. C: John Gilbert, Renée Adorée, Hobart Bosworth, Claire McDowell, Claire Adams, Robert Ober, Tom O'Brien, Karl Dane, Rosita Marstini, Dan Mason (uncredited).

Synopsis: As World War I breaks out, Jim Apperson enlists in the American army and is sent to France. He and his buddies are billeted on a farm where Jim falls in love with the young woman, Melisande. When Jim is sent to the front, his buddies are killed and Jim is wounded. He is rescued from no man's land and ends up in a hospital where he learns that Melisande's village has been the center of a battle. He leaves the hospital, finds the farmhouse damaged and Melisande missing, and collapses. He is returned to the hospital where he recovers. After the war, he is sent home but soon returns to look for Melisande. When he finds her working on the farm, she rushes into his arms. (Dan Mason played the part of a French peasant in this film.)

Wages for Wives. (FOX, 13 December 1925) 7 reels. D: Frank Borsage. C: Jacqueline Logan, Creighton Hale, Earle Fox, Zasu Pitts, Claude Gillingwater, David Butler, Margaret Seddon, Margaret Livingston, Dan Mason, Tom Ricketts.

Synopsis: Nell Bailey agrees to marry Danny Kester if he agrees to turn over half his paycheck to her. However, after they are married, he reneges on his promise and she goes on strike in protest. Nell also persuades her mother and sister to do the same, thus leaving three husbands in the lurch. The three men valiantly try to hold out against their wives' demands, while floundering in their attempts to cope on their own. Meanwhile, the kindly stationmaster, Mr. Tevis (Mason), who minds everyone's business, is successful in getting the three couples to reconcile.

Filmography

Hearts and Fists. (HCW, 3 January 1926) 6 reels. D: Lloyd Ingraham. C: John Bowers, Marguerite De La Motta, Alan Hale, Dan Mason, Lois Ingraham, Howard Russell, Jack Curtis, Kent Mead, Charles Mailes.

Synopsis: Larry Pond inherits a nearly bankrupt lumber company from his father and hopes to turn it around. But the owner of the bank which has made loans to the failing firm has other ideas. He wants to take over the company himself. Meanwhile, a rival lumberman goes about sabotaging Pond's attempts to revive his business, blowing up a bridge in the process. Complicating matters, Pond falls in love with the banker's daughter, who is also his rival's fiancée. Fighting back against the odds, and with the help of Tacitus Harper (Mason), a cagy old employee he promotes to partner, Pond manages to drive away his rival and marry his sweetheart.

A Desperate Moment. (BP, 19 January 1926) 6 reels. D: Jack Dawn. C: Wanda Hawley, Theodore von Eltz, Sheldon Lewis, Leo White, Dan Mason, James Neill, Bill Franey.

Synopsis: Virginia Dean is enjoying a yachting trip with her father, all the more so for the fact that she has fallen in love with the captain, John Reynolds. However, a gang of thugs, hidden on board, highjack the yacht and set her father and his crew adrift. They hold onto Virginia and John, however. When the boat catches fire, all abandon the craft and end up on a remote desert island populated by cannibals. Blackie Slade, the leader of the thugs, incites the natives to attack the others, but John rescues Virginia and they eventually fight their way back to civilization. (Dan Mason played the role of Jim Warren in this film.)

Rainbow Riley. (CCB, 7 February 1926) 7 reels. D: Charles Hines. C: Johnny Hines, Brenda Bond, Bradley Barker, Dan Mason, John Hamilton, Harlan Knight, Herbert Standing, Ben Wilson, Lillian Ardell.

Synopsis: Steve Riley, a cub reporter from Louisville, is sent out to cover a feud in eastern Kentucky. Blissfully unaware of the local culture, he takes along his golf clubs, tennis racket and baseball bat. He soon falls in love with Alice Ripper, the local schoolteacher, who is also the sweetheart of Tilden McFields, leader of one of the fighting clans, and a notoriously bad man of the mountains. The whole Ripper clan is offended by Riley's attentions to Alice, while the other clan, the Whites, are offended that he doesn't like pretty Becky White. As a result, Riley manages to make the feud between the two families even worse and gets caught in the middle. The only friend he makes, aside from Alice, is the doctor and undertaker, Lem Perkins (Mason). When Alice is kidnapped by a half-wit and taken to a cabin on a mountaintop, Riley goes to rescue her. But when he overcomes the halfwit and tries to flee with Alice, he finds a mob of mountain men coming up the hillside after him. Riley defends himself with volleys of golf balls, tennis balls, pumpkins, and boomerangs until his supply runs out. In the end, he is rescued by the army and navy of the United States, who have received a telegram from Dr. Perkins telling them, with considerable exaggeration, that the president is in danger.

Forbidden Waters. (MPC, 21 March 1926) 6 reels. D: Alan Hale. C: Priscilla Dean, Walter McGrail, Dan Mason, Casson Ferguson, De Sacia Mooers.

Synopsis: Nancy Lee Bell, a newly divorced woman, is arrested for speeding and has no money to pay the fine. To avoid jail, she calls her ex, J. Austin Bell, to bail her out, and he comes to her assistance. Later, Nancy discovers that Austin is about to marry an adventuress who is planning to swindle him for his money. Nancy disguises herself as an old woman and kidnaps Austin at gunpoint. She takes him to a deserted island just off the coast, where she reveals her true identity. The couple are eventually reconciled and remarry, albeit once again at gunpoint. (Dan Mason played the role of a prospector, Nugget Pete, in this film.)

Hard Boiled. (JGB/FOX, 6 June 1926) 6 reels. D: John G. Blystone. C: Tom Mix, Helene Chadwick, Charles Conklin, Phyllis Haver, W.E. Lawrence, Emily Fitzroy,

Filmography

Dan Mason, Spec O'Donnell, Ethel Grey Terry, Eddie Sturgis, Eddie Boland, Emmett Wagner.

Synopsis: Abner Boyden (Mason), a successful Chicago businessman, is exasperated with his carefree nephew, Jeff. As a last resort, he sends him out west to find out why his dude ranch isn't making money. There, Jeff meets Abigail Gregg, the manager, and her attractive niece, Marjorie, who catches Jeff's eye. Masquerading as a doctor, having stolen a physician's clothes, Jeff discovers a plot by New York crooks to steal the jewelry from the safe at the ranch. Jeff thwarts the crooks' plans, fights the whole gang atop a moving train car, and puts them all in jail. When he and his wonder horse, Tony, rescue Marjorie from a charging steer, his conquest of the west is complete.

*So This Is Paris.*** (WB, 31 July 1926) 7 reels. D: Ernst Lubitsch. C: Monte Blue, Patsy Ruth Miller, Lilyan Tashman, George Beranger, Myrna Loy, Sidney D'Albrook, Max Barwyn, Dan Mason (uncredited).

Synopsis: Dr. Paul Giraud is so dull that his wife Suzanne daydreams about romancing a sheik. When she thinks she spots a sheik next door, she begins pining for him. The sheik is, however, just Maurice Lalle, an ordinary guy in costume, rehearsing with his wife Georgette and their piano accompanist (Mason) for a dance performance. But when Paul goes to scold Maurice for appearing at his window shirtless, he discovers that the "sheik's" wife is an old flame of his and they enjoy a little reunion. When he forgets his cane in the Lalle's apartment, Maurice returns it to Giraud's wife, and sparks fly between them. The flirtations between the two couples become increasingly complicated. Paul and Georgette go to a fancy dress ball without their spouses' knowledge and Maurice, mistaken for Paul while visiting the Giraud's apartment, goes to jail for Paul's speeding offense. After Suzanne hears on the radio that Paul and his date have won a prize at the ball, she retrieves the drunken Paul from the ball, and drags him home. The next morning, all is wedded bliss once again between the doctor and his wife.

Stepping Along. (CCB, 14 November 1926) 7 reels. D: Charles Hines. C: Johnny Hines, Mary Brian, William Gaxton, Ruth Dwyer, Edmund Breese, Dan Mason, Lee Beggs.

Synopsis: Johnny Rooney sells newspapers but hopes to run for political office in New York City. His sweetheart, Molly, dreams of a Broadway career as a dancer. Their lives become complicated when Boss O'Brien backs Johnny to run for assemblyman against Frank Moreland, the man who is sponsoring Molly's attempt to break into show business. Molly's debut with the George White's Scandals is a disaster and she leaves town. Concerned by Johnny's growing popularity, Moreland steals Johnny's birth certificate and tries to claim that he is ineligible for office. Johnny ultimately prevails, exposes Moreland, and gets elected. He and Molly are reunited. (Dan Mason played the role of Mike in this film.)

Tin Hats. (MGM, 28 November 1926) 7 reels. D: Edward Sedgwick. C: Conrad Nagel, Claire Windsor, George Cooper, Bert Roach, Tom O'Brien, Eileen Sedgwick, Dan Mason.

Synopsis: Jack, Lefty, and Dutch, three rookies of the American Expeditionary Force, have landed in France just as the armistice is signed. They spend so much time in a café that they don't realize their unit is moving on. Unsure where to go, they steal three bicycles and try to follow their unit. They encounter a German girl, Elsa, waiting for her chauffeur to fix her car. After a brief conversation and flirtation, they follow her when she drives on and come to a German village where they are welcomed by the mayor who thinks they are the occupying American army. Elsa invites them to her father's castle, where they all encounter strange and frightening activity during the night. Then Elsa is kidnapped by Bolsheviks who hold her in the dungeon hoping to pry the castle's secrets out of her. Elsa is rescued by the Americans, whereupon she and Jack find a hidden cache of jewels. Elsa agrees to become Jack's wife, but their celebration is interrupted by the arrival of Jack's commanding officer. (Dan Mason played the role of a flamboyant French photographer in this film.)

Filmography

The Fire Brigade. ** (MGM, 20 December 1926) 9 reels. D: William Nigh. C: May McAvoy, Charles Ray, Holmes Herbert, Tom O'Brien, Eugenie Besserer, Warner Richmond, Bert Woodruff, Vivia Ogden, DeWitt Jennings, Dan Mason, Erwin Connelly, James Bradbury, Sr.

Synopsis: Young Terry O'Neill decides to follow in the footsteps of his father and grandfather and become a fireman. The three generations argue about whether or not to keep the old horse drawn apparatus along with the modern fire trucks. Terry's sweetheart is Helen Corwin, but their relationship becomes complicated when Terry learns that Helen's father, James Corwin, a powerful Politician, has made some crooked deals that resulted in people living in unsafe buildings. Some of his structures are firetraps. Terry's criticism of James Corwin leads to a split-up with Helen. When the orphanage burns, all units, including the horse drawn apparatus, are pressed into action. Terry risks his life to save the children. Finding one toddler on the roof, he jumps from the roof into a net, with the baby in his arms. Terry and Helen are reconciled, and Terry receives public praise for his heroism. (Dan Mason played an old fireman, Peg Leg Murphy, in this film.)

The Price of Honor. (CP, 3 March 1927) 6 reels. D: Edward H. Griffith. C: Dorothy Revier, Malcolm McGregor, William V. Mong, Gustav von Seyffertitz, Erville Alderson, Dan Mason.

Synopsis: Dan Hoyt is convicted of murder he did not commit, on the basis of circumstantial evidence. He spends twenty years in prison before his sentence is commuted. When he returns home, embittered, he discovers that his niece, Carolyn, is engaged to marry Anthony Fielding, son of the District Attorney who framed and convicted Hoyt. Fielding, Sr., is opposed to this marriage. Hoyt commits suicide, but first arranges that evidence will suggest it was murder and that Anthony is the suspect. He also arranges that Anthony will be acquitted and through it all hopes to show the District Attorney that a man shouldn't be convicted on circumstantial evidence. But the evidence for acquittal never reaches the man for whom it was intended and Anthony is sentenced to hang. Only at the last minute does the truth emerge and Anthony is saved. (Dan Mason played the part of Roberts, a faithful butler, in this film.)

A Hero on Horseback. ** (UP, 10 July 1927) 6 reels. D: Del Andrews. C: Hoot Gibson, Ethlyne Clair, Edwards Davis, Edward Hearn, Dan Mason.

Synopsis: Billy Garford, a happy go lucky cowboy, loses his ranch and all but fifty dollars gambling. He gives his remaining fifty to an old prospector, Jimmie Breeze (Mason), as a grubstake. Billy goes to work for J.B. Starbuck, the man who won his ranch, but gets fired for paying too much attention to Starbuck's daughter, Ollie. When Jimmie strikes it rich, he splits his winnings with Billy, who buys the bank. Billy loans money to his friends, then wins it back at poker. But a crooked cashier, also in love with Ollie, absconds with both the funds and Ollie, and Billy must follow them in hot pursuit. Meanwhile, the townsfolk invade the bank and threaten to hang Jimmie Breeze. In the end, Billy rescues Ollie and the money, Jimmie is saved, and the cashier and his henchman get justice.

The Elegy. (PP, 6 August 1927) 2 reels. D: Andrew Stone. C: Tyrone Power, Sr., Gladys Brockwell, Phillipe De Lacy, Dan Mason.

Synopsis: In a tiny French village, a child of the streets plays his violin as his only means of income. His only companion is his pet dog. A cruel policeman kicks the pet dog and kills it. When the young violinist plays an elegy for his lost friend, the policeman is overcome with remorse and tries to make amends. But the child dies, leaving the policeman to reconsider how to live his own life. (Dan Mason's role in this film is unknown.)

Out All Night. (UP, 4 September 1927) 6 reels. D: William A. Seiter. C: Reginald Denny, Marian Nixon, Wheeler Oakum, Dorothy Earle, Dan Mason, Alfred Allen, Robert Seiter, Ben Hendricks, Jr., Billy Franey, Harry Tracy, Lionel Braham.

Synopsis: John Graham, a wealthy young man, meets and marries a cute little showgirl, Molly O'Day. When her

169

Filmography

show, "Sweet Daddy," embarks for London, he goes along. However, Molly discovers a clause in her contract that prevents her from marrying. To avoid her having to forfeit one hundred thousand dollars, the newlyweds must hide the fact that they are man and wife, and stay in separate staterooms. They devise a series of awkward strategies by which they can see each other while trying to keep their secret. When John poses as the ship's doctor making a sick call to her cabin, he finds himself obligated to treat other passengers and prescribes castor oil for all ailments, with predictable results. Ultimately, his treatment for the captain's gout makes it clear he is no doctor. Meanwhile, the manager of the show proposes to Molly. When she refuses, citing the non-marriage clause in her contract, he invalidates the document by tearing it up. Moments later, John, who has taken refuge in a ventilator shaft to escape the outraged crew, slides down into Molly's room and they embrace. (Dan Mason played the role of Uncle McDermott in this film.)

The Chinese Parrot. (UP, 23 October 1927) 7 reels. D: Paul Leni. C: Marian Nixon, Florence Turner, Hobart Bosworth, Edmund Burns, Albert Conti, Sojin Kamiyama, Fred Esmelton, Edgar Kennedy, George Kuwa, Slim Summerville, Dan Mason, Anna May Wong, Etta Lee, Jack Trent.

Synopsis: A valuable pearl necklace is given to Sally Phillimore when she jilts Phillip Madden to marry her father's wealthy friend. Years later, when a widowed Sally finds herself penniless with a young daughter, Phillip, now a millionaire, offers to buy the pearls. He wants them delivered to New York. Sally sends Charlie Chan from her home in Honolulu to the mainland to meet Bob Eden, the son of a jeweler who has brokered the deal. But Bob is shadowed at the docks and when Madden suddenly insists the pearls come to his California desert home, Charlie senses that something is wrong. He delays turning over the pearls and arrives at the ranch posing as a cook, to do some investigating. Finding some suspicious evidence, Chan and Bob suspect a murder has taken place. But there is no body. They try to figure out who the victim was and who did the killing. A parrot that speaks English and Chinese provides a clue, but the bird is poisoned. An old prospector, William Cherry (Mason), thinks he witnessed a murder, but his account is questionable. In the end, Chan determines that an imposter, Jerry Delaney, a known jewel thief, has replaced Madden. Delaney wounded the millionaire during his kidnapping, an event witnessed by the parrot. After a confrontation and a struggle, the truth is revealed and Delaney is arrested. The pearls are delivered to the real Madden, who has been rescued by Bob Eden.

*The Valley of the Giants.*** (FNP, 4 December 1927) 7 reels. D: Charles Brabin. C: Milton Sills, Doris Kenyon, Arthur Stone, George Fawcett, Paul Hurst, Yola d'Avril, Phil Brady, James A. Marcus, Erville Alderson, Dan Crimmins, Otto Hoffman, Lucien Littlefield, Dan Mason, Charles Sellon, Johnny Downs, Lon Poff.

Synopsis: Bryce Cardigan returns home from years of travel to find that his father, a pioneering lumberman, has since gone blind, and is being ruined financially. His rival, Colonel Pennington, refuses to allow Cardigan to use his railroad to transport his logs. Bryce suggests they build their own railroad, goes about getting financing, and hires a crew. Meanwhile, Bryce has met and fallen in love with Shirley Pennington, daughter of the rival lumberman. To build their railroad, the Cardigans must secretly cross the Pennington line at night. But Pennington hears about it and assembles his forces to attack them. Shirley sides with Bryce and warns him of the impending battle. After a bitter struggle, the Pennington forces are routed and the crossing is successfully made. Bryce's father blesses his son's marriage to his rival's daughter and urges them to carry on the work he began years before. (Dan Mason played one of the town's councilmen in this film.)

*Hop Off.*** (BCC, 1 July 1928) 2 reels. D: Charles R. Bowers, Harold L. Muller. C: Charles R. Bowers, Yvonne Howell, Dan Mason, Robert Graves.

Synopsis: Charley makes his living by running a flea circus. His fleas perform a series of acrobatic feats. At one point, they skate on the head of a bald man (Mason). Charley also stumbles upon a fluid that transforms everything back to its original state of being. He uses it on a variety of objects such as cigars and sausages, and eventually on himself.

Lilac Time. ** (FNP, 3 August 1928) 11 reels. D: George Fitzmaurice. C: Colleen Moore, Gary Cooper, Eugenie Besserer, Burr McIntosh, Dan Mason, Kathryn McGuire, Cleve Moore, Arthur Lake, Richard Jarvis, Jack Stoney, Dan Dowling, Dick Grace, Stuart Knox, Jack Ponder, Harlan Hilton, George Cooper, Edward Dillon, Emile Chautard, Eddie Clayton, Philo McCullough, Nelson McDowell, Paul Hurst, Yolanda Kruger, Harold Lockwood.

Synopsis: Jeannine Berthelot lives on a farm in France with her widowed mother and grandfather (Mason). When the First World War begins, their farm is used as an airbase and English pilots are billeted in their home. In the spring, Jeannine sets their table with bouquets of lilacs. When she takes a special interest in one of the flyers, Captain Phillip Blythe, he becomes increasingly appreciative of her. When the air corps is sent off on a mission, Philip professes his love and promises to return to Jeannie. She promises to wait for him. Soon after, the Germans advance and Jeannine and her family become refugees forced to flee. But Jeannine, who has promised to wait for Phillip's return, soon runs back to her village, only to find it in ruins. Suddenly, Phillip appears overhead, the only survivor of his squadron. Jeannine watches in horror as he is attacked by a German pilot and shot down. She rushes to the crash site and flags down an ambulance in a passing convoy. The medics take Phillip away but won't let Jeannine go along. She travels to Paris, hoping to find him in a military hospital. At first she is mistakenly informed that he is dead. She finds a bouquet of lilacs in the market and asks an officer to bring them to Phillip as a memorial. When Phillip sees them, he realizes that Jeannine has been to the hospital. He struggles to the window and calls out to her. When she finally hears him, she rushes to his side and they are reunited.

The Awakening. (SGC, 17 November 1928) 9 reels D: Victor Fleming. C: Vilma Banky, Walter Byron, Louis Wolheim, George Davis, William Orlamond, Carl von Haartman, Jack McDonald, Dan Mason (uncredited).

Synopsis: Just before the First World War, Marie Ducrot, a lovely and naïve Alsatian peasant girl, falls in love with a German army officer, Count Karl von Hagen, who at first sees her only as a passing fancy. When she innocently visits him in his quarters, the townspeople assume the worst and attack her with stones. Her peasant suitor, Louis, whips her from the village in disgust and tries to kill Karl. Marie goes into exile. Karl, who realizes too late that he loves her, assumes she is dead. But Marie has entered the religious life as a novice. During the war, the convent is under siege and Karl is sent to rescue the nuns. He arrives, badly wounded, and finds Marie about to take her vows as a nun. While the other nuns evacuate, Marie stays behind to care for Karl's wounds. But a French officer, Marie's former suitor in the village, finds them and determines to kill the German. Instead, Marie persuades him to help her carry Karl to safety, and she and Karl are saved by their former enemy.

The Bellamy Trial. (MGM, 23 January 1929) 9 reels. D: Monta Bell. C: Leatrice Joy, Betty Bronson, Edward J. Nugent, George Baraud, Margaret Livingston, Kenneth Thomson, Margaret Seddon, Charles Middleton, Charles Hill Mailes, William H. Tooker, Cosmo Kyrle Bellew, Robert Dudley, Jacqueline Gadsden, Dan Mason, Jack Raymond, Polly Ann Young.

Synopsis: Mimi Bellamy, a prominent Long Island society matron, is found murdered in an old gardener's cottage. Since Mimi once had an affair with Patrick Ives, and the two had recently been meeting secretly in the cottage where Mimi was found dead, suspicion falls upon Mimi's husband, Stephen Bellamy, and Pat's wife, Sue Ives. Assuming a motive of jealousy, prosecutors put Stephen and Sue on trial. Prosecutors present an abundance of evidence, all of it circumstantial. The two defendants tell one story, then another. They finally admit to having been to the cottage on the day of the crime, but insist that they found Mimi already dead. As the trial is wrapping up, a surprise witness appears and gives testimony that corroborates the alibis of Stephen and Sue, clearing them of suspicion. Just as the jury is about to return with a verdict, Patrick's mother suddenly rises to address the courtroom and confesses that she killed Mimi Bellamy, claiming it was self-defense. When the jury comes in with the verdict of not guilty, the stress is too much for old Mrs. Ives and she dies of a heart attack.

Chapter Notes

Chapter 1

1. William James Grassman and Mary Brown, Affidavit for License to Marry, Town of Courtland, West Chester County, New York, 29 August 1910, "New York, County Marriage Records, 1847–1849, 1907–1936," https://www.ancestry.com (hereinafter cited as Ancestry.com).
2. Dan Mason, *Fifty Years A Trouper*, notes for a planned memoir, handwritten manuscript, p. 1, Dan Mason Papers, Daniel Gelfand Collection, Woodstock, New York. (hereinafter cited as Gelfand Collection).
3. "Local News," *The Journal* (Syracuse), 16 May 1868, p. 8; "Local News," *The Journal*, 20 May 1868, p. 8; *Fifty Years A Trouper*, p. 2.
4. *Fifty Years A Trouper*, p. 2.
5. C. H. Williams, "Observations," *The Marcellus Observer* (Marcellus, NY), 10 July 1929, p. 1; *Fifty Years a Trouper*, p. 3; "This, That, and T'other," *The Syracuse Standard*, 23 January 1887, p. 5.
6. *Fifty Years A Trouper*, pp. 3–5.
7. *Fifty Years A Trouper*, pp. 5–8; Franklin H. Chase, "Just a Moment," *Syracuse Journal*, 18 October 1924, p. 8.
8. *Fifty Years A Trouper*, pp. 5–8; For a full discussion of Concert Saloons, See: Gillian M. Rodger, *Champagne Charlie and Pretty Jemima* (Champaign: University of Illinois Press, 2010), Chapter Three; "Veteran Actor Tells of Old Days," *Syracuse Herald*, 2 June 1918, unpaginated clipping, Gelfand Collection.
9. *Fifty Years A Trouper*, pp. 8–10, 14; "Daily Squint At Movie Stars," *Star Gazette* (Elmira, NY), 15 September 1922, p. 10; The modern value of dollar amounts cited here and throughout the book have been determined using the calculator provided by Samuel H. Williamson on his website, Measuring Worth: https://www.measuringworth.com.
10. *Fifty Years A Trouper*, p. 10.
11. Advertisement for Washburn's Last Sensation, *Pittston Gazette* (Pittston, Pennsylvania), 18 July 1872, p. 3; *Fifty Years A Trouper*, p. 15.
12. *Fifty Years A Trouper*, p. 16.

Chapter 2

1. Dan Mason, "The Variety Theater," supplemental notes for *Fifty Years A Trouper*, unpaginated, Gelfand Collection.
2. Trav S. D., *No Applause—Just Throw Money* (New York: Faber and Faber, 2005), pp. 67–68.
3. As noted by theatrical impresario, Richard D'Oyly Carte, in London in 1881: "The greatest drawbacks to the enjoyment of the theatrical performances are, undoubtedly, the foul air and heat which pervade all theaters. As everyone knows, each gas-burner consumes as much oxygen as many people, and causes great heat beside." See Walter Hamilton, *The Aesthetic Movement in England* (London: Reeves and Turner, 1882), p. 38; Hunton Sellman and Merrill Lessley, *Essentials of Stage Lighting. 2nd ed.* (Englewood Cliffs, NJ: Prentice-Hall, 1982), pp. 14–17; Louis Hartman, *Theatre Lighting: A Manual of the Stage Switchboard* (New York: DBS Publications, 1970 [1930]), p. 173.
4. Based on the number of handwritten poems found in Dan Mason's personal papers, it appears that reciting poetry was an important part of his early acts. He

Notes—Chapter 3

appears to have traded poems with his fellow troupers, some of whom autographed the pieces they gave him. See Dan Mason's collection of poems, Gelfand Collection.

5. "Variety Halls," *The New York Clipper* (hereinafter *NYCl*), 17 November 1877, p. 271; Dan Mason's collection of theater programs, 1877–78, Gelfand Collection.

6. "Variety Halls," *NYCl*, 16 October 1875, p. 231; "Capital City Brevities," *The Daily Arkansas Gazette* (Little Rock, Arkansas), 28 March 1876, p. 4; Flora Frawley had first appeared on stage at age sixteen in Chicago's Academy of Music in 1873. See "Theatrical Record," *NYCl*, 30 August 1873, p. 174.

7. "Theatrical Record," *NYCl*, 1 July 1876, p. 111; "Baries Opera House," *Daily Courier* (Syracuse, New York), 26 July 1876, p. 3.

8. "Variety Halls," *NYCl*, 30 December, 1876, p. 311; "From the Workshop to the Stage," unattributed, unpaginated clipping in Millie La Fonte scrapbook, Gelfand Collection.

9. "Variety Halls," *NYCl*, 20 October, 1877, p. 239; "Variety Halls," *NYCl*, 28 September 1878, p. 215; "Variety Halls," *NYCl*, 4 January 1879, p. 327.

10. "Variety Halls," *NYCl*, 19 April 1879, p. 31; Advertisement for The Coliseum, *The Cincinnati Enquirer*, 19 November 1878, p. 5; "The Coliseum," *Cincinnati Enquirer*, 26 November 1878, p. 7.

11. "Dan Sully Says Something And Saws Wood," *The Brooklyn Daily Eagle*, 6 August 1905, p. 20; "Ocelia C. Wallmatin," *Cincinnati Enquirer*, 11 July 1877, p. 2l; "Theatrical Chit-Chat," *Reynold's Newspaper* (London, England), 29 July 1877, p. 8; Ocelia's name is also given as Wallanatia; Irish and German dialect comedians predominated in the mid to late nineteenth century due to the numbers of immigrants from those cultures that the average American encountered in daily life. Later on, Jewish and Italian comedians would begin to appear as those ethnic groups grew in numbers. Though they did ultimately prevail, humorists of African American heritage were slower to find favor in the mainstream and were at a disadvantage, having to break through the stereotypes being reinforced in Minstrel Shows.

12. "Variety Halls," *NYCl*, 5 June 1880, p. 87.

13. "Variety Halls," *NYCl*, 20 December 1879, p. 307.

14. "Variety Halls," *NYCl*, 25 December, 1880, p. 815.

15. Dan Mason, *Unneighborly Neighbors*, partial hand written manuscript in seven sections, c. 1880, Gelfand Collection; *A Crowded Hotel*, partial hand written manuscript in five sections, c. 1880, Gelfand Collection.

16. "Took Him For A Gentleman," *Star Tribune* (Minneapolis, Minnesota), 6 October 1902, p. 2.

17. "Variety Halls," *NYCl*, 25 December 1880, p. 815; "Variety Halls," *NYCl*, 1 January 1881, p. 323; Notice of copyright infringement, *NYCl*, 26 March 1881, p. 15.

18. "John D. Griffin, Comedian, Dead," *The Boston Globe*, 10 August 1910, p. 11.

19. Dan Mason, *All Fools Day*, c. 1881, hand written manuscript in bound notebook, Gelfand Collection. *All Fools Day* is the only one of Mason's afterpieces or plays to survive completely intact.

20. "Variety Halls," *NYCl*, 10 June 1882, p. 195; "Variety Halls," *NYCL*, 16 December 1882, p. 638.

21. "Variety Halls," *NYCl*, 2 December 1882, p. 598; "A Vocalist Shot," *The Times* (Philadelphia, Pennsylvania), 10 December 1882, p. 1.

22. Armond Fields, *Tony Pastor, Father of Vaudeville* (Jefferson, North Carolina: McFarland and Company, 2007), pp. 105–108; "Amusements: Park Theater," *The Detroit Free Press*, 20 May 1883, p. 15; "Amusements," *Cincinnati Enquirer*, 1 May 1883, p. 2.

23. "Peck's Bad Boy," *The Daily Review* (Wilmington, North Carolina), 31 December 1884, p. 1; "The Corner Grocery," *Vicksburg Herald*, p. 4; "Peck's Bad Boy," reprint from *The Boston Herald* in *The Richmond Item* (Richmond, Indiana), 22 January 1884, p. 2.

24. "Rhode Island," *NYCl*, 13 June 1885, p. 203.

Chapter 3

1. Jefferson De Angelis and Alvin E. Harlow, *A Vagabond Trouper* (New York: Harcourt Brace & Company, 1931), pp.

Notes—Chapter 3

50, 51, 87, 103. Millie La Fonte's name is sometimes given as Lafonte, La Font, or La Fount.

2. "Really Too Too," *The Brooklyn Daily Eagle*, 31 December 1883, p. 2; To distract from the sad drama of her actual early life, when asked to provide a biographic profile to the press Millie was inspired to embellish her story with fanciful tales of abduction, incarceration in a French convent, singing in the streets of Paris, and discovery by an English impresario who whisked her away to London to make her debut at the Alhambra. See "Miss Millie La Fonte, Serio-Comic vocalist—A Handsome Girl With an Eventful History," unattributed, unpaginated item, Millie La Fonte Scrapbook, Gelfand Collection.

3. "Dedicated to Millie La Font," unattributed and unpaginated clipping, c. 1884, Millie La Fonte Scrapbook, Gelfand Collection; Advertisement for Gaylord and Sullivan's Mastodons, *Xenia Daily Gazette* (Ohio), 24 April 1883, p. 3.

4. "A Handsome Girl With an Eventful History," Gelfand Collection; John J. Jennings, *Theatrical and Circus Life: Or, Secrets of the Stage, Green Room and Sawdust* (Brandon, Vermont: Sidney M. Southard, 1884) p. 85.

5. "Variety," *NYCl*, 26 January 1885, p. 767; "Virginia," *NYCL* 18 July 1885, p. 281; "Rhode Island," *NYCl*, 20 June 1885, p. 219; Marriage Certificate # 48996, "New York, New York, Extracted Marriage Index, 1866–1937," Ancestry.com.

6. "Academy of Music," *The Buffalo Commercial*, 7 September 1885, p. 3; "Show Gossip," *The Cincinnati Enquirer*, 14 September 1885, p. 4; "Theatrical Gossip," *The Buffalo Morning Express*, 6 September 1885, p. 5; "At Crawfords,'" *The Daily Commonwealth* (Topeka, Kansas), 24 October 1885, p. 4; Armond Fields, *Eddie Foy: A Biography of the Early Popular Stage Comedian* (Jefferson, North Carolina: McFarland and Company, 1999), p. 63; Mason would later claim to have "discovered" Eddie Foy and given him his first real part. See "Dan Mason and Harry Kelley Renew Acquaintance in Picture Studio," *NYCl*, 26 April 1915, p. 6.

7. "Music Hath Charms," *The Pittsburgh Dispatch*, 8 February 1891, p. 4.

8. 'Theatrical Gossip," *The Inter-Ocean* (Chicago), 7 February 1886, p. 13; Death Certificate for Daniel Mason Grassman, 11 February 1886, "Cook County, Illinois, Deaths Index, 1878–1922," Ancestry.com; Wilna Hervey, notes for proposed memoir, J-2, Gelfand Collection.

9. "New York," *NYCl*, 13 February 1886, p. 757.

10. "This, That, T'other," *Syracuse Daily Standard*, 23 January 1887, p. 5; Since Mason's wig for his role as Dietrich was made by Helmer and Lietz in Manhattan, an engraving of "Mr. Dan Mason as Capt. Dietrich" found its way into *The Illustrated Hairdresser* as a "specimen illustration of wigs and coiffures." See unpaginated clipping from *The Illustrated Hairdresser* (New York: Helmer and Lietz, 1889); Cabinet card of Dan Mason as Captain Dietrich, Gehrig Photography, Chicago, c. 1886; Unattributed, unpaginated and undated partial clipping in Millie La Fonte Scrapbook, Gelfand Collection.

11. "Amusement," *The Inter Ocean* (Chicago, Illinois), 30 May 1887, p. 13; "News of the Theaters," *The New York Sun*, 24 April 1887, p. 13.

12. "Coulisse Chat," *St. Louis Dispatch*, 7 May 1887, p. 10; "New York," *NYCl*, 21 May 1887, p. 150; Also known as *The Sideshow by the Seashore*. The other shows were *In A Fix*, *A Boy Wanted*, *Winkle's Fix*, and *Two Widowers*; "Rhode Island," *NYCl*, 6 August 1887, p. 323; "New York," 16 October 1887, *NYCl*, p. 490; Advertisement for The Boston Musical Hall, *The Boston Globe*, 30 Oct 1887, p. 11; "Greenroom Chat," *NYCl*, 26 March 1887, p. 21; "Amusements," *St. Louis Dispatch*, 1 January 1888, p. 1.

13. "Rhode Island," *NYCl*, 1 September 1888, p. 391; "Over the Garden Wall," *New York Dramatic Mirror*, 15 September 1888, p. 8; "This, That, T'other, " *Syracuse Daily Standard*, 23 January 1887, p. 5.

14. "Dramatic and Musical Notes," *NYCl*, 2 February 1889, p. 749.

15. "Dramatic and Musical Notes," *NYCl*, 3 August 1889, p. 340; "Court Street Theater," *The Buffalo Courier*, 8 December 1889, p. 11.

16. "Continental," *The Times* (Philadelphia, Pennsylvania), 18 November 1890, p. 4; "Kansas City Globe," *The Fort Scott Daily Monitor* (Fort Scott, Kansas), 11 March

Notes—Chapter 4

1890, p. 3; "Connecticut," *NYCl*, 16 August 1890, p. 354; Advertisement for *A Clean Sweep*, *Poughkeepsie Eagle News* (Poughkeepsie, New York), 8 September 1890, p. 4; "Made a Clean Sweep," *New York Herald*, 20 October 1890, p. 6; "Over The Garden Wall," *The Pittsburgh Dispatch*, 5 May 1889, p. 4.

17. "New York City," *NYCl*, 17 January 1891, p. 709; "Funny Little Stories," *The Sunday Morning Star* (Wilmington, Delaware), 19 August 1917, p. 7.

18. "The Hustler," *The Pittsburgh Press*, 3 February 1891, p. 3; Advertisement for *The Hustler*, *The Tennessean*, 19 January 1891, p. 8.

19. "Last Night's Plays," *The Philadelphia Inquirer*, 10 March 1891, p. 5.

20. "Academy of Music," *The Buffalo Commercial*, 7 May 1891, p. 8.

21. "An American Boy," *NYCl*, 19 September 1891, p. 473; "An American Boy," *The Salt Lake Herald*, 10 April 1892, p. 12.

22. Advertisement for *An American Boy*, *The Salt Lake Tribune*, 18 April 1892, p. 8.

23. 'The World of Players," *NYCl*, 1 August 1891, p. 348; "Town Talk," *The Rock Island Argus* (Davenport, Iowa), 20 November 1891, p. 6; "Music and Drama," *The Chicago Tribune*, 5 October 1891, p. 4; "Items In Brief," *Quad City Times* (Davenport, Iowa), 11 November 1891, p. 1; "The World of Players," *NYCl*, 28 November 1891, p. 634.

24. Advertisement for *An American Boy*, *The Salt Lake Herald*, 10 April 1892, p. 12.

25. "City and Neighborhood," *Salt Lake Tribune*, 18 April 1892, p. 8; "Wonderland," *The Salt Lake Herald*, 20 April 1892, p. 5.

26. "World of Players," *NYCl*, 14 May 1892, p. 148.

Chapter 4

1. Draft card for Harry G. Mason, 1917, "U.S., World War I Draft Registration Cards, 1917–1918," Ancestry.com; "Daddy Nolan," *The Daily Tribune* (Great Falls, Minnesota), 20 August 1892, p. 5; Advertisement for *The Tigers*, *St. Joseph Herald*, 24 March 1892, p. 2; "The Stage," *Los Angeles Times*, 17 July 1892, p. 10.

2. Daniel Sully's plays include: *Peck's Bad Boy and his Father* (1883), *The Corner Grocery* (1885), *Capital Prize* (1885), *Con Conroy and Co.* (1889), *Daddy's Darling* (1889), *The Country Grocery* (1899), *The Millionaire* (1890), *Mr. Dooley of Chicago* (1890), *Auld Lang Syne* (1893), *A Social Lion* (1894). See Alf Evers, *Woodstock: History of an American Town* (Woodstock, NY: Overlook Press, 1897), p. 386.

3. "Daddy Nolan," *The Great Falls Tribune* (Montana), 20 August 1892, p. 5; "Daniel Sully at the Bush," *The San Francisco Examiner*, 18 September 1892, p. 8; "Amusements," *Duluth Evening Herald*, 29 November 1892, p. 2; "The Stage," *Detroit Free Press*, 6 January 1893, p. 4.

4. CassStudio6 Theatre History, "Theater Lighting Throughout History," https://cassstudio6.wordpress.com/lighting/change-over-to-electricity/

5. Advertisement for The Howard Theater, *The Boston Post*, 18 August 1895, p. 8; Promissory note from Daniel Sully to Dan Mason, May 1893, Gelfand Collection.

6. "Local Intelligence," *The Alexandria Gazette* (Virginia), 28 August 1893, p. 3; "Pennsylvania," *NYCl*, 9 September 1893, p. 431; "Amusements," *The Tennessean* (Nashville), 3 October 1893, p. 6; "City News," *Lawrence Daily Gazette* (Lawrence, Kansas), 28 November 1893, p. 3; "Havlin's," *Cincinnati Inquirer*, 8 October 1894, p. 7; "Manager's Troubles," *Cincinnati Inquirer*, 16 April 1895, p. 8.

7. "Sully and Mason," *The St. Paul Globe* (Minnesota), 13 October 1895, p. 13; "The Theatre, " *The Star Tribune* (Minneapolis, Minnesota), 20 October 1895, p. 25; "A Day In June," *The San Francisco Call*, 15 December 1895, p. 22.

8. "Dan Sully's New Play," *The Anaconda Standard*, 13 November 1895, p. 3; "A Bachelor's Wives," *The Courier* (Lincoln, Nebraska), 4 January 1896, p. 8; Dan Mason, Handwritten inventory of dates and corresponding box office receipts, four pages, 23 December 1895- 30 April 1896, Gelfand Collection.

9. "Actor Dan Sully Bankrupt," *The Sun* (New York, NY), 19 May 1899, p. 7; Willis E. Boyer, Manager of Daniel Sully Company, to Dan Mason, Esq., 23 February 1898, Gelfand Collection.

10. "Chicago Opera House," *Chicago*

Notes—Chapter 5

Daily Tribune, 30 August 1897, p. 29; "Evangeline Is In Tears," *The Leader-Democrat* (Springfield, Missouri), 2 February 1897, p. 5; Advertisement for Hopkins Grand Opera House, *The St. Louis Dispatch*, 28 March 1897, p. 23; "World of Players," *NYCI*, 22 May 1897, p. 188.

Chapter 5

1. Advertisement for Bijou theater, *The Washington Times* (Washington, D.C.), 4 April 1897, p. 17; "The Man from Mexico," *The Illustrated American*, Volume 21, 1 May 1897, p. 596.
2. Henry A. Du Souchet, *The Man from Mexico: A Farcical Comedy in Three Acts* (New York: Samuel French, 1897); "Music and Drama," *Sacramento Daily Union*, 1 May 1898, p. 8; "Theatrical Notes," *The Pittsburgh Press*, 8 May 1898, p. 18.
3. "Madison Square Theater," *NYCI*, 14 October 1899, p. 674; "Why Smith Left Home," *The Boston Globe*, 8 May 1900, p. 8; "Amusements," *Indianapolis News*, 8 February 1900, p. 3.
4. "Entertainments," *The Hartford Courant*, 9 November 1900, p. 7; "Amusements," *Omaha Daily Bee*, 21 January 1901, p. 5; "Theatrical," *Arkansas Democrat* (Little Rock), 10 December 1901, p. 6.
5. "Briefly Told," *The Washington Post*, 28 July 1901, p. 9; "At the Theaters," *The Los Angeles Times*, 29 September 1901, p. 36.
6. "The Best of All," *The Junction City Sentinel* (Kansas), 10 January 1902, p. 4; "Last Night's Play," *The Wilkes-Barre Times*, 12 April 1902, p. 5; "Amusements," *San Bernardino County Sun*, 28 September 1901, p. 6; "Tomorrow Night," *Austin American-Statesman* (Austin, Texas), 13 January 1903, p. 8; "Amusements," *The Times* (Richmond, Virginia), 29 August 1901, p. 2.
7. "Professional Doings," *New York Dramatic Mirror*, 19 July 1902, p. 10; Advertisement for The Lilas, *The Washington Post*, 8 July 1906, p. 32; *Gopsill's Atlantic City Directory*, 1907, p. 341, "U.S. City Directories, 1822–1995," Ancestry.com; It appears that Millie avoided controversy by never mentioning to her boarding house guests that she and her often absent husband were theatrical folks. When the census of 1910 was taken, she listed Dan Mason as a traveling salesman. See 1910 United States Census for Atlantic City, "Atlantic City Ward 4, Atlantic, New Jersey," Ancestry.com.
8. "Nervy Mr. Mason," *New York Morning Telegraph*, 18 May 1903, p. 12; "Dan Mason Claims a Double," *New York Morning Telegraph*, 16 May 1903, p. 7.
9. "Plays and Play People," *News-Journal* (Mansfield, Ohio), 24 September 1904, p. 6.
10. It should be noted that the word "gay" as used here must be understood in the older sense of "light hearted" or "carefree."
11. "He's in 'Gay New York,'" *New York Morning Telegraph*, 11 August 1905, p. 10; "Gay New York," *The Philadelphia Inquirer*, 24 October 1905, p. 4; "Telegraphic News," *New York Dramatic Mirror*, 21 October 1905, p. 12; "Dan Mason Hits Mark with Gay New York," *The Morning Telegraph* (New York City), 6 February 1906, p. 10.
12. "Syracuse," *New York Dramatic Mirror*, 26 August 1906 p. 6; "Elmira Likes 'In Norland' [sic]," *Star-Gazette* (Elmira, New York), 5 September 1906, p. 7; "It Happened In Nordland," *The Montgomery Advertiser* (Montgomery, Alabama), 31 October 1906, p. 10; "Theatrical," *Leavenworth Post* (Kansas), 7 January 1907, p. 8.
13. "Amusements," *The Charlotte News* (Charlotte, North Carolina), 13 January 1908, p. 6, 14 January 1908, p. 6; "Musical Notes," *Democrat and Chronicle* (Rochester, New York), 26 January 1908, p. 12; "The Prince of Pilsen," *Kansas City Globe*, 11 February 1908, p. 6.
14. The 1910 Census for Atlantic City shows Dan Mason's sister, Jane, in household. See "1910 United States Federal Census, Atlantic City Ward 4, Atlantic, New Jersey," Ancestry.com; "Gay New York," *The Morning Herald* (New York City), 4 November 1908, p. 2; "Connecticut," *Billboard*, 9 January 1908, p. 24; "A Revival of The Man from Mexico at the Garrick," *New York Times*, 9 May 1909, p 60.
15. "Miss Patsy," *Press and Sun Bulletin* (Binghamton, New York), 4 January 1910, p. 4; "Miss Patsy," *Chicago Tribune*, 30 January 1910, p. 2; "Two Plays Given First Night Productions Here," *Press and Sun Bulletin* (Chicago, Illinois), 11 January 1910, p. 3;

Notes—Chapter 6

"Veteran Dan Mason," *The Allentown Democrat* (Pennsylvania), 22 August 1910, p. 7; "Offerings At The Theaters This Week," *The Washington Post*, 4 October 1910, p. 5; "Notes of the Stage," *The Washington Post*, 23 October 1910, p. 3.

16. "The Passing Show," *The Victoria Daily Times* (Victoria, British Columbia), 1 September 1911, p. 15; "Lansing Theaters," *Lansing State Journal* (Michigan), 5 December 1911, p. 6; "Amusements," The York Daily (York, Pennsylvania), 11 April 1911, p. 2; The idea of a man falling into a coal chute and wandering up into the house was a concept Dan Mason first used in an afterpiece, *Keintz's Visit to O'Harra*, in the 1880s. See hand written script in Gelfand Collection; Asked by a reporter in Detroit whether he was actually eating anything during the luncheon scene in the play, Mason replied: "You can't fake eating and make it seem real.... My repast consists of a banana sliced up ... one or two at every performance." See "An Old Timer Is Here," unattributed, unpaginated clipping, c. 1911, Gelfand Collection.

17. Advertisement for *The New Chauffeur*, Kingston *Daily Freeman* (Kingston, New York), 2 January 1911, p. 2; "Vaudeville Notes," *NYCl*, 28 January 1911, p. 1253; "At the Orpheum," *The Allentown Democrat* (Allentown, Pennsylvania), 6 April, 1911, p. 6.

Chapter 6

1. "New York State," *NYCl*, 16 February 1889, p. 782; "Amusements," *The Times* (Richmond), 29 August 1901, p. 2; "The Stage," *Detroit Free Press*, 16 August 1905, p. 4; Dan Mason Cigars were manufactured by J. J. Ambrose in Mount Carmel, Pennsylvania.

2. "Dan Mason," *Motion Picture Magazine*, February 1915, p. 112; Andrew A. Erish, *Colonel William N. Selig; The Man Who Invented Hollywood* (Austin: University of Texas Press) p 89; "Chicago," *New York Dramatic Mirror*, 14 August 1909, p. 24; Dan Mason's three films for Selig, *Winning a Widow* (1909), *Our German Cousin* (1909), and *The Crowded Hotel* (1910), do not survive. Some sources say he made one film for Vitagraph, *The Drop of Blood*, just before coming to Edison, although there is no indication of Mason's involvement in the film.

3. "Amusements," *The Times* (Richmond, Virginia), 29 August 1901, p. 2; Descriptions of the Selig films, *A Crowded Hotel* and *Winning a Widow* sound very much like the plots of Mason's sketches, *The Crowded Hotel* and *All Fool's Day*.

4. "Paragraphs About the Photoplayers," *The News Herald* (Franklin, Pennsylvania), 26 July 1913, p. 7; Advertisement for *Professor William Nutt* (1913), *Belvidere Daily Republican* (Belvidere, Illinois), 31 July 1913, p. 6; "The Theaters," *The Daily Missoulian* (Missoula, Montana), 20 June 1913, p. 2; Don H. Eddy, "Dan Mason, 52 Years With Show World, In Movies," *El Paso Times*, 30 March 1924, p. 21; Mason's surviving Edison films include: *Why Girls Leave Home* (1913), *A Millinery Mix-up* (1914), *A Double Elopement* (1914), and supposedly *Stickin' Around* (1915), though no Edison release bulletin for such a title can be found. He can be seen as an extra in *Andy Goes On The Stage* (1913).

5. "Brief Biographies of Popular Players: Dan Mason," *Motion Picture Magazine*, February 1915, p. 112; Leonhard H. Gmuer, *Rex Ingram: Hollywood's Rebel of the Silver Screen* (Berlin: epubli GmbH, 2013), p. 65; "News, Notes, and Gossip About Plays and Players," *Boston Globe*, 7 January 1917, p. 35; Ruth Barton, *Rex Ingram: Visionary Director of the Silent Screen* (Lexington: University Press of Kentucky, 2014), p. 32.

6. "About Photoplays and Photoplayers," *The Anaconda Standard* (Anaconda, Montana), 15 February 1914, p. 39; "Austin and Stones," *The Boston Post*, 12 May 1895, p. 11; Dan Mason, *Dinkelspiel's Baby, Comedy with a Touch of Sentiment*, typescript, c. 1914, Gelfand Collection.

7. George C. Warren, "Actor Enters Fiftieth Year on Stage," *San Francisco Chronicle*, 4 June 1922 p. 4.

8. Edison Motion Picture Company, *The Kinetogram*, Vol. 10, July 1914, p. 22, https://books.google.com/books.

9. Wilna Hervey, "Incident—The Original Katrinka," *The Original Katrinka*, unpaginated fragment, Gelfand Collection.

10. "Brief Biographies of Popular

178

Notes—Chapter 7

Players," *Motion Picture Magazine*, February 1915, p. 112; "The Path of the Picture Play," *Arizona Republic* (Phoenix) 24 August 1913, p. 17.

11. "Notes Written On The Screen," *New York Times*, 23 May 1915, Section S, p. 6; "Harry Kelley and Dan Mason Together" *Syracuse Journal* May 24 1915, p. 14; "Dan Mason and Harry Kelly Renew Acquaintance in Picture Studio," *NYCl*, 24 April 1915, p. 6; The Edison Company was a significant participant in the Motion Picture Patents Company which was sued by the Federal Government as an illegal trust in 1912 and ordered dissolved in October 1915.

12. "With the Pictures," *Syracuse Journal*, 20 September 1915, p. 11; Adam Tawfik, *The Elusive Eastern Film Corporation of Providence, Rhode Island; Resurrecting a Footnote in Film History*, Honors Project Paper, Rhode Island College (2013), pp. 22, 27, https://digitalcommons.ric.edu/honors_projects/76; Dan Mason, *All Fools Day*.

13. Mae Tinee, "Tragic Story Makes Good But Sad Picture," *Chicago Daily Tribune*, 17 February 1917, p. 10; "False Face Fringe Pride of Actor's Life," *The Winnipeg Tribune* (Winnipeg, Manitoba), 20 January 1917, p. 26.

14. "Jack Spurlock, Prodigal," *Motography*, 23 February 1918, p. 375.

15. "Theatre," *The Wilmington Dispatch* (Wilmington, NC), 16 October 1917, p. 2; "Stuart Holmes in 'The Derelict' at the Strand Today," *San Bernardino Sun*, 22 August 1917, p. 10; "Lyric," *Reading Times* (Pennsylvania), 11 June 1917, p. 6; "George Walsh wins Billion and Girl in Fast Photoplay," *The Ottawa Citizen* (Ottawa, Canada), 21 September 1918, p. 11.

16. The George M. Perry Motion Picture Service was located at 101 W. 46th Street, New York City; "Next Week's Amusements," *The Marion Star* (Marion, Ohio), 4 May 1918, p. 15.

Chapter 7

1. Marriage Certificate for Harry Grossman [sic] Mason and Barbara Charlotte Kuester, 10 April 1915, "New York, New York, Extracted Marriage Index, 1866–1937," Ancestry.com; "Movie Notes," *Atlanta Constitution*, 30 December 1917, p. 2; Harry Mason, Draft Registration Card, 5 June 1917, U.S., "World War I Draft Registration Cards, 1917–1918," Ancestry.com.

2. Paul Kupperberg, *The Influenza Pandemic of 1918-1919* (New York City: Chelsea House, 2008), p. 49; Millicent Grassman Mason, Certificate of Death, #1487, "Department of Health of the City of New York, Department of Records," Ancestry.com; "Deaths of the Week," *NYCl*, 13 February 1919, p. 33.

3. "Dan Mason and Company," *Variety*, April 1919, p. 10; "Vaudeville," *NYCl*, 25 April 1919, p. 12; "Movie Gossip," *Syracuse Journal*, 21 July 1919, p. 9; Aubrey Solomon, *The Fox Film Corporation, 1915–1935* (Jefferson, North Carolina: McFarland and Company, 2011), p. 259; As Sylvester Dolan, Mason played the father of Bara's character, Olga Dolan.

4. Joseph P. Eckhardt, "Clatter, Sproing, Clunk, Went the Trolley," *Pennsylvania Heritage*, Quarterly of the Pennsylvania Historical and Museum Commission, vol. 18, no. 3, Summer, 1992, pp. 24–31.

5. Ibid.

6. *The Original Katrinka*, pp. 27–30, Gelfand Collection.

7. Ibid.

8. *The Original Katrinka*, p. 61; Dan Mason to Wilna Hervey, 14 June 1923, HMP, box 3, folder 10; Also see: Joseph P. Eckhardt, *Living Large: Wilna Hervey and Nan Mason* (Woodstock, NY: Woodstock-Arts, LLC, 2015), pp. 26–33

9. "The Skipper's Treasure Garden," *Moving Picture World*, 19 March 1921, p. 270.

10. "The Majestic Theater," *Reno Gazette Journal* (Reno, Nevada), 19 February 1921, p. 12; "Skipper Rivals Barrymore," *The Wichita Beacon* (Wichita, Kansas) 16 June 1921, p. 2.

11. Four surviving Toonerville Trolley films in 16mm format are part of the Betzwood Film Archive collection at Montgomery County Community College in Blue Bell, PA: *The Skipper's Narrow Escape* (1920), *The Skipper's Flirtation* (1920), *Toonerville's Boozem Friends* (1921), and *Toonerville Follies* (1922); "Clatter, Sproing, Clunk," p. 28.

12. *The Original Katrinka*, 6B-7B, Gelfand Collection; "$ 750 for Family of Electricity Victim," *The Ambler Gazette* (Ambler, Pennsylvania), 25 August 1921, p. 3.
13. "Metropolitan—'Why Girls Leave Home,'" *Washington Times*, 7 November 1921, p. 19; Production stills from *Why Girls Leave Home* (1921), Gelfand collection.
14. *Living Large*, p. 41.
15. Each Toonerville release earned the studio $14,000 from First National, an amount worth c. $175,000 today. This sum had to be balanced against the considerable costs of making the films and keeping the studio in operation. See Contract between Betzwood Film Company and First National, 20 February 1920, Princeton University Library; *Living Large*, p. 44.

Chapter 8

1. See photograph of a homemade Toonerville Trolley in a Lafayette, Indiana, parade, *Exhibitors Herald*, 6 August 1921, p. 43, and photograph of the Kansas Theater in Wichita, Kansas, with Skipper and Katrinka impersonators, Cinema Treasures, http://cinematreasures.org/theaters/17987.
2. Advertisement for Dan Mason appearing in Vaudeville, *The Philadelphia Inquirer*, 19 November 1921, p. 13.
3. Dan Mason to Wilna Hervey, 29 July 1923, Wilna Hervey and Nan Mason Papers (hereinafter HMP), Archives of American Art, box 3, folder 10; "With the Film Folks," *The Journal News* (Hamilton, OH), 7 December 1921, p. 5: "Daily Squint at the Movie Stars," *Star Gazette* (Elmira, New York), 28 January 1922, p. 4.
4. "Clean Movies Public Demand, Says Producer," *San Francisco Chronicle*, 19 September 1921, p. 2; "Dan Mason to Make More Comedies," *Detroit Free Press*, 15 December 1923, p. 4; "Clean, Heart Interest Features," *Moving Picture World*, 6 May 1922, p. 49.
5. Although Robert Eddy is officially credited with only one of the Toonerville films, Wilna Hervey remembered him as directing the entire second series of films begun in 1921. As he appears in several production stills, it is possible that he worked under Ira Lowry as an assistant and got no public credit for his efforts. See *The Original Katrinka*, p. 3-c, p. 6-c, p. 68; Joseph McBride, *Frank Capra: The Catastrophe of Success* (New York: Simon & Shuster, 2011), pp. 135–136; "Los Angeles," *Billboard*, 27 December 1913, p. 18; Email from J. Flint Baumwirt, granddaughter of Robert Eddy, to author, 19 February 2019; Photograph of director Robert Eddy, signed to Dan Mason, July 1922, Gelfand Collection.
6. "Dan Mason Gets License For Bus," *San Francisco Chronicle*, 21 February 1922, p. 10.
7. "Jitney Bus Comedy To Be Made Here," *San Francisco Examiner*, 18 February 1922, p. 12; Wilna Hervey, contract with Paul Gerson Pictures Corporation, 9 February 1922, HMP, box 11, folder 7.
8. *The Original Katrinka*, p. 7-c.
9. Frank Capra, *The Name Above the Title: An Autobiography* (New York: Macmillan, 1971), p. 35.
10. "First Run Of Pictures Is Set For September," *San Francisco Examiner*, 14 July 1922, p. 11; "Plum Center Comedies Make Hit," *San Francisco Examiner*, 16 September 1922, p. 11; Advertisement for *Pop Tuttle's Movie Queen*, *The Republic* (Columbus, Indiana), 2 December 1922, p. 8; "Said to Eclipse his Former Efforts," *Buffalo Enquirer*, 2 September 1922, p. 3.
11. "Flashes from Frisco," *Camera Magazine* 5, no 42, 1923, 20; "Toonerville Skipper Sued," *San Francisco Chronicle*, 4 May 1923, p. 3; Nothing seems to have come of this law suit. It may have been settled out of court.

Chapter 9

1. "Dan Mason Joins Hollywood Colony," *The Baltimore Sun*, 8 July 1923, p. 69.
2. Dan Mason to Wilna Hervey, 6 June 1923, 14 June 1923, HMP, box 11, folder 7; "Picture People," *Oakland Tribune*, 22 July 1923, p. 64; Dan Mason, "An Article of Agreement of Cooperation," typed and signed contract, undated, Gelfand Collection.
3. Dan Mason to Wilna Hervey, 14 June 1923, 29 July 1923, HMP, box 11, folder 7.

Notes—Chapter 10

4. *Conductor 1492* (1924), DVD edition, Alpha Home Entertainment, Narberth, PA; "Lad From Ireland Makes Fame and Fortune Here," *New York Daily News*, 8 March 1924, p. 5; "The Passing Show," *Journal and Courier* (Lafayette, Indiana), 15 March 1924, p. 4; "Dan Mason, of Toonerville Trolley Fame, in 'Conductor 1492,'" *Calgary Herald* (Calgary, Canada) 19 March 1924, p. 5. The copy in this Calgary item was repeated in several other newspapers, suggesting it came from a studio press release.

5. Wilna Hervey, chronology for *The Original Katrinka*, unpaginated typescript, p. 1, HMP, box 11, folder 1.

6. Dan Mason to Nan Mason and Wilna Hervey, 14 June 1924, HMP, box 3, folder 11; For the detailed story of Nan and Wilna's fifty-nine year love affair, see Joseph P. Eckhardt, *Living Large: Wilna Hervey and Nan Mason* (WoodstockArts: Woodstock, New York, 2015).

7. "Dan Mason in 'The Plunderer' at the Strand Monday and Tuesday," *The Chillicothe Constitution-Tribune* (Missouri), 16 August 1924, p. 7.

8. "Chatter of the Make Believers," *Oakland Tribune*, 28 March 1924, p. 30; Don H. Eddy, "In and About Hollywood," *Indianapolis Star* (Indiana), 30 March 1924, p. 2; "Comedy Congress," *Los Angeles Times*, 6 April 1924, p. 50; "At The Queen," *Austin American-Statesman* (Austin, Texas), 11 August 1924, p. 2; Jack Jungmeyer, "Movie Notes," *Muncie Evening Press*, 4 July 1924, p. 2.

9. "Darwinian Theory Basis For Film Play," *Baltimore Sun*, 25 May 1924, p. 52; "Darwin Was Right," *The Morning Call* (Allentown, Pennsylvania), 19 September 1925, p. 4.

10. Dan Mason to Nan Mason and Wilna Hervey, 18 July 1924, HMP, box 3, folder 11; "State," *Dayton Daily News* (Dayton, Ohio), 25 February 1926, p. 25.

11. Dan Mason to Wilna Hervey, 14 June 1924, Dan Mason to Nan Mason and Wilna Hervey, 18 June 1924, HMP, box 3, folder 11; Dan Mason to Wilna Hervey, 31 March 1926, Gelfand Collection; "Rudolph and Adolph," *The Scranton Republican* (Scranton, Pennsylvania), 9 April 1902, p. 3.

12. Dan Mason to Nan Mason and Wilna Hervey, 9 October 1924, HMP, box 3, folder 11.

13. Minnich and Sons Cigars to Dan Mason, 13 December 1922, Gelfand Collection.

14. Dan Mason to Nan Mason, 21 June 1921, HMP, box 3, folder 11.

15. "'Sally' Goes Into Production As Cast Is Rounded Out," *The Orlando Sentinel*, 14 December 1924, p. 21; "Colleen Moore Shining Star In 'Sally,'" *Calgary Herald*, 1 June 1925, p. 7; "Sally a la Film," *Los Angeles Times*, 25 March 1925, p. 9–11.

16. Wilna Hervey, chronology for *The Original Katrinka*, p. 2, HMP, box 11, folder 1; Dan Mason to Nan Mason and Wilna Hervey, 21 October 1928, Gelfand Collection.

Chapter 10

1. Dan Mason to Wilna Hervey, 22 December 1925, HMP, box 4, folder 1.

2. "George Walsh Finishes 'American Pluck,'" *Sioux City Journal* (Iowa), 24 May 1925, p. 20; "American Pluck At The Strand Opening Monday," *Republican and Herald* (Pottsville, Pennsylvania), 29 August 1925, p. 2; "George Walsh Wins Billion and Girl in Fast Photoplay," *The Ottawa Citizen* (Ottawa, Canada), 21 September 1918, p. 11; *American Pluck*, 1925, DVD edition, Grapevine Video, Phoenix, Arizona.

3. Photograph of Harvey C. Weaver, inscribed to Dan Mason: "One who I have come to love like a father," c. 1922, Gelfand Collection; Tacoma Library NW History, "A Snowy Day in May," www.tacomalibray.org; Mick Flaaen, *Weaver Studios, Tacoma, WA, 1924–1928*, Mariposa Productions, 2014, https://vimeo.com/122159276; Peter Monaghan, "Reopening The Eyes of the Totem," *Moving Image Archive News*, 30 June 2015, http://www.movingimagearchivenews.org/reopening-the-eyes-of-the-totem/.

4. "John Bowers Makes Perilous Journey In Making Pictures," *The Montgomery Advertiser* (Montgomery, Alabama), 19 December 1926, p. 34; "At The Theaters: Patio," *Tampa Bay Times*, 2 October 1926, p. 12; "Franklin Showing Real He-Man Film," *The Tampa Times*, 7 May 1926,

Notes—Chapter 10

p. 15; "Newlyweds Funmakers," Los Angeles Times, 12 April 1926, p. 25; Dan Mason to Nan Mason, 20 January 1926, Gelfand Collection.

5. "Fox Crew in Mountaineer Garb Embark For Big Basin Work," *Santa Cruz Evening News*, 26 June 1925, p. 3; "Old Trouper Boots Wore by Mason in Thunder Mountain," *Minneapolis Star*, 24 October 1925, p. 23; "Dan Mason Appears At Unique Tomorrow," *Santa Cruz Evening News*, 8 July 1925, p. 2.

6. "Panzer Arrives," *Santa Cruz Evening News*, 2 July 1925, p. 1; "Fox Players Put Out Forest Fire," *Billings Gazette* (Montana) 6 September 1925, p. 16.

7. "Marie Sparkles Like Champagne," *Los Angeles Times*, 12 July 1926, p. 60; "Unbilled Stars of The Big Parade," *University Life* (Wichita, Kansas), 14 December 1926, p. 5. This item appeared in numerous newspapers, indicating it was a studio press release; "At The Park Tonight," *The News Herald* (Franklin, Pennsylvania), 22 January 1926, p. 16; A copy of *The Wall Street Whiz* (1926) is reported to exist on nitrate in Paris.

8. "Wages for Wives Picture is Based on Home Problem," *The Sedalia Democrat* (Missouri), 27 January 1926, p. 4; "Wages For Wives Players Get Roses," *Sioux City Journal*, 1 November 1925, p. 28; "'Wages for Wives' From John Golden's 'Chicken Feed,'" *The Journal News* (Hamilton, Ohio), 20 March 1926, p. 8; "Vivid Portrayals Feature Comedy," *Los Angeles Times*, 10 May 1926, p. 27; "Colonial—Wages For Wives," *The Indianapolis Star*, 31 May 1926, p. 5; "Wages For Wives End Showing Gaiety Tonight," *Santa Maria Times* (California), 30 August 1926, p. 2.

9. "State," *Dayton Daly News* (Dayton, Ohio), 25 February 1926, p. 25; Q.E.D, "For Film Fans," *Baltimore Evening Sun*, 12 October 1926, p. 9; Jerry Wayne Williamson, *What the Movies did to the Mountains and What the Mountains did to the Movies* (Chapel Hill: University of North Carolina Press, 1995), p. 39; A trailer for this film survives in the Library of Congress.

10. Dan Mason to Wilna Hervey, 17 October 1925, Dan Mason to Wilna Hervey, 19 October 1925, HMP, box 3, folder 11.

11. "A Desperate Moment," *Variety*, 27 January 1926, p. 42.

12. Dan Mason to Nan Mason, 24 December 1925, Gelfand Collection; Dan Mason to Wilna Hervey, 22 December 1925, HMP, box 3, folder 11; "Saenger Theater," *The Times* (Shreveport, Louisiana), 3 April 1926, p. 17.

13. "Forbidden Waters," *The Huntington Press* (Huntington, Indiana), 27 February 1927, p. 8; "Priscilla Deans' New Picture Fine Story," *Calgary Herald* (Canada), 16 April 1926, p. 8.

14. Dan Mason to Nan Mason, 11 January 1926, Dan Mason to Nan Mason, 12 January 1926, Dan Mason to Nan Mason and Wilna Hervey, 31 January 1926, Dan Mason to Nan Mason, 1 February 1926, Gelfand Collection; "The Strand," *The Daily Record* (Long Branch, NJ), 22 September 1926, p. 4.

15. Dan Mason to Nan Mason and Wilna Hervey, 28 February 1926, Dan Mason to Wilna Hervey, 2 March 1926, Dan Mason to Wilna Hervey, 10 March 1926, Gelfand Collection.

16. Dan Mason to Nan Mason, 17 March 1926, Gelfand Collection; "Strand," *The Scranton Republican*, 7 November 1927, p. 10; Kristin Thompson, *Herr Lubitsch Goes to Hollywood: German and American Film After World War I* (Amsterdam: Amsterdam University Press, 2005), p. 27; Dan Mason to Nan Mason, 29 March 1926, Gelfand Collection.

17. Dan Mason to Nan Mason and Wilna Hervey, 19 May 1926, Gelfand Collection; Dan Mason to Nan Mason, 23 June 1926, HMP, box 12, folder 7.

18. Dan Mason to Nan Mason, 18 May 1926, Gelfand Collection; "The Fire Brigade" *Shamokin News-Dispatch* (Shamokin, Pennsylvania), 5 May 1927, p. 3; "Fire Prevention Pictured," *The South Bend Tribune* (Indiana), 12 May 1926, p. 18; Dan Mason to Nan Mason and Wilna Hervey, 19 May 1926, Gelfand Collection; Dan Mason to Nan Mason, 23 June 1926, HMP, box 12, folder 7.

19. Dan Mason to Nan Mason and Wilna Hervey, 2 July 1926, HMP, box 12, folder 7; "Francis X., Jr., is Winner," *Los Angeles Times*, 5 July 1926, p. 25.

20. Dan Mason to Nan Mason and Wilna Hervey, 5 August 1926, Dan Mason to Nan Mason and Wilna Hervey, 8 August

Notes—Chapter 11

1926, HMP, box 12, folder 7; "Hudson," *The Richmond Item* (Richmond, Indiana), 18 November 1926, p. 3.

21. *Living Large*, p. 62.

22. "Harris," *The Pittsburgh Press*, 29 May 1927, p. 30.

23. Nan Mason to Dan Mason, 15 November 1926, Nan Mason to Dan Mason, 20 November 1926, HMP, box 12, folder 7.

24. Wilna Hervey to Dan Mason, 9 December 1926, Nan Mason to Dan Mason, 9 December 1926, HMP, box 12, folder 7.

25. Nan Mason to Dan Mason, 7 January 1927, HMP, box 12, folder 8.

26. Dan Mason to Nan Mason, 7 December 1926, Dan Mason to Nan Mason, 1 January 1928, Gelfand Collection; "Organizations," *Neworld* (Los Angeles, California: Inner City Cultural Center), Vol. 2, Fall 1975, p. 49; "Troupers Meet at Fourth Rehearsal," *Los Angeles Times*, 20 February 1926, p. 27; "The Old Troupers Club," *Billboard*, 23 April 1927, p. 41; Dan Mason, "New Year's Thoughts of an Old Trouper," *The Vaudeville News and New York Star*, 1 January 1927, p. 11.

27. *Fifty Years A Trouper*, p. 1.

28. Dan Mason to Wilna Hervey, 16 May 1927, Dan Mason to Nan Mason and Wilna Hervey, 17 May 1927, HMP, box 4, folder 3.

29. "Ship On Land Rare Sight in Rialto Film," *The Morning Call* (Allentown, Pennsylvania), 20 November 1927, p. 10; "Ship Built For Denny to Float On Dry Land," *The Mansfield News-Journal* (Ohio), 25 November 1927, p. 14.

30. "Hero Of Films, Gibson, Modest In Real Life," *The Times* (Shreveport, Louisiana), 17 July 1927, p. 15; Q.E.D., "A Hero On Horseback, *The Evening Sun* (Baltimore, Maryland), 2 September 1927, p. 18.

31. Dan Mason to Nan Mason, 3 May 1927, Gelfand Collection; Dan Mason to Nan Mason, 15 December 1927, HMP, box 4, folder 3.

32. Dan Mason to Nan Mason, 14 June 1927, HMP, box 4, folder 3; Harry English, "Billy Gould and Sam Collins in 'Come Back,'" *Vaudeville News*. 2 July 1927, p. 8; "To-Day's Radio Programme: WODA," *The Herald News* (Passaic, New Jersey), 26 August 1927, p. 5; Oliver W.

Tuttle, "Comedian To Put Jokes On Radio Waves," *San Francisco Examiner*, 21 July 1922, p. 4.

33. Dan Mason to Nan Mason, 1 January 1928, Gelfand Collection; "Dan Mason In Revival," *Vaudeville News*, 5 November 1927, p. 6; Dan Mason to Wilna Hervey, 25 October 1927, HMP, box 4, folder 3; Dan Mason to Nan Mason and Wilna Hervey, 28 March 1928, Gelfand Collection.

34. Dan Mason to Wilna Hervey, 25 October 1927, HMP, box 4, folder 3; Dan Mason to Nan Mason, 20 April 1928, Gelfand Collection; Dan Mason to Nan Mason and Wilna Hervey, 27 April 1928, HMP, box 4, folder 4.

35. Dan Mason to Nan Mason and Wilna Hervey, 9 April 1928, HMP, box 4, folder 4.

Chapter 11

1. Donald Crafton, *The Talkies: American Cinema's Transition 7o Sound, 1926–1931* (New York: Simon & Schuster, Macmillan, 1997), pp. 76–82.

2. *Ibid.*, p. 280.

3. While the entirety of *Lilac Time* survives, the substantially truncated 16mm version most often seen in recent years in VHS transfer does not contain any footage of Dan Mason's performance.

4. Dan Mason to Nan Mason, 14 February 1928, HMP, box 4, folder 4.

5. "Mason in Bellamy Trial," Rochester Times-Union, 2 May 1928, p. 3; "Vilma Banky Has First Star Role," *The Gazette* (Montreal, Canada) 26 November 1928, p. 12; Richard Mason, "The New Films," *The Standard Union* (Brooklyn) 29 December 1928, p. 38.

6. "Magnificent Flirt Due Tomorrow," *The Daily Star* (Queens, New York), 18 July 1928, p. 5; The author is grateful to film historian and author, Steve Massa, for his description of Mason's final film, *Hop Off*, on nitrate at the Library of Congress.

7. Dan Mason to Nan Mason, 29 July 1928, HMP, box 4, folder 4.

8. *Ibid.*

9. Dan Mason to Nan Mason and Wilna Hervey, 13 October 1928, Gelfand Collection; "Dan Mason, City Native, To

Notes—Chapter 11

Tour R-K-O Circuit," *Syracuse Herald*, 20 December 1928, p. 22; "Dan Mason Dies At Woodstock," *Kingston Daily Freeman* (Kingston, New York), 8 July 1929, p. 1.

10. Dan Mason to Nan Mason, 29 April 1929, HMP, box 4, folder 4; Fred Grassman to Dan Mason, 8 June 1929, Gelfand Collection; Death Certificate for Daniel G. Mason, 8 July 1929, County Clerk's Office, Kingston, New York; "Dan Mason, Famous Syracuse Actor, Dies at Home on Hudson," *Syracuse Journal*, 6 July 1929, p. 3.

11. Woodstock Reformed Church, Record Book, 6,7, July 1929, *U.S., Dutch Reformed Church Records in Selected States, 1639–1989*, Ancestry.com; In a letter of 28 March 1928, Dan Mason conveyed his final arrangements to his daughter. See Dan Mason to Nan Mason, 28 March 1928, Gelfand Collection.

12. "Friends Here Mourn Mason, Toonerville Trolley Pilot," *Syracuse Herald*, 7 July 1929, Second Section, p. 3.

13. *Ibid.*

Bibliography

Public Collections

Betzwood Film Archive, Brendlinger Library, Montgomery County Community College, Blue Bell, PA.
George Eastman House, International Museum of Photography and Film, Rochester, NY.
Historical Society of Montgomery County, Norristown, PA.
Historical Society of Woodstock, Woodstock, NY.
Montgomery County Courthouse, Property Records, Norristown, PA.
UCLA Film and Television Archive, Los Angeles, CA.
Ulster County Courthouse, Kingston, NY.
Wilna Hervey and Nan Mason Papers, Archives of American Art, Smithsonian Institution, Washington, D. C.

Private Collections

Daniel Gelfand Collection, Woodstock, NY.
Robert S. Birchard Collection, Los Angeles, CA.

Books

Birchard, Robert S. *Cecil B. DeMille's Hollywood*. Lexington: University of Kentucky Press, 2004.
Blanke, David. *Cecil B. DeMille, Classical Hollywood, and Modern American Mass Culture, 1910–1960*. New York: Palgrave Macmillan, 2018.
Bordman, Gerald, and Norton, Richard. *American Musical Theater: A Chronicle*. New York: Oxford University Press, 2010.
Briggs, Jody. *Encyclopedia of Stage Lighting*. Jefferson, NC: McFarland, 2015.
Capra, Frank. *The Name Above the Title: An Autobiography*. New York: Macmillan, 1971.
Crafton, Donald. *The Talkies: American Cinema's Transition to Sound, 1926–1931*. New York: Simon & Schuster, Macmillan, 1997.
De Angelis, Jefferson, and Harlow, Alvin E. *A Vagabond Trouper*. New York: Harcourt Brace, 1931.
Eckhardt, Joseph P. *Living Large: Wilna Hervey and Nan Mason*. Woodstock, NY: WoodstockArts, LLC, 2015.
Erish, Andrew A. *Colonel William N. Selig; The Man Who Invented Hollywood*. Austin: University of Texas Press, 2012.
Evers, Alf. *Woodstock: History of an American Town*. Woodstock, NY: Overlook Press, 1987.
Fields, Armond. *Eddie Foy: A Biography of the Early Popular Stage Comedian*. Jefferson, NC: McFarland, 1999.
_____. *Tony Pastor, Father of Vaudeville*. Jefferson, NC: McFarland, 2007.
Gebhardt, Nicholas. *Vaudeville Melodies: Popular Musicians and Mass Entertainment in American Culture, 1870–1929*. Chicago: University of Chicago Press, 2017.
Hartman, Louis. *Theatre Lighting: A Manual of the Stage Switchboard*. New York: DBS Publications (1930) 1970.
Jennings, John J. *Theatrical and Circus Life: Or, Secrets of the Stage, Green Room and Sawdust*. Brandon, VT: Sidney M. Southard, 1884.
Kattwinkel, Susan. *Tony Pastor Presents: Afterpieces from the Vaudeville Stage*. Westport, CT: Greenwood Press, 1998.
Koszarski, Richard. *An Evening's Entertain-*

Bibliography

ment: *The Age of the Silent Feature Picture, 1915–1928*. Berkeley: University of California Press, 1994.

_____. *Fort Lee: The Film Town*. East Barnet, UK: John Libbey Publishing, Ltd., 2004.

Lewis, Robert M., ed. *From Traveling Show to Vaudeville: Theatrical Spectacle in America, 1830–1910*. Baltimore: Johns Hopkins University Press, 2003.

Lowry, Ed. *My Life in Vaudeville: The Autobiography of Ed Lowry*. Carbondale: Southern Illinois University Press, 2011.

McArthur, Benjamin. *Actors and American Culture, 1880–1920*. Iowa City: University of Iowa Press, 2000.

McBride, Joseph. *Frank Capra: The Catastrophe of Success*. New York: Simon & Shuster, 2011.

Marston, William Moulton, and Feller, John Henry. *F. F. Proctor: Vaudeville Pioneer*. New York: Richard R. Smith, 1943.

Rice, Edward LeRoy. *Monarchs of Minstrelsy, From "Daddy" Rice to Date*. New York: Kenny Publishing Company, 1911.

Rodger, Gillian M. *Champagne Charlie and Pretty Jemima*. Champaign: University of Illinois Press, 2010.

Sellman, Hunton D., and Lessley, Merrill. *Essentials of Stage Lighting*. 2nd ed. Englewood Cliffs, NJ: Prentice-Hall, 1982.

Slide, Anthony. *The Encyclopedia of Vaudeville*. Westport, CT: Greenwood Press, 1994.

Solomon, Aubrey. *The Fox Film Corporation, 1915–1935*. Jefferson, NC: McFarland, 2011.

Springhall, John. *The Genesis of Mass Culture: Show Business Live in America, 1840 to 1940*. New York: Palgrave Macmillan, 2008.

Tawfik, Adam. *The Elusive Eastern Film Corporation of Providence, Rhode Island; Resurrecting a Footnote in Film History*. Providence: Rhode Island College, 2013.

Thompson, Kristin. *Herr Lubitsch Goes to Hollywood: German and American Film After World War I*. Amsterdam: Amsterdam University Press, 2005.

Trav S. D. *No Applause—Just Throw Money*. New York: Faber & Faber, 2005.

Williamson, Jerry Wayne. *What the Movies Did to the Mountains and What the Mountains Did to the Movies*. Chapel Hill: University of North Carolina Press, 1995.

Journal and Magazine Articles

Eckhardt, Joseph P. "Clatter, Sproing, Clunk Went the Trolley." *Pennsylvania Heritage Magazine* 18, no. 3 (Summer 1992), 24.

_____. "The Toonerville Trolley Films of the Betzwood Studio." *Griffithiana* 53 (May 1995).

Johnson, Ray. "Tricks, Traps, and Transformations," *Early Popular Visual Culture* 5 (2007) 151.

MacFarlane, Peter Clark. "William Collier, Laugh Builder." *Everybody's Magazine* 32 (January to June 1915), 474.

Newspaper Articles

"Clean Movies Public Demand, Says Producer." *San Francisco Chronicle*, 19 September 1921, p. 2.

"Dan Mason and Harry Kelley Renew Acquaintance in Picture Studio." *The New York Clipper*, 26 April 1915, 6.

"Dan Mason Dies at Woodstock." *Kingston Daily Freeman* (Kingston, New York), 8 July 1929, p. 1.

"Dan Mason, Famous Syracuse Actor, Dies at Home on Hudson." *Syracuse Journal*, 6 July 1929, 3.

"Dan Mason Gets License For Bus." *San Francisco Chronicle*, 21 February 1922, p. 10.

"Dan Mason Joins Hollywood Colony." *The Baltimore Sun*, 8 July 1923, p. 69.

"Friends Here Mourn Mason, Toonerville Trolley Pilot." *Syracuse Herald*, 7 July 1929, Second Section, p. 3.

"Made a Clean Sweep." *New York Herald*, 20 October 1890, 6.

Mason, Dan. "New Year's Thoughts of an Old Trouper." *The Vaudeville News and New York Star*, 1 January 1927, p. 11.

"Really Too Too." *The Brooklyn Daily Eagle*, 31 December 1883, p. 2.

"Sully Says Something and Saws Wood." *The Brooklyn Daily Eagle*, 6 August 1905, 20.

Bibliography

"Veteran Actor Tells of Old Days." *Syracuse Herald*, 2 June 1918.

Warren, George C. "Actor Enters Fiftieth Year on Stage," *San Francisco Chronicle*, 4 June 1922, p. 4.

Online Resources

Ancestry.com. Lehi, Utah: https://www.ancestry.com.

Betzwood Film Archive. Blue Bell, Pennsylvania: Montgomery County Community College. http://mc3betzwood.wordpress.com.

California Digital Newspapers Collection. Riverside, California: University of California. https://cdnc.ucr.edu.

Chronicling America: Historic American Newspapers. Washington, D.C. The Library of Congress. https://chroniclingamerica.loc.gov.

Colorado Historical Newspapers Collection. Denver, CO: Colorado State Library. https://www.coloradohistoricnewspapers.org.

The Edison Kinetogram. Orange, NJ: Thomas A. Edison, Inc., 1909–1916. https://catalog.hathitrust.org/Record/000534937.

Illinois Digital Newspaper Collection. Urbana: University of Illinois. https://idnc.library.illinois.edu.

International Movie Data Base. http://www.imdb.com.

Measuring Worth. https://www.measuringworth.com.

Newspapers.com. http://www.newspapers.com.

Old New York State Historical Newspapers. http://www.fultonhistory.com/Fulton.html.

Rhode Island College, Providence: Jane P. Adams Digital Library Commons. https://digitalcommons.ric.edu/honors_projects.

Index

Numbers in **_bold italics_** indicate pages with photos

Adorée, Renée 104, 166
afterpiece 10, 13–14, 17–18, **_20_**–22, 45, 57, 59, 62, **_64_**, 126, 129, 131
Algeria 115
All Fools Day (afterpiece) 21, 62, **_64_**, 129, 130, 157, 174*n*19
An All Fools Day Affair (film) 62, **_64_**, 130, 157
Alley Inn Café 99, 165
Alphonse and Gaston 49
The Alps 114
An American Boy 33–**_35_**, 37, 49, 130
The American Consul 101, 166
American Pluck 101, 166, 181*n*2
Anaconda, Montana 40
Anderson, W.C. 39
Andrew Arbuckle Agency 101
Andrews, Del 116, 169
Arbuckle, Roscoe "Fatty" 80, 83
Archainbaud, George 94, 164
Associated First National 74, 99, 118, 122, 141, 180
The Associated Press 126
Astra Film Company **_68_**, 151
Atkinson, Charles 22–23, 27, 33
Atlantic City 48, 51, 53, 56, 60, **_63_**
Atlantic Garden Theater (Fort Wayne, Indiana) 16
Audubon, Pennsylvania 74, 79, 82, 85, 91, 100, 111, 113, 118–119
The Awakening 123, 171

A Bachelor's Wives 40, 130
The Bad Man 124
Baldwin, Henry 95, 164
Banky, Vilma 123, 171
Banner Productions 105, 141
Bara, Theda 71, 158
Baries Opera House (Syracuse) 15
Barrymore, John 69, 121
Barrymore, Lionel 75
Barton, Charles C. 54
Bearsville, New York 91, 98, 110, 114; *see also* Woodstock, New York

Beaudine, William 95, 164
Belasco, David 45, 126
Bell, Monta 122, 171
Bellamy, Madge 103, 165
The Bellamy Trial 171–172, 183
Belmont, California 86
Betzwood Film Company 1–2, 71–73, 75–76, 78–79, 141, 180
The Big Parade 104, 166
Biggers, Earl Derr 116
Bijou Theater (NYC) 48
Bijou Theater (Washington, DC) 43
The Biograph 41
Biskra, Algeria 115; *see also The Sheik*
blackface 9, 12, 14, 25, 133
Blatz, Peter 33
Blue Ridge Mountains 106
Blystone, John G. 108, 141, 167
Bonnie Brier Productions 92
Borzage, Frank 104
Boston 22, 27, 33, 57
Bowers, Charles R. "Charley" 123, 141, 170
Bowers, John 102, 181
Boyden, Abner 108–**_109_**, 168
Brabin, Charles 118
Brave and Bold 67, 156
Breeze, Jimmy 116–**_117_**, 169
Broadhurst, George H. 44–45, 47–48, 53
Broadway 1, 27–28, 43, 45–47, 49, 51, 53–55, 69, 95
The Broadway Sport 67
Brockwell, Gladys 110, 169
The Bronx 57–58, 60, 64–64, 70, 74, 105–106, 111
Brooklyn, New York 30
Bryan, William Jennings 95
Buchowetzki, Dmitri 95, 164
Bunny, George 62, 155
Bunny, John 62
Burr, C.C. 111, 141
Busch, Aniser 31
Butler, Gen. Benjamin 25, 28
Butler, Richard 165

189

Index

The Camel's Back 93
Cameo Comedies 62, 141
the can-can 135
Capra, Frank **84**, 88, 180, 185–186
Captain Dietrich 28–29, 41, 175n10
Carlos Productions 104
Carmel-by-the-Sea 114
Cator, Thomas V. 114
Catskill Mountains 91, 106, 124
Chadwick Pictures Corporation 101, 141
Chan, Charlie 116
Chaplin, Charlie 80
Cherry, William 116, 170
Chester County, Pennsylvania 77
Chicago 14, 16, 27–28, 33, 53–54, 57, 141, 168
Chickenfeed **104**
Chillingheim, Otto 85
Chillingworth, Roger 65–**66**, 153
The Chinese Parrot 116, 170
Christian Science 97, 115–117, 123, 125
chuck wagon 108
cigars 11–12, 57, 98, 126, 145, 171
Cincinnati 17, 51, 135
A Clean Sweep 30–31, 33, 49, 55, 130, 139
Cloudburst Fire Company 86, 162
The Coliseum (Cincinnati) 17
Collier, Willie 43–44, 54
Collins, Walt **67**, 154
Colonial Motion Picture Corporation 62, 141; *see also* Cameo Comedies
Columbia Pictures 113, 141
concert saloons 8, 11, 15
Concord, New Hampshire 33
Conductor 1492 92–94, 105, 163
costumes and make up: 14, 28–29, 32, 38, 53, 58, **61**–63, 72, 74, **78**, 86, 95, 103, 111, 126; *see also* blackface
Crone's City Garden (Indianapolis) 16
cross dressing 9, 18, 60
A Crowded Hotel (film) 142
The Crowded Hotel (afterpiece) 18–19, 21, 129–134
Cruze, James 82, 161
Culver City 107, 110

Daddy Nolan 37–38, 40
Dan Mason Cigars 57, 178
Dan Mason Comedies 91
Dan Mason Company 55
Darwin Was Right 95, 164
Dawn, Jack 106, 167
A Day in June 40, 130
Dean, Priscilla **107**–108, 167
The DeAngelis Family 24
De La Motte, Marguerite 102
Delaware Water Gap 106
DeMille, Cecil B. 107
The Derelict 67, 153–154

A Desperate Moment 106–107, 167
Detroit, Michigan 16, 22, 38, 178n16
dialect comedians 9, 17, 104, 174n11
Dinkle and Maginty's Racket 22, 129
Dinklespiel, Rudolph 45, **47**–48, 53, 57–58, 81, 126, 137
Dinkelspiel's Baby 130, 147
Dizzy, the Dancing Elephant 27, 30, 34
Dodo, the lounge lizard **78**–79, 160
Dolt, the German Butler 44
Don Juan 121
Dooley, Johnny 158
D'Oyly Carte, Richard 173ch2n3
Dudley, Robert 115
Duffy's Blunders 39–40
Durant automobile 99
Durning, Bernard J. 82, 160
Du Souchet, H.A. 43, 177
Dutch Reformed Church 125
The Dutch Shoemaker 17, 129

Eastern Film Corporation 62, 64–65, 69, 141; *see also* Jaxon Comedies; Sparkle Comedies
Eddy, Mary Baker 97
Eddy, Robert 83–**84**, 88, 90, 158, 161–163, 180n5
Edison Motion Picture Company 57–63, **68**, 70, 141, 179ch6n11
Educational Pictures 80
Edward Small Agency 101
Eichler, Frederick 38
The Elegy 109–110, 169
Emmett, J.K. "Fritz" 6
Essanay Film Manufacturing Company 95
Evangeline, or the Belle of Arcadia 28–30, 41
Every Girl's Dream 66

Famous Players 68, 70
Famous Players-Lasky 82, 108, 141
farmers' hotels 8, 10
Fat Ladies on Bicycles 60
Female Mastodons **24**–25
Fenton, Leslie 103, 165
Fields, Lew 51; *see also* Weber and Fields
Fifty Years a Trouper 115
Film Booking Offices of America 86, 90–91
The Fire Brigade 110–**112**, 169
First National Pictures 74, 99, 118, 122, 141, 180n15
Fitler, Edwin Henry 32
Fitzgerald, F. Scott 93
Fitzhew, Benjamin 43–**44**
Fitzmaurice, George 171
Fleming, Victor 123, 171
Florence, Italy 114
Forbidden Waters **107**–108, 167
Fort Lee, New Jersey 64, 66–68, 79, 101, 110, 118

190

Index

Fourteenth Street Theater (NYC) 28
Fox, Fontaine 71–72, 74–75, 77, 81, 88
Fox, William 94
Fox Film Corporation 64, *66–67*, 82, 94–95, 101, 103–104, 108–*109*, 141
Foy, Edwin "Eddie" 27
France 58, 113, 157, 166, 168, 171
France, Charles H. 143–147, 150–151, 153
Franco-Prussian War *122*
Franklin, Pearl 103
Frawley, Flora 114–16, 21, 26, 174*n*6

Galveston, Texas 36
Garrick Theater (NYC) 54
gas table 12; *see also* theater lighting
Gay New York 49–51, 54, 57, 157*n*10
George M. Perry Motion Picture Service 667, 179*n*16
George White's Scandals 111, 168
Germany 5, 114
Gerson, Paul 83–*84*, 86–*88*, 90, 141
Gibson, Hoot 116–118
Giebler, Alfred H. 86
Gilbert, John 104, 166
Golden, John *104*, 154
Goldwyn Studio 68, 141
Grand-Asher Studio 92
Grand Central Theater (Philadelphia) 18
Grand Opera House (St. Louis) 41
Grassman, Daniel "Dannie" Mason 26, 28
Grassman, Fred 125–126
Grassman, Jacob 5–6
Green, Alfred E. 99, 165
Grenier's Lyceum Theater (Chicago) 28
Griffin, John D. 21–22
Griffith, Edward H. 113, 169
Griffith Park, Los Angeles 82

Hackensack, New Jersey 70, 126
Hale, Alan 102, 107–108, 167
Hale, Creighton 104, 166
Hamilton, Lloyd 95, 164
Hamilton, Mark 96
Harbaugh, Carl 64–65, 153–157
Hard Boiled 108–*109*, 167–168
Hawley, Wanda 106, 166–167
H.C. Weaver Productions 102, 141; *see also* Weaver, Harvey C.
Hearts and Fists 102–103, 107, 167
Hearts and Harpoons 62, 155
Heath, George W. 33–34
Henley, Hobart 156–157
Herbert, Victor 51
A Hero on Horseback 116–*117*, 169
Hervey, Wilna 72–74, *76*–88, 90–94, 97–101, 106, 108–110, 113–117, 120, 124–125, 159–163; *see also* Wilde, Wilna
Hill, Gus 49, 54

Hilliker, Katherine 77
Hillyer, Lambert 97, 165
Hines, Charles 93, 163, 167–168
Hines, Johnny 92–93, 96, *105*–106, 11–113, 121, 163, 167–168
"Hinkey Dee" 49–*50*
Hollywood 1, 12, 77, 83, 89, 91–101, 113–114, 118–121, 123, 125–126
Hollywood Pictures Corporation 92
Holmes, Stuart 65, 69, 153–154
Hooley's Theater (Chicago) 29
Hop Off 123, 170
Hopper, Tacitus 102, 167
Hotel St. George (Santa Cruz, California) 103
Howdy Folks 103
Howell, Helen 83
Howell, William A. 83
Hoyt Theater (NYC) 43
Hugh S. Jeffrey Agency 101
Hulette, Gladys *68*, 143, 146, 149–152, 155
Humboldt County, California 118
The Hustler 31–32

Idle Hour Theater 86, 88–*89*
Idle Tongues *96*, 98, 165
influenza pandemic 70
Ingraham, Lloyd 102, 167
Ingram, Rex 59
Ireland 5, 96, 164
Iron to Gold 82, 160
Is Matrimony a Failure? 82, 161
It Happened in Nordland 51–*52*, 103
Italy 113–114

Jack Spurlock, Prodigal 66, 101, 156
The Janitor's Flirtation 60, 130, 146
The Janitor's Quiet Life 59, 130, 145
Jardin Mabille 135
Jaxon Comedies 64, 156–157; *see also* Colonial Motion Picture Corporation
The Jazz Singer 121
Jolly Old Chums 39–40

Kaufman, Joseph 155
Keaton, Buster 80
Kelley, Dan 39
Kelly, John T. 26, 139
Kentucky 16, 103, 106, 167
Knickerbocker Theater (Louisville) 19
Knight, George S. 9
Krousemyer's Elevation (The Ladies Archery Club) 129, 136
KUO (radio station) 118

La Fonte, Millie 23–26, 29–31, 34–35, 37, 39–41, 48 51, 54, 56–57, 60, 62–63, 70, 72, 97, 107, 126,175*n*2, 177*n*7; *see also* Page, Millicent

191

Index

Las Vegas, Nevada 124–125
The Last Warning 123
Laughing Bill Hyde 70, 157
Lawrence, Edmund 71, 158
Leavitt, Michael Bennett 22
Leavitt-Pastor Combination 22
Leni, Paul 116, 123, 170
"Liberty Cabbage" 59
"Liberty Hounds" 59
Lilac Time 122, 171, 183ch11n3
The Lilas 48, 51
Livingston, Margaret 105, 166, 171
Lloyd, Harold 80
lobby cards 2, 88
Logan, Jacqueline 104–105, 166
Long, John Luther 45
Los Angeles 55, 82, 91–92, 94, 98–100, 103, 108, 115, 123
Louisville, Kentucky 16–17, 19, 71, 167
Lowry, Ira M. 71–72, 74, 83, 158–162, 180
Lubin, Siegmund 71
Lubitsch, Ernst 110, 168
The Lure of Ambition 71, 158
Lyceum Theater (Brooklyn) 30

Madame Butterfly (story, afterpiece) 45
The Man from Mexico 43–44, 54
Marble, Scott 29, 31
Marsh, Mae 69, 156
Martin, Mary 65, 153
Mason, Charles 47, 137
Mason, Clinton Winford 29, 33–27
Mason, Harry Grassman 337, 39–40, 56, 60–**61**, 70, 92, 98, 110, 124–125, 149
Mason, Nan (Anna) 41, 56, 60, 62–**63**, 72, 74, 79, 82–83, 85–86, 88, 91–92, 95, 97–101, 103, 106, 108–122, 125–126
Massanet, Jules 110
Mathis, June 99
Maximilian, Robert 78, 159–161
Mayo, Frank 94, 164
McKinley, William 43
McMullen, Nancy 5
Men 95
Metro Goldwyn Mayer 104, 110–**112**, 141, 166, 168–171
Metropolitan Studio **107**, 141
Milestone, Lewis 104, 166
Millarde, Harry F. 154–155, 157
The Millionaire 37–38, 41
minstrel shows 6, 9, 12–14, **24**–25, 115, 133, 136, 174n11
Miss Patsy 54, 57
Mr. Smooth 44
Mr. Tevis, the stationmaster **104**–105, 166
Mix, Tom 108–**109**, 167
Montgomery County, Pennsylvania 1, 71
moonshine 75–76, 88, **96**, 158–159, 162

Moore, Colleen **99**, 122, 165, 171
Motion Picture Magazine 59
Motion Picture Patents Company 179n11
motion pictures 2, 28, 42, 57–60, 61, 77, 81–82, 121, 123, 145
Motography 66
Mount Rainier 102
MovieTone 121, 123
Myers' Opera House (Memphis) 14
Mynheer de Haas 66

Nancy Brown 48
Nashville, Tennessee 31
Natchez, Mississippi 135–136
National Theater (Cincinnati) 135
National Vaudeville Artists 111
Naughty Anthony 45
Neal, Rev. Timothy **68**, 156
Negri, Pola 95, 164
Nelson, Jack 104, 165
The New Butler 104, 165; see also *The Wall Street Whiz*
The New Chauffeur 54–57, 64, 70, 130, 178n16; see also *Via The Coal Hole*
New Orleans, Louisiana 15
New Rochelle, New York 68
New York City 23, 26, 29, 37, 28–30, 41, 43, 48, **50**, 54, 57, 62, 67–68, 70, 72, 74, 82, 121, 138
The New York Clipper 14, 21, 25–26, 29, 31, 34, 51, 131
Newhall, California 108
Niblo, the French clown 135
Nigh, William 64, 79, 110–111, 154–15, 158, 160, 169
Nilsson, Anna Q. 79, 160
Norcross, Frank 92
Norristown, Pennsylvania 74, 78, 185
North Africa 115
North Stanley Avenue, West Hollywood **100**, 119
Novelty Theater (NYC) 30
Nugget Pete **107**, 167
Nutt, William 58

olio 9, 12–14
Olson, Tillie 82, 86–**88**, 90–91, 162–163; see also Hervey, Wilna
Onondaga County, New York 5
Opera House (Chicago) 54
Opera House (Newark, NJ) 31
orthochromatic film stock 61
O'Toole, Mike **93**, 96, 163
Our Uncles 21, 129
Out All Night 116, 169
Over the Garden Wall 29–30, 57
Over the Hill **68**, 155

Index

"Pa" MacBirney 103
Pacific Ocean 107–108
Page, Millicent 24, 26, 29, 41, 54, **63**, 70; *see also* La Fonte, Millie
Palace Hotel, Plum Center 86, 163
Paramount Pictures 109, 141
Paris, France 53, 110, 114, 164, 168, 171, 175, 182n7
Park Theater (Detroit) 22
Parke, William 155–156
Parks, Bells 94, 96, 164
Parmele's Novelty Theater (Louisville) 16
Partridge, Hattie 138
Pastor, Tony 22, 37, 126
Paterson, New Jersey 118
Pathé Film Company 68
Paul Gerson Pictures Corporation 83–**84**, 86–**88**, 90, 141, 161
Payson, Henry Ward Beecher **96**, 165
Peck, George Wilbur 22
Peck's Bad Boy 22–23, 26–28, 33, 126
Peepfogel, Hubert 51–**52**, 103
Peg Leg Murphy 110–**112**, 169
Perkins, Abe 149
Perkins, Lem **105**–106, 167
Philadelphia, Pennsylvania 1, 18, 22, 31–32, 54 71, 82
Phoenixville, Valley Forge and Strafford Railway 77
photoplayer 62
Pickford, Mary 94
Pidgeon, Eddie 138
Pitts, Zasu 103, 105, 161, 165–166
Pittsburgh, Pennsylvania 25, 32, 44, 156
Plum Center 81–91, 102, 114, 162–163
Plum Centerpedes **84**, 86
The Plunderer 94–96, 98, 164
poetry 173–174
Pop Tuttle 82, 86–91, 161–163
Pop Tuttle, Detekative 87, 89, 162
Pop Tuttle, Fire Chief 87–88, 159, 162
Pop Tuttle's Lost Control 163
Pop Tuttle's Movie Queen 87–**88**, 161
Pop Tuttle's Russian Rumors 91, 163
Pops Shendorf **99**, 165
popular price houses 34, 38, 47, 54, 95
Potel, Vic 95, 164
Power, Tyrone, Sr. 110, 169
The Powerful Katrinka 71–72, 76–77, 81, 90–91, 158–161; *see also* Hervey, Wilna
The Price of Honor 133, 169
The Prince of Pilsen 51, 53
Proctor, F.F. 29–30
Professor William Nutt 58, 142
prohibition **75**–77, 93, 144, 146, 150, 158
Providence, Rhode Island 21, 23, 39, 136, 139
Prynne, Hester 65, 153
Pumpernickel, Hans 49

Rainbow Riley 106, 167
Rapf, Harry **78**–79, 141
Rex Beach Pictures 68, 141
Rheims Cathedral 114
Riverdale Studio 106
R-K-O (Radio-Keith-Orpheum) 124
Rogers, Will 69–70, 157
Rolph, James, Jr. 86
Rome, Italy 114
Rosen, Lew 31
Rosita 94
rube comedies 82–83
Rudolph and Adolph 45, **47**–48, 53, 57–58, 81, 126, 137
Ryan, Arthur 72, 79
Ryan, James 5, 103–104, 108–109

Sacramento, California 40, 44
St. Joseph, Missouri 37, 137
St. Louis, Missouri 41
St. Paul, Minnesota 26, 39–40
Sally 98–**99**, 165
Salt Lake City, Utah 34, 36
San Francisco 24, 40, 55, 83, 85–86, **88**, 90–91, 102, 114
Sans Souci Theater (Providence) 23
Santa Cruz, California 103
Savage, Henry H. 51, 53–54
The Scarlet Letter 65–**66**, 153
Schmidt, Otto **55**
Schmidt, Von Bulow Bismarck 43–**44**, 54
Schultz, Hermann 49–**50**
Schultz, Max 22–23, 47, 81
Schuylkill River 71
Scopes "Monkey Trial" 95
Seay, Charles M. 144–153
Sedgwick, Edward 111, 168
Seiler, Lewis 95
Seiter, William 116, 169
A Self-Made Failure 95, 164
Selig Polyscope Company 57, 141
Seller, Lewis 164
Selwyn Theater (NYC) 111
serio-comic 21, 24, 38, 60, 70, 99
Seven Sinners 104, 166
Shakespeare Hall (Syracuse) 6
The Sheik 115
Sherrill, Friedman, Schuessler, Inc. 101
Shertzinger, Victor 103
The Sideshow by the Seaside 29, 130
Sienna, Italy 114
The Skipper's Flirtation **76**, 159, 179ch7n11
The Skipper's Narrow Escape 74, 76, 158, 179ch7n11
The Skipper's Scheme 77, 159
The Skipper's Treasure Garden 75, 158
Smith's Tavern 92
Snitz, Julius 30

193

Index

So This Is Paris 110, 168
A Social Lion 39–40
The Society Opposed to Everything **89**, 161
Sonora, California 94
sound films 121, 123
Sparkle Comedies 64–**65**, 141, 155; see also Colonial Motion Picture Corporation
spiritualism 97, 150
Stanton, Richard 166
Stepping Along 11, 121, 168
stock company 34, 41
Stone, Andrew 110, 169
Sully, Dan (Daniel Sullivan) 16–21, 27, 37–41, 129–131, 133, 176n2
Switzerland 114
Syracuse, New York 5–7, 9–12, 15, 91, 98, 111, 118, 125–127

Tacoma, Washington 102–103, 108–109
Talmadge, Richard 104, 141, 165
Tec-Art Studios 105
Thanhouser Film Corporation 68
That Heavenly Cook 62, 153
theater lighting 7, 12, 32, 38, 121; see also gas table
theaters 6, 14–19, 21–23, 26, 28–32, 34, 37, 41, 43, 48, 51, 54
Theatre Comique (Providence) 21
Theatre Comique (St. Paul) 26
Theatre Comique (Toledo) 15
Theatre Vendome (Nashville) 31
Theatrical and Circus Life 26
Thomas Ince Corporation 96, 141
Thunder Mountain 103, 165
The Tigers 26–27, 30, 33, 130; see also *A Clean Sweep*
Tin Hats 111, 168
Titlow Beach, Tacoma, Washington 102
Todd, Harry 95, 164
Tony Pastor's Theater (NYC) 37
The Toonerville Skipper 1, 71–79, 81–82, 90–91, 93, 95, 103, 158–162
Toonerville Follies 159, 179ch7n11
Toonerville Tactics 77, 160
Toonerville Trolley: cartoons 71–72, 81, 88; characters 71, 76–78, 86, 158–160; comedies 1–2, **73**–83, 86–91, 93, 95, 103, 126, 158–162, 179ch7n11, 180n15; replica trolley constructed for films 71, 74–78; see also Fox, Fontaine
The Toonerville Trolley That Meets All The Trains 74
Toonerville's Boozem Friends 76, 78, 159, 179ch7n11
Toonerville's Fire Brigade 75, 159
Topeka, Kansas 27
trained fleas 123, 170
Treasure Farm 110, 113, 116, 118, 125

The Trip to Egypt 49
The Troupers Club 115
tuberculosis 16, 125

Uncle Dudley comedies 62, 153
Uncle McDermott 116, 170
United Booking Offices 55
Universal Studios 116–**117**, 141
Unneighborly Neighbors 18, 21, 129
An Up to Date Courtship 60–**61**, 149

Valley Forge 71, 77
The Valley of the Giants 118, 170
Variety 1–2, 6–7, 9, 11–16, 22, **24**, 27, 30, 32, 34, 56, 59, 69–70, 78, 126
variety halls 11, 14–15, 69
vaudeville 1–2, 11, 22, 27, 29, 41, 43, 48–49, 51, 54–57, 60, 64, 69, 70, 74, 78, 82–83, 95, 111, 115, 119, 121, 131
The Vaudeville News 115
Vaughan, Gus 52
Venice, Italy 114
Via the Coal Hole 70, 78, 130; see also *The New Chauffeur*
Victor Herbert Theater (NYC) 51
Vidor, King 104, 166
Vitaphone 121–**122**
von Eltz, Theodore 106, 167
von Guggenheim, Count 44, **46**
von Schoenthan, Franz 54
von Steinberger, Baron 38

Wages for Wives **104**–105, 166
Wagner, Hans 51
The Wall Street Whiz 104, 165, 182n7; see also *The New Butler*
Walnut Street Theater (Philadelphia) 32
Walsh, George 66, 69, 101, 156, 166
Ward, Fannie 69, 156
Warner Brothers 92, 104, 108, 110, 121, 141
Warranty Trust Company 119
Warren, Jim 106, 167
Washburn, E.S. 7–12, 86
Washburn's Last Sensation 7–8, 86
Washington D.C. 23, 43, 54
Weaver, Harvey C. 82–83, 102–103, 108–109, 141; see also Weaver, H.C.
Weber and Fields 45
Westwood Park, San Francisco
Why Girls Leave Home 78–79, 143, 160, 178n4
Why Smith Left Home 44–46
Wieting's Opera House (Syracuse) 6
Wilde, Wilna 72, 158–162; see also Hervey, Wilna
Wildfire (horse) **84**, 86, 162–163
Williams, C.J. 57–58, 142–144, 150
Williams Corner 77

194

Index

Wilson, Mollie 21–22, 26
Winkle, Julius 30–31
Wiswell, Lewis C. 54
Withey, Chester 157
The Witness to the Will 59, 146
WODA (radio station) 118
Wolf Brothers, Inc. 71, 80

Wonderland Theater (Salt Lake City) 34
Woodstock Artists Association 106
Woodstock, New York 2, 91, 94, 97–98, 101–102, 110–111, 113, 116, 118–119, 121, 125
World War I 58, 70, 104, 111, 123, 166, 171

Young, Clara Kimball 68–69, 141

www.ingramcontent.com/pod-product-compliance
Lightning Source LLC
Chambersburg PA
CBHW032045300426
44117CB00009B/1198